DATE DUE

SIRINGO

NUMBER THIRTY-ONE

The Centennial Series

of the Association of Former Students,

TEXAS A&M UNIVERSITY

Charles A. Siringo in Boise City, Idaho,
during the trial of "Big Bill" Haywood in
1907 (from the author's collection).

SIRINGO

By Ben E. Pingenot

✳

*The true story
of Charles A. Siringo, Texas cowboy,
longhorn trail driver, private detective,
rancher, New Mexico Ranger, and author.
Revealing highlights of his action-filled life,
with a behind-the-scenes account of his romances,
his successes and failures,
and his intermittent battles with
Pinkerton's National Detective Agency
that became the focus of nearly
one-third of his life.*

TEXAS A&M UNIVERSITY PRESS
College Station

The quotation in chapter 5 from *Desperate Men: Revelations from the Sealed Pinkerton Files,* by James D. Horan (Garden City, N.Y.: Doubleday, 1962), is reprinted by permission of the publisher.

The paper used in this book meets the minimum requirements of the American National Standard for Permanence of Paper for Printed Library Materials, z39.48-1984. Binding materials have been chosen for durability.

Library of Congress Cataloging-in-Publication Data

Pingenot, Ben E.
  Siringo : the true story of Charles A. Siringo, Texas cowboy, longhorn trail driver, private detective, ranger, New Mexico ranger, and author . . . / by Ben E. Pingenot.—1st ed.
    p.   cm.—(The Centennial series of the Association of Former Students, Texas A&M University ; no. 31)
  Bibliography: p.
  Includes index.
  ISBN 0-89096-381-9 (alk. paper)
    1. Siringo, Charles A., 1855–1928. 2. Cowboys—Texas—Biography. 3. Detectives—Texas—Biography. 4. New Mexico—Biography. 5. Frontier and pioneer life—Texas. 6. Texas—History—1846–1950. 7. Texas—Biography. I. Title. II. Series.
F391.S625P56 1989
976.4'061'0924—dc19   88-29511
[B]   CIP

To
ROZETTA
My life's companion and best friend

To a surprising degree, the men and women who were engaged in this movement West over the North American Continent, were conscious of their place in history. . . . So those that could write or remember—from the mountain men in the vanguard, to the builders of railroads and towns and cities—kept a record, a memory of their experiences which has become the shared inheritance of the American people.

—William H. Goetzmann and William N. Goetzmann,
The West of the Imagination

CONTENTS

ILLUSTRATIONS

frontispiece
Charles A. Siringo in 1907

following page 48
W. C. ("Outlaw Bill") Moore
Siringo's store in Caldwell, Kansas
Mamie Lloyd Siringo and daughter Viola
Broadside announcing Haymarket meeting
Siringo in 1893
Family portrait of Siringo, Lillie, and Lee Roy

following page 133
Frontispiece from *A Texas Cowboy*
Two Evils Isms front cover
Siringo and film star William S. Hart
Advertisement for *A Cowboy Detective*
Siringo and old friends in 1927
Siringo, Evelyn Ramey, and Charles Smith

PREFACE
AND ACKNOWLEDGMENTS

Siringo is not a book that was purposely planned, but, rather, it evolved over a long period of time. What began more than thirty years ago as a casual interest in Charles A. Siringo, and then grew as the insatiable appetite of a collector grows, finally developed into a minor obsession. I wanted to know more about this man who wrote about himself so much, who knew and was known by so many people, both famous and infamous, whose public life was autobiographically displayed, but whose private life was controversial and shrouded. I had few clues to go on and many early leads turned out to be dead ends. Over a period of years I made numerous trips and traveled thousands of miles in my quest for information about Siringo. I wrote to colleagues and friends, to scholars whose own research related to Siringo, and I visited libraries and public-record repositories in three states. By the time I completed my term as president of the Texas State Historical Association, I had assembled enough information to write a paper entitled "Charlie Siringo and the Pinkertons." I presented it as my presidential address at the Association's annual meeting in El Paso, March 6, 1981, held jointly that year with the Historical Society of New Mexico. It is from these beginnings that this book has grown.

Because so many years were consumed in research and in collecting, I have become indebted to many individuals without whose assistance this story of Siringo's life could not have been written. Since my search began in New Mexico, it seems appropriate that my acknowledgments should begin there as well. Jack Rittenhouse, a rare-book dealer in Albuquerque, and Bruce Ellis, in Santa Fe, called my attention to the Renehan Papers in the History Library of the Museum of New Mexico, Santa Fe. A friend and colleague, Santa Fe bookman Robert Kadlec, drove me through what used to be the Sunny Slope Ranch and pointed out the adobe house that was Siringo's home. Kadlec also searched for surviving acquaintances of Siringo and ran down leads, some of which proved invaluable. James H. Purdy, historian for the New Mexico State Records Center and Archives in Santa Fe, directed me to pertinent papers in that institution. Clarence Siringo Adams, of Roswell, told of the circumstances surrounding his special relationship with Charlie Siringo. Harlan P. Euler, of Sandia Park, related memories of his childhood on Siringo's Sunny Slope Ranch and recalled interesting details of the early 1920s, when Siringo's fortunes in Santa Fe were failing. Necah Stewart Furman, once a high-school student of mine, years later the biographer of Walter Prescott Webb, and now corporate historian at Sandia National Laboratories in Albuquerque, was generous in making recommendations. Stephany Eger, formerly librarian at the Museum of New Mexico History Library, and the staff at the New Mexico State Library, both in Santa Fe, were very courteous and helpful.

Among those who aided my research in California were Valerie Franco, formerly assistant curator, and William P. Frank, associate curator, of Western manuscripts at the Huntington Library, San Marino. Doyce Nunis, professor of history at the University of Southern California, Los Angeles, discussed Dr. Henry F. Hoyt, whom he had researched, and Frank Putnam, whom he had known, as well as assisting me in other ways. Veteran Los Angeles rare-book dealer Glen Dawson recalled his dealings with Viola Reid and gave me a copy of their 1940 catalogue that offered for sale books from Siringo's library. Richard Mohr of International Bookfinders, Pacific Palisades, shared his expertise concerning early editions of *A Texas Cowboy*. Both of these bookmen suggested leads that were helpful.

The late Loring Campbell of Burbank, well-known magician and enthusiastic collector of Western Americana, not only invited me to be his guest at the Magic Castle but drove to Inglewood Park Cemetery to make a photograph of Siringo's gravesite. Nancy N. Nakasone, at the time a USC graduate student, assisted by researching Los Angeles area newspapers of the 1920s for articles about Siringo. From San Francisco, Keith Lummis, son of Charles Fletcher Lummis and personal friend of Henry Herbert Knibbs, told of his father's reaction to news of Siringo's death and sent me a facsimile copy from the house book at El Alisal. My thanks go to Errol Stevens, head of the Seaver Center for Western History Research at Natural History Museum of Los Angeles

County, for permission to quote from the William S. Hart letters, and to Raymond Thorp, Jr., Placentia, California, who kindly permitted me to quote from his father's article, "Cowboy Charley Siringo."

I am especially indebted to historian W. H. Hutchinson of Chico, California. Hutch not only made suggestions that led to important discoveries, he later read an early draft of the manuscript and made constructive recommendations. One of the pleasures of historical research was discovering the whereabouts and making the acquaintance of Siringo's granddaughters, Carol Siringo McFarland, of Whittier, California, and Betty Siringo Kent, of Westlake Village, both daughters of Lee Roy Siringo. These ladies were very generous in sharing their family memorabilia and information with me. For this as well as permission to quote from their grandfather's letters, I am especially grateful.

Austin Olney, manager, trade division, at Houghton Mifflin Company, in Boston, recalled in an interview his early years with that publisher. His reminiscences provided valuable insights into the character of both Ferris Greenslet, whom he knew, and Ira Rich Kent, who had died shortly before Olney joined the firm. Stella Easland, an associate editor at Houghton Mifflin, made available biographical data on these editors and company personnel of half a century ago. Noted historian J. Evetts Haley of Midland, Texas, gave his own assessment, in an interview, of editors Ferris Greenslet and Ira Kent, whom he had personally known. Haley also recalled his meeting with Siringo in an overheated room in Venice, California, during the winter of 1928, while doing research for his biography of Charles Goodnight that Houghton Mifflin later published. W. H. Bond, librarian, the Houghton Library, Harvard University, Cambridge, Massachusetts, where the Houghton Mifflin Company records are archived, was courteous and helpful. To the Houghton Mifflin Company, who allowed me permission to quote from their letters and company files, I am especially indebted.

In Austin, Texas, colleagues Michael Heaston, Ray Walton, and Kevin MacDonnell all provided assistance in various ways, as did Tuffly Ellis, formerly director of the Texas State Historical Association, and Joe Austell Small, publisher of *True West* magazine. Byron Price, executive director of the National Cowboy Hall of Fame, Oklahoma City, Oklahoma, called my attention to the Cal Polk manuscript in the Panhandle-Plains Historical Museum, Canyon, Texas. Claire Kuehn, archivist-librarian at that institution, was knowledgeable and helpful.

My neighbor and friend of many years, Charles Downing, assisted by keeping a keen eye peeled for anything that might be useful in my research. Harwood P. Hinton, formerly editor of *Arizona and the West* at the University of Arizona, Tucson; George F. O'Neill, assistant vice president, Pinkerton's Inc., New York City; Ruth H. Pierce, Blessing, Texas; Mrs. Arnold Burton, Palacios, Texas; and Mary Armer Earwood, Sonora, Texas, assisted by granting interviews and answering inquiries.

Others to whom I owe thanks are John Terrell Hoyt, Jr., Stockbridge, Massachusetts, grandson of Dr. Henry F. Hoyt, who granted me permission to quote from Dr. Hoyt's letters. William H. Goetzmann, Pulitzer Prize–winning historian at the University of Texas at Austin, allowed me to quote from his and his son's book, *The West of the Imagination*. The excerpt from James D. Horan's *Desperate Men: Revelations from the Sealed Pinkerton Files* is by permission of Doubleday, Inc., New York City, and those portions of Charles Badger Clark, Jr.'s poem, "The Old Cow Man," which Siringo used as an epigraph in *Riata and Spurs,* are quoted by permission of Westerners International, Oklahoma City, Oklahoma.

I am especially grateful to Robert A. Calvert, associate professor of history at Texas A&M University, who read an early draft of the manuscript and, later, a much revised and expanded version. His recommendations and constructive criticism were invaluable. I am also indebted to him for his suggestions concerning populism, social Darwinism, and the early labor movement, all Gilded Age factors that Siringo was not only a part of, but the product of as well. John O. West, professor of English at the University of Texas at El Paso, offered advice and positive recommendations helped make the book a reality. Special thanks are reserved for Orlan Sawey, my English professor at Texas A&I, now a longtime friend and fellow Siringo researcher. Orlan generously shared his own Siringo material with me and allowed me to quote from his fine study, *Charles A. Siringo.* Finally, I thank my wife, Rozetta, for her confidence, encouragement, and long-suffering patience. To all those who have assisted in so many ways I owe whatever success this work might enjoy. Its shortcomings and failures are mine alone.

INTRODUCTION

I might as well ... become educated into
the ways of free America, where all men and
women are considered kings and queens, and
the children kinglets and queenlets.

—from *Two Evil Isms*

IN late August, 1907, a small wiry man, accompanied by his young
bride, alighted from a train at Santa Fe, New Mexico Territory, to
begin a new life on his ranch located just southwest of the city. He
was Charles A. Siringo, a noted lawman, who had recently resigned his
position with Pinkerton's National Detective Agency. Although in his
fifty-third year, Siringo still appeared youthful, thanks to a slender
body and boyish countenance that belied the fact he had lived past the
half-century mark.[1]

Siringo had worked for the Pinkertons since 1886, having begun his
detective career in Chicago with an assignment to the Haymarket anarchist case.[2] Soon thereafter he had been sent to Denver, Colorado,
where the agency needed a detective to work out of its newly opened
office in tracking down lawbreakers. During the next two decades Siringo worked all over the West and Southwest, and even chased outlaws
from as far north as Alaska to as far south as Mexico City. His career
had been predicted by a phrenologist who told him that he had a "fine
head" for becoming a detective.[3]

Siringo did earn a reputation as a determined and tenacious Pinkerton detective, thus bearing out the phrenologist's prediction. Yet, even
before that, he was recognized for his accomplishments as an author.
In 1885 he had written and published his life story in a book entitled *A
Texas Cowboy or, Fifteen Years on the Hurricane Deck of a Spanish
Pony*. The book was immensely popular, particularly with the cowboy
trade, and passed through several publishers during the more than
thirty years it remained in print.[4]

He was born Charles Angelo Siringo on February 7, 1855, in the
"Dutch Settlement" on Matagorda Peninsula in southeast Texas of immigrant parents. His father, an Italian, died when Siringo was one year
old, leaving his Irish mother, Bridgit, the task of supporting Charlie

and his older sister, Catherine.[5] In *A Texas Cowboy* Siringo recounted his experiences as a youth on the Texas coastal plain, the remarriage of his mother and their removal to Illinois, his separation from his mother and sister and his search for them, his several trips on the Mississippi between Saint Louis and New Orleans, his eventual return to Texas and his work as a cowboy on the Rancho Grande for Jonathan and Abel "Shanghai" Pierce, his experiences driving longhorn cattle up the Chisholm Trail to Kansas, and his meeting with and later pursuit of Billy the Kid.[6]

Siringo was barely thirty years old when he completed *A Texas Cowboy*, his first autobiography. Between then and his death forty-three years later, his desire to relate his life's adventures in print was fully realized in four books and partially in two others. Few men were ever as possessed by the autobiographical urge, and for Siringo it seemed to be a never-ending compulsion, his *raison d'être*.[7] It was Siringo's attempt to publish his detective experiences, following his resignation from the agency, that brought the ire of the Pinkertons down on him. Legal confrontations between them raged, on and off, for nearly eighteen years. The intensity of the controversy between Siringo and the Pinkertons now seems puzzling, especially when viewed from the perspective of today's more liberal interpretation of First Amendment rights. However, what may first appear as a strangely curious feud begins to assume form and dimension when it is examined within the context of the times, and with an understanding of the background and the mindset of the principals in the dispute.[8]

It is difficult in our time to appreciate the importance of the Pinkerton Agency and the extent of its power and influence during the late nineteenth century. At that time the most effective crime-fighting organization in the United States was neither the federal government nor the state or local police but a firm of private detectives run by a Scottish immigrant named Allan Pinkerton. Founded in 1850, Pinkerton's National Detective Agency grew over the succeeding decades to become the most respected, the most hated, the most feared, and, above all, the most powerful investigative organization in the country.

In mid-nineteenth-century America there was no statewide or national system for tracking the movements of criminals, and police methods for solving crimes were primitive and haphazard. Crime, in fact, had become a national threat affecting many large cities, where police department effectiveness was frequently vitiated by political corruption. Soon after Allan Pinkerton opened his office in Chicago, his services were sought by business houses, express agencies, banks, and railroads both within and beyond the state of Illinois. He pioneered in the development of modern police investigative methods, including the use of a "rogues' gallery" and the maintenance of a complete file, or dossier, on every suspect investigated. The agency built such a solid reputation for solving major thefts that Chicago's harried thieves began referring to the company as "The Eye" because of the never-sleeping eye that it adopted as a trademark. Eventually, the phrase "private eye" became a universal synonym for all private detectives.

In 1861 Pinkerton became a national hero by foiling an assassination attempt against President-elect Abraham Lincoln. During the Civil War he was called upon to set up the government's first secret service, and his agents uncovered a notorious spy ring in the nation's capital. At war's end Pinkerton resumed his detective agency operations and, as demand for his services increased, he opened offices in Philadelphia and New York. By 1870 his detective agency had become the world's largest. Pinkerton's two sons followed in their father's footsteps, and both made illustrious names for themselves as detectives. William led in linking the agency with the major police forces in Europe in a cooperative exchange of information and assistance that was a forerunner of Interpol. By the time of Robert Pinkerton's death in 1907, London newspapers were referring to the Pinkertons as "America's Scotland Yard."[9]

The rapid growth and prosperity of Pinkerton's National Detective Agency following the Civil War was a microcosm of what was happening to the nation at large. It was a time of enormous economic expansion in the United States, of continuing western migration and settlement, of pacification of the Plains Indians, and of increased European immigration. Out of such diverse channels of human endeavor arose a multitude of problems, and the Pinkertons were involved in many of them.

An intense nationalism pervaded the country, but at the same time the fabric of society was being torn by cynicism and chicanery, by corruption and rampant abuses in the legislative process, and by fraudulent business practices. The jury system was threatened, as it had become common practice to bribe jurors. The civil service was demoralized and corrupt, and abuses abounded in suffrage. Even the White

House was tainted with scandal during the administration of Ulysses S. Grant with the exposure and national disgrace of the Crédit Mobilier. It seemed at times that the entire federal government was for sale, if anyone wanted to buy it, especially Congress. James Russell Lowell alluded to the widespread revelations of moral sickness and decay as the "festering" tidings of "public scandal, private fraud." The American humorist Samuel L. Clemens (Mark Twain) described the times as an "era of incredible rottenness." Clemens and his Hartford, Connecticut, neighbor, Charles Dudley Warner, co-authored a satirical novel on the national character wherein a compendium of all of the more dubious business practices of the times was presented. Its title, *The Gilded Age,* gave the name that has been applied to those years.[10]

As industry flourished and grew, a struggling movement to organize workers into labor unions was also growing and gaining public notice. Strikes frequently led to riots and bloodshed, and it was not uncommon for state militia or armed strikebreakers to be used to quell union-fomented labor unrest. The Pinkertons became involved with labor in the early 1870s when Irish coal miners in Pennsylvania's anthracite counties organized a secret society called the Molly Maguires and perpetrated terrorist activity in the region. Allan Pinkerton sent James McParlan (he would later spell his name McParland) to infiltrate the Mollies so as to put a stop to the killing and destruction of property. Using the name McKenna, McParlan worked undercover for two and a half years until sufficient evidence had been obtained to convict and hang twenty of the terrorists. Although the Molly incidents did not settle the basic labor disputes or have any real effect on conditions in the coal fields, neither has any evidence been produced to indicate that the Molly Maguires were motivated by social injustice. Nevertheless, Pinkerton's participation in a labor case that would become legendary suggested to some an antilabor bias. This belief was reinforced throughout the 1870s and 1880s because of the agency's practice of supplying guards and watchmen for factories where labor disputes were in progress.[11]

During the mid-1880s the unions, including a number of railroad brotherhoods, began to campaign for an eight-hour working day. Most notable was the Knights of Labor, which won impressive strike victories over Jay Gould's southwestern railroad system and other employers. Nowhere was the struggle for the eight-hour day more aggressive than in Chicago, which at that time was a hotbed for convinced anarchists who were playing a prominent role in the movement. It was the detonation of a bomb in Chicago's Haymarket that inflamed Siringo with a desire to help stamp out anarchism.

The Haymarket incident occurred on May 4, 1886, two days after the eruption of violence at the McCormick Reaper Works between locked-out unionists and nonunion workers. After the police were summoned, several of the workers were killed and others injured. Local anarchists, incensed at what they believed was police brutality, called a meeting of workers in the Haymarket to voice their protest. August Spies, a leader among the local anarchists advocating the eighthour day, spoke first and was followed by Albert Parsons, who delivered a longer address. Before the last speaker had finished, a sudden biting wind and drizzle came up, causing many of the 1,200 to 1,300 people to leave for shelter. Those who remained were startled by the appearance of a column of 180 police with orders for the meeting to disperse. Abruptly, and without warning, a bomb was thrown; it exploded near the first rank of police, killing one policeman and injuring sixty-seven others. Of the injured officers, six later died as a result of the bomb explosion. In the confusion and police gunfire that followed, according to official reports, one citizen was killed and twelve others were wounded. The unofficial estimate was five or six times that number.[12]

Siringo, along with his wife and baby daughter, had recently moved to Chicago from Caldwell, Kansas, and had found accommodations with a family on Harrison Avenue. The Haymarket was just a few blocks away, and when Siringo witnessed the scene of carnage the next morning, he began wishing he was a detective so that he could ferret out the bomb thrower and his cohorts. Siringo felt that the proper way to become a lawman was to enter "the greatest detective school on earth—Pinkerton's National Detective Agency." Arming himself with a letter of introduction from a local banker who knew him, he entered the Pinkerton agency offices and submitted his application to William A. Pinkerton. When asked to provide additional references to establish his qualifications, Siringo offered the name of his former employer, David T. Beals, and those of two friends, James H. East, a popular Texas sheriff, and Pat F. Garrett, the slayer of Billy the Kid.[13]

Siringo was hired by William A. Pinkerton and immediately began his training as a detective. The trial of the Haymarket anarchists, his first assignment, opened his eyes as to how anarchism was being fought.

It was an experience, he said, that gave him his first lesson in learning the ways of the world. Siringo was repelled by the false reports being written about anarchists by agency operatives; he said they "would make a decent man's blood boil." There were other evils—perjured testimony, "third degree" brutality, and padded expense accounts—to round out his education in disillusionment. Years later he would write: "The lessons of injustice learned during my first month in the big agency almost caused me to throw up my position in disgust. But I argued in my own mind that the corruption was a sore on the body politic, which no one man could cure—hence, I might as well remain and become educated into the ways of free America, where all men and women are considered kings and queens, the children kinglets and queenlets." [14]

Siringo criticized the Pinkertons for their part in convicting the Haymarket anarchists and sending most of them to their deaths on the basis of flimsy and insufficient evidence. Albert Parsons, George Engel, Adolph Fischer, and August Spies were found guilty and executed simply for being anarchists, and not because the evidence presented proved they had committed a heinous crime. This was Siringo's introduction to what has been described as social Darwinism, or a consequence of it, that nineteenth-century tooth-and-claw philosophy characterized by ruthless business rivalry and unprincipled politics. [15]

From the beginning of his work as a Pinkerton detective, Siringo was obliged to walk a narrow pathway, sometimes choosing assignments that were morally acceptable to him and eschewing those that offended his conscience. However, there were not many of the latter, as most of the time Siringo was able to put aside his personal feelings and perform even those duties he found distasteful. Having once considered the Pinkertons "a model institution," Siringo would eventually denounce the agency as "a school for the making of anarchists, and a disgrace to an enlightened age," but he offered an explanation for having been able to turn his head and continue working for the agency for so many years.

> The question might be asked why I did not show my manhood
> by resigning and exposing this crooked agency in the beginning.
> Exposing it to whom, pray? Not to the officers of the law, I hope.
> In my cowboy simplicity I might have been persuaded to do so
> at the time. But I am glad I did not, for, with my twenty-two years

behind the curtains, I can now see the outcome. It would have resulted in many "sleeps" in the city bullpen, and a few doses of the
"third degree" to try and wring a confession for blackmailing this
notorious institution.[16]

Siringo was aware of the hierarchy within the agency that separated
himself, an obscure cowboy detective at the bottom, from William and
Robert Pinkerton, both nationally prominent and financially secure at
the top. He believed that only a person of consummate financial ability
and prestige could successfully go against the system to oppose its in-
equities. "A man without wealth and influence," he wrote, "trying to
expose the dastardly work of Pinkerton [*sic*] National Detective Agency
would be like a two-year old boy blowing his breath against a cyclone
to stop its force."[17]

The culmination of the Pinkertons' power and influence came in
1892 with the Homestead strike six miles from Pittsburgh. When the
Amalgamated Association of Iron and Steel Workers called a strike the
year before, Henry Frick attempted to continue operation of the Carnegie steel mill. More than one hundred deputy sheriffs were sent to
the site; however, pickets refused to allow them to enter the plant. The
union struck again in 1892, and Frick ordered 300 armed guards from
Robert Pinkerton, having concluded that "it would be necessary to
protect our own property and secure new workmen."

Approaching the Homestead works by boats on the Monongahela,
the Pinkerton men were detected by the strikers, who broke through a
fence the company had erected. Shooting broke out, and after three
unsuccessful assaults, the Pinkerton men surrendered and were held
captive by the strikers who had taken over the plant. Thirteen men
were killed, with many more injured, before the governor sent 7,000
troops to subdue the strikers and remove them from the premises.
During the tumult an anarchist shot and stabbed Frick but failed to
kill him. Eventually, Homestead reopened but with nonunion workers.

Although the Pinkertons came out losers in this encounter, they sustained an even greater loss from the adverse national publicity, which
dealt a severe blow to their prestige and influence. At best, labor activists for years had regarded the Pinkerton agency with suspicious hos-
tility if not outright distrust. If there remained a shred of doubt that the
agency was the bête noire of the labor union movement, Homestead
erased it completely and earned the Pinkerton agency organized la-

bor's everlasting enmity. Robert Pinkerton offered the excuse that they had "never looked for any strike work; it was something which has grown up about our shoulders." It had been a costly lesson for the Pinkertons, and thereafter they never again would furnish guards or become engaged where a labor dispute was involved.[18]

Siringo perceived, and probably correctly, that the Homestead riot, with the wave of moral reform that swept the land immediately afterward, was the high-water mark in the agency's power and influence. Until that time, he said, "A word from W. A. Pinkerton or one of his officers would send any 'scrub' citizen to the scrap heap, or even to the penitentiary. This is no joke, for I have heard of many innocent men being 'railroaded' to prisons, and my information came from inside the circle."[19] In spite of all of the abuses and corruption in the agency that Siringo complained about, he grudgingly admitted: "With all of the agency's faults, I must confess that they do a lot of good work in running down crime for money. If they did not, they could not keep their head above the dirty water in which they constantly flounder."[20]

Siringo's concession was, understandably, a reluctantly confessed understatement. The Pinkerton achievements are very impressive, considering the agency's record against outlaws and train robbers on the Great Plains or their pursuit of international rogues of the Victorian Age. The Pinkerton detectives became so effective as crime fighters that their techniques and pioneering methods are now the fundamentals of modern police procedure worldwide.[21]

Perhaps it was inevitable that Pinkerton's National Detective Agency, born out of a nationwide need for law and order, should itself become ensnared in the same corrupting influence and moral decadence that so pervaded the era. Charlie Siringo and the Pinkertons were all victims, in one way or another, of that strange Victorian morality that characterized the Gilded Age. It was an ethical concept that extolled virtue, that demanded the strict observation of enshrined mores and the avowed profession of community piety, while it ignored the moral chaos being engendered and the social injustices that abounded.

As for anarchism, the political ideology that led Siringo to become a Pinkerton man in the first place, its recondite origin remained remote and of little interest to him. Both Siringo and the Pinkerton brothers probably had only a dim understanding of its revolutionary tenets, though they were certain that anarchism was a destabilizing threat to society. It is interesting and perhaps ironic that Siringo, a first-generation American like his employers, William and Robert Pinkerton, regarded anarchists as bomb-throwing foreigners, even though Albert Parsons, one of the Haymarket eight, had ancestors in this country before the American Revolution.[22]

The irony goes further. Allan Pinkerton—once a fugitive radical in his native Scotland, a friend of anarchist George Julian Harney, a champion of labor and what he believed was the exploited working man—quickly switched to the side of the Establishment following his taste of financial success and his rise to prominence in the United States. His sons, in like manner, were awed by the powerful corporations they represented and were wedded to the notion that the end justifies the means. Although the Pinkertons were true believers in the Horatio Alger success stories, they were also charter members in the savage world of social Darwinism. As such, they tended to distort the principles of free enterprise by resisting any changes in the status quo and by attempting to deny the equal opportunities of freedom to those with whom they disagreed.[23]

By the time of Siringo's open conflict with the Pinkertons, only William remained as head of the agency, assisted by his nephew Allan. William was autocratic to a degree, strong willed, ultra-conservative, sometimes unbearably touchy, opinionated, and a staunch advocate of nineteenth-century economic orthodoxy. The "Big Eye," as he was known to his employees, was not the type of man to look tolerantly on the public revelations of company affairs by a former subordinate.[24]

Charlie Siringo, by contrast, was an impetuous man, sometimes simplistic in his thinking, and yet shrewd in his perception of human nature. His views of the economic and political issues of the day were often pragmatic, if not outright populist, and therefore typical of many working men in the West. Like William Pinkerton, Charlie could be stubborn, obstinate, and somewhat opinionated, but these qualities were balanced by a cowboy's honesty, a keen sense of humor, and a free-spirited, devil-may-care lust for life.

Although Siringo marched in concert with most nineteenth-century ideas, he seemed in some ways cut from the same cloth as Mark Twain's Huckleberry Finn. Like "Huck," Charlie was sometimes torn between obeying the inclinations of "a sound heart" or conforming to the dictates of "a deformed conscience." This similarity was due to Siringo's having to reconcile his conscience to his sometimes distasteful duties as a Pinkerton detective. In the *Adventures of Huckleberry Finn* both the author and the central character sought to reject the community, or at least maintain a critical distance from it, in order to win freedom from the tyranny of conscience.

Siringo could maintain his distance from the abuses of his colleagues and the corruption sanctioned within the agency by mounting his horse and pursuing outlaws on his own terms. Many times, however, his choices were not clear-cut. The one dark blot on his conscience, he said, was caused by having to work against coal miners in their fight for equity. Although he only reported the facts, he considered what he did to be a disgrace, knowing that "the truth would be used to retard justice" to a class of men who were poorly paid and who risked their lives every time they entered "a dirty coal mine." Unlike Huck Finn, whose "deformed conscience" in the novel continually suffers defeat, Siringo often managed to bend his conscience by simply looking the other way.[25]

The Pinkertons, on the other hand, and especially William, never wavered in their commitment to the ethos of the times. Their very nature as well as their business achievements were the product of an elemental tenacity, restlessness, drive, and especially an intense partisanship. As their biographer, James Horan, wrote: "you were either with them, completely, entirely, absolutely, without question—or you were against them and their world. The reward for unquestioning loyalty was their unswerving, never ending friendship." But cross them, and they could unleash a venom and a fury that could numb most any adversary. It seems inevitable, in retrospect, that Charlie Siringo and the Pinkertons, all dynamic, determined, and intensely individualistic, would come into conflict with one another.[26]

Siringo's arrival in Santa Fe in 1907 essentially marked the end of his Pinkerton association and the beginning of his new career as a resident New Mexico rancher, writer, and free-lance detective. Nearly one-third of his life still lay ahead of him, and it was during the next twenty years that he would do most of his autobiographical writing. From Siringo's perspective, his youthful adventures as a frontier cowboy and subsequent experiences as a Pinkerton detective were the areas in which he believed readers would be most interested. At the time he probably was right.

Siringo's fame during this later period rested on two of his autobiographies: *A Texas Cowboy* (1885), describing his life to age thirty, and *A Cowboy Detective* (1912), which followed his detective career through age fifty-two. *Riata and Spurs* (1927), a mature composite of the two preceding titles and his only book issued by a major publisher, came near the end of his life. It was *Riata and Spurs* that brought him national recognition as an authentic western character. In the more than sixty years since Siringo's death, all of the biographies and biographical sketches about him have been based almost exclusively on his own writings. These, of course, describe only the first two-thirds of his life. His years after leaving the Pinkerton agency, which were almost as many as his years with the company, are usually given only perfunctory mention or, at best, a brief treatment.

Part of the reason for Siringo's popularity is that he wrote in a natural, amusing, and unassuming style. The image he created is a self-serving portrait of a bold, gregarious, and engaging man of the West. One interpreter of the cowboy wrote that if "Siringo is to be 'explained' the explanation lies in a paradox: a richly sentimental mind expressing itself in reticence, reserve, sententiousness, [and] apparent indifference." Though this may be sufficient to characterize Siringo the cowboy, it only scratches the surface of Siringo the man. A more complete picture does show Siringo as a unique individual, but it also reveals that he was a man flawed in ways common to the human condition, and that his character was not only complex but sometimes even contradictory. Samuel Clemens's statement, that "everyone is a moon and has a dark side which he never shows to anybody" seems especially appropriate when considering the puzzling and enigmatic aspects of Siringo's nature. An occasional glimpse at Siringo's dark side does indeed provide insight into his character. These glimpses show, that although his books made him appear larger than life, he was in fact an ordinary man endowed with unusual qualities and traits, some of which, to say the least, were less than noble. If the revelation of his imperfections and shortcomings diminishes his image as an admirable figure, it certainly does not make him a less interesting one.[27]

However, the purpose of *Siringo* is not to debunk or psychoanalyze, but to follow Charlie Siringo as he evolved from a twenty-two-year-old wild and carefree cowboy into a clever, audacious, and purposeful cowboy detective. It traces the high points of his career with the Pinkerton agency and examines his adventures, along with his attitudes and personal convictions, setting these against the political, social, and moral background of American thought in the late nineteenth and early twentieth centuries. It is also the story of Siringo's life after leaving the

Pinkerton agency, of his conflicts with them, of his years as a Santa Fe rancher and a New Mexico Ranger. It is a personal story of love and romance, of human understanding and humane tenderness, of enduring and compassionate friendships, and of success, disappointment, and failure. Finally, it is the story of an ill and aging frontiersman struggling for survival in an urban environment, a nineteenth-century man who had become an anachronism in a twentieth-century world that had passed him by.

PART I
THE EARLY YEARS, 1877–1890

Oh, I am a jolly cowboy,
From Texas now I hail,
Give me my saddle and pony
And I'm ready for the trail.
I love the rolling prairie
Where we are free from care and strife,
And behind a herd of long-horns,
I will journey all my life.

—from *The Song Companion of a Lone Star Cowboy*

1 / GENESIS OF A
COWBOY DETECTIVE

C HARLIE SIRINGO always claimed that the pathway that led him to a career with Pinkerton was revealed one evening in Caldwell, Kansas, with the amusing declarations of a blind phrenologist. On that occasion the phrenologist made his determination after pronouncing, much to the enjoyment of those present, that Siringo had a "mule's head" because he had felt a large "stubborn bump" that indicated him to be as stubborn as a mule. The phrenologist then made his prediction that Siringo would find success as a detective, a newspaper editor, or a stock raiser. It was toward the detective work that Siringo leaned the most.

Years later, when Siringo rewrote his autobiography for the last time under the title *Riata and Spurs,* he still offered this experience with the phrenologist as the incident that turned him from cowboy and cowboy-merchant to a career as a cowboy detective.[1] In reality, curiously enough, it was his decision to celebrate a national holiday in Dodge City seven years earlier that marked a turning point in his life and ordained his destiny. At the same time, a near-fatal incident in a Dodge City saloon and dancehall came uncomfortably close to terminating that destiny.

It was July 4, 1877, and Siringo had ridden into Dodge the day before with one of the Littlefield cattle herds from Texas that was bound for Nebraska, or possibly Montana. Although this was his second trip up the Chisholm Trail, it was his first visit to Dodge City, which, he said, had become the "long-horn cattle center of the Universe." Siringo drew his pay and left the herd so that he could help celebrate the nation's Independence Day in "the toughest cattle town on earth."

Dodge had already earned its reputation for toughness, and its citizens, in fact, seemed proud of their graveyard in Boot Hill cemetery where eighty of its eighty-one occupants had died with their boots on.

The Atchison, Topeka & Santa Fe Railway was building west from Dodge at that time, and the town was filled with the boisterous frontier roustabouts and drifters who generally followed the path of a new railroad. Five miles distant was the government post of Fort Dodge, and its soldiers added color and frequently mischief to the town's raucous character. Dodge was also the outfitting center for buffalo hunters within a radius of hundreds of miles, and these men, mostly greasy, long-haired, and bearded, provided a conspicuous and often odoriferous contrast in a town teeming with tough characters.[2]

One of the largest watering holes south of the tracks was the Lone Star Dancehall. It was tremendously popular with the Texan cowboy trade, as its name would indicate, and it was managed by the noted William Barclay ("Bat") Masterson along with his partner, Ben Springer. On this occasion Masterson was working as the night barkeeper. Siringo, joined by Wess Adams, an old cowboy friend, observed that the festivities in a number of dancehalls were in full swing, but they settled on the Lone Star because the girls there seemed better looking and the name had a Texas flavor. Once inside, Siringo and Adams found "the hall was jammed full of free-and-easy girls" and wild and woolly cowboys.

About 11:00 P.M. Adams called Siringo outside and told him how he had been insulted by a big long-haired buffalo hunter. Adams thought this fellow ought to be taught a lesson to show him that the killers of buffalo are not in the cowboy class. He then asked Siringo if he would stay with him in case a fight resulted. Charlie thought it would be a disgrace for a cowboy to quit his chum in time of danger, so he told Adams that in case of trouble he would stay with him "till Hades froze up solid."

In anticipation of having to make a hurried exit, the two cowboys took their horses out of the livery stable and tied them in front of the Lone Star Dancehall. Adams and Siringo reentered the Lone Star, both wearing their Colt .45 pistols. When the fight started, Bat Masterson, who was behind the bar, began throwing heavy beer glasses in Siringo's direction. One beer glass glanced off the side of Charlie's head and hit a wall nearby. Siringo said later that the glass "clipped [him] behind the right ear and didn't feel like a mother's kiss, either." The glass that struck Charlie shattered against the wall, and a shard hit him in the face, drawing blood. Although about a dozen cowboys and buffalo hunters were engaged in the brawl, there wasn't a shot fired, but in two instances pistols were used as clubs to knock men down.

During the melee one of the smelly hide hunters rammed a skinning knife into Adams's back, inflicting a severe stab wound. Siringo had to help drag his friend outside through a side door of the hall to their horses. After they mounted up, Joe Mason, a city policeman, confronted the pair and tried to arrest them. Mason was at a disadvantage, being on foot, and the two cowboys ran him into an alley. Then they galloped out of town, yelling cowboy fashion and shooting off their pistols, or, as Siringo put it, "we cut sticks out of there a-helling." Charlie later claimed that both he and Adams were half-drunk from the poisonous liquor that Bat Masterson had passed to them over the bar.[3]

When the two men reached the stockyard a mile east of town, they dismounted and went into a little board shanty to determine the severity of Wess Adams's injury. Siringo laid Adams on his stomach, pulled his shirt over his shoulders, and found a horrible knife cut under his right shoulder blade. The knife had been thrust in and then brought around in a semicircle in the shape of a large horseshoe. His clothing was saturated with blood, and the flesh stood out from the wound several inches. Siringo told Adams to lie there until he could ride back into town to get medicine, along with a needle and thread to sew up the wound.

Mounting his pet horse, Whiskey Pete, Siringo rode fast, but nearing town he became "foxy," thinking the officers might be watching for their return. So instead of proceeding directly toward Dodge, he diverted south, riding in a deep arroyo, until he struck the railroad tracks, which he followed into town. After purchasing needles, thread, sticking plaster, and a candle, he returned to the stockyard the same way he had come.[4]

Siringo did not know it at the time, but his foxiness probably saved his life. Bat Masterson, along with several officers, had followed Siringo and Adams to the edge of town, and thinking they might return, they concealed themselves from view. Armed with rifles and shotguns, they intended to make angels of these two wayward cowboys and thus increase the population of Boot Hill cemetery.[5]

Siringo managed to avoid Masterson's posse and made it back to the shanty, where he found Adams groaning with pain. Adams "kicked like a bronco steer" when Charlie put his knee to the wound to force the swollen flesh back into place so that it could be sewn up. Try as he might, he could not get the protruding flesh pushed back level with the surrounding flesh, so he discarded his needle and thread and patched poor Adams up as best he could with the sticking plaster.

Somehow, Charlie then managed to get his companion back on his horse. After an eighteen-mile ride, with Siringo having to hold Adams in the saddle the last few miles because of his loss of blood, the two foolish cowboys arrived at the steer camp of David T. Beals. It was well after sunup when the two celebrants dismounted, with Adams weak from his injury and both exhausted by their ordeal. Adams was laid up for two weeks but eventually recovered.

David Beals and his partner, W. H. "Deacon" Bates, were wealthy shoe manufacturers from Boston who had been operating a ranch on the Arkansas River near Granada, Colorado. Beals hired Siringo to accompany a herd of steers into the Texas Panhandle where the LX, a new and larger ranch, was to be established. Deacon Bates was to accompany the trail drive for the purpose of selecting the new range, while Beals remained in Dodge City with Erskine Clement, another partner, to purchase more cattle.[6]

The next morning Siringo, along with ten other men including Bates, struck out in a southwesterly direction driving a herd of 2,500 steers. Bill Allen of Corpus Christi bossed the herd while "Owl Head" Johnson cooked and drove the wagon. After six days they crossed the Cimarron River and sighted the first large herd of buffalo. Upon reaching Blue Creek, a tributary to the South Canadian River, they set up a temporary camp. Bates, taking Siringo with him, struck out to hunt the range, which had to be large enough for at least 50,000 cattle. Three days later they landed in Tascosa, a quiet little town on the Canadian consisting of half a dozen Mexican families and a store owned by Howard and Rinehart. Following the river downstream some twenty-five miles, they arrived at the mouth of Pitcher Creek, where a small trading post was located. With some apprehension, Bates and Siringo observed an estimated three hundred Apache Indians camped across the river from them. About a mile east of Pitcher Creek, Bates selected the site that would be the center of the LX Ranch.

After returning to the camp at Blue Creek, the herd was moved by the cowboys to the Canadian River and turned loose. "Sign camps" were established around a vast range, which extended twenty miles up the river and the same distance down the stream, then twenty miles south to the foot of the Llano Estacado (Staked Plains), and another twenty miles north to the foot of what was called the North Staked Plains. About October 1 four more herds arrived: three from Dodge and one from the company's ranch near Granada, Colorado. Siringo said that "by the time snow began to fall this grassy LX range contained thousands upon thousands of cattle." Bill Allen returned home to the balmy brush country of south Texas and was replaced by W. C. "Bill" Moore.[7]

It was during these years as an LX cowboy that Siringo met the young outlaw William H. Bonney, better known as Billy the Kid. Although his association with the Kid lasted only a few weeks, it made a profound and lifelong impression on him. His meeting with Billy occurred in the fall of 1878 at LX Ranch headquarters. Charlie had just ridden 225 miles from Dodge City, after having transported 400 head of cattle that had been shipped by rail to Chicago.

> I arrived at the headquarters ranch late in the evening. A crowd of strangers were playing cards under a cottonwood tree near by. The cook informed me that they were Billy the Kid and his Lincoln County, New Mexico, warriors.
>
> When the cook rang the supper bell, these strangers ran for the long table. After being introduced, I found myself seated by the side of good-natured Billy the Kid. Henry Brown, Fred White and Tom O'Phalliard [*sic*] are the only names of this outlaw gang that I can recall. . . . During the next few weeks Billy the Kid and I became quite chummy. After selling out the band of ponies he and his gang had stolen from the Seven River Warriors, in New Mexico, he left the Canadian River country, and I never saw him again.[8]

Two years later Siringo was ordered by LX manager W. C. Moore to lead a posse of "fighting cowboys" into New Mexico to recover cattle the Kid had stolen from the LX and other Panhandle ranches. Bill Moore, who was also known as "Outlaw Bill" because he was a fugitive from two widely separated ranges, had not reformed but instead was rustling LX calves and had already enlisted two LX cowboys to join him in throwing the wide loop. Siringo had high regard for Moore as a cowman and said he "was a natural leader of men," but he refused when invited to participate in these thefts. It is believed that

Moore was not so much interested in the recovery of stolen cattle, or the apprehension of Billy the Kid, as he was in getting rid of the LX cowboys who disapproved of what he was doing.

Siringo's fighting crew consisted of Frank "Big Foot Wallace" Clifford, James H. East, Cal Polk, Lon Chambers, and Lee Hall. On November 16, 1880, the group left the ranch and headed for Tascosa, where they were joined by five riders from the Littlefield crew, led by Bob Roberson, with a mess wagon and a cook. Frank Stewart, a man hired by Canadian River ranchmen to locate stolen cattle, and three other men also joined the group. Although the Kid's capture or death may have mattered little to Bill Moore, it was important to other Panhandle outfits that had lost a great many cattle.

At San Lorenzo, New Mexico Territory, Siringo sent his men on ahead to Anton Chico on the Pecos River, where they were to lay over until he rejoined them. In the meantime he went to Las Vegas to buy a supply of corn, food, and ammunition. Charlie found Las Vegas to be "a swift dancehall town," and the first night of his arrival he began playing monte and did not stop until he had gambled away all $300 of his LX expense money plus another $100 Bob Roberson had given him to buy supplies for his group. Fortunately, according to Siringo, a Las Vegas merchant by the name of Van Houton extended credit to the LX Company and provided some of the goods he needed.[9]

Meanwhile, Charlie's posse had gone on to Anton Chico where, according to Jim East, they spent all the money they had "buying whiskey, playing monte, betting on rooster fights and horse races, and going to *bailes* with the Mexican girls—thinking Charlie would soon be in with the grub." Ten days later, when Charlie arrived in Anton Chico, his men told him that a few nights earlier Billy the Kid and his gang had slipped into town and stolen some fresh horses. They had come from the White Oaks country, 105 miles south.

The morning after Siringo and his men pulled out for White Oaks, Pat Garrett, the sheriff of Lincoln County, along with his brother-in-law, Barney Mason, rode into their camp. They had heard the Texans were coming and had ridden to intercept them. Garrett asked for volunteers to join his posse to go after the Kid, whom he believed to be at Fort Sumner with three or four hundred head of cattle. Jim East observed that Garrett "was a man of few words and said what he wanted." Garrett warned that there was likely to be some fighting and he wanted only those to go who were willing. Lee Hall, Jim East, and Lon Chambers volunteered from Siringo's group, while Tom Emory, Louis Boze-man, and Bob Williams agreed to go from the Littlefield outfit. Frank Stewart, who was on his own, also opted to join Garrett's posse.

Siringo, in relating the incident, said that Garrett asked him for some of his men to help him go after the Kid, but he made no explanation as to why he did not volunteer himself. Instead, Siringo, Rober-son, and the remaining cowboys struck out for White Oaks in a raging snowstorm to await the return of Garrett's posse. Jim East claimed that Siringo, "after gambling off the money for our chuck," was asked to go along but "backed down" without giving a reason. "We didn't want him to," commented East peevishly, as "we were [all] a little huffy, and would have been ashamed not to go with Garrett our-selves." Siringo later maintained that his orders from Moore were spe-cific: "Stay over there until you get those cattle or bust the LX Com-pany," Moore had told him. Then he added, "You can hire all the men you need; but don't undertake . . . [the Kid's] capture until you have first secured the [stolen LX] cattle." [10]

The first word they received concerning Billy the Kid came with the arrival from Fort Sumner of Lee Hall, Lon Chambers, and Louis Boze-man. They related how Garrett and his men had captured the young outlaw after a chase from Fort Sumner to Stinking Springs and a suc-cession of gunfire exchanges in which Tom O'Folliard and Charlie Bowdre were killed. Tom Emory and Jim East accompanied the sheriff and his prisoners to Las Vegas, where the railroad conveyed Billy to the penitentiary at Santa Fe for safekeeping.

As a member of Garrett's posse, Jim East liked his taste of law en-forcement, and upon his arrival in White Oaks he told Siringo he wanted to return to Tascosa so he could run for sheriff of Oldham County. Siringo, meanwhile, had received permission from LX man-ager Bill Moore to stay in the White Oaks area to gather up any LX cattle that might be in the country.

Charlie knew that Billy the Kid had been selling stolen cattle to Pat Coghlan, a fiery, muscular Tularosa rancher with an unsavory reputa-tion for dealing in rustled beef. When he found a number of LX hides, some freshly butchered, in Coghlan's slaughterhouse, he sought out the old Irishman, known as the "King of the Tularosa," and warned him that he planned to search his range for more stolen LX cattle. In an attempt to throw Siringo off guard, Coghlan told him he would not butcher any more cattle bearing the LX brand. Instead, he set a trap to murder Siringo so as to avoid being prosecuted for the LX hides found in his slaughterhouse. Siringo managed to foil this assassination attempt and eventually made his way back to Texas and the LX Ranch with 2,500 head of cattle he and his men had rounded up. Upon his return he learned that Outlaw Bill Moore had quit the LX company so that he could attend to his own cattle. Beals commended Siringo for his seven months' work in New Mexico and said he planned to recommend that he be promoted to replace Moore as manager. Beal's partners, however, objected to Siringo, as they considered him too wild for a position of responsibility.[11]

While Siringo was dealing with Coghlan and rounding up LX cattle, Billy the Kid was transferred to Mesilla, in Doña Ana County, to stand trial for the murder of Sheriff William Brady. In less than two weeks Billy was tried and found guilty, and his execution date was set for May 13, 1881. He was moved to Lincoln County and delivered to Sheriff Pat Garrett to await his fate. On April 28, while Garrett was collecting taxes in White Oaks, Billy managed to escape, killing his two guards in the process. Garrett immediately began a relentless pursuit of the Kid, whose notoriety by then had begun attracting attention throughout the Southwest.

On July 14, 1881, less than one month after Siringo's return to the LX Ranch, Billy the Kid was shot and killed by Sheriff Pat Garrett at Fort Sumner, New Mexico Territory. Charlie liked the exuberant Billy, and during his seven-month "pursuit" had shown a disinclination, for whatever reason, to participate in the capture of the young outlaw. In fact, to the consternation and dismay of some of his saddlemates, he had spurned an opportunity to ride with Pat Garrett's posse. Instead, he concentrated his efforts, as he claimed he had been instructed to do, in searching the country for stolen LX cattle.[12]

That fall, Charlie and Lon Chambers returned to New Mexico to appear as witnesses at Lincoln against Pat Coghlan. Upon their arrival they learned that a change of venue to Doña Ana County had shifted the site of the trial to Mesilla on the Rio Grande. The trial date was not until the first Monday in April, 1882, so Siringo managed to pass the time in a characteristic odyssey of adventures. One was his meeting with Ash Upson, an itinerant newspaperman, who was then living at Pat Garrett's ranch near Roswell.

Siringo and Upson traveled in a buggy together to Pecos, Texas, to meet Garrett, who was due to arrive on the Texas Pacific Railroad. It was on this trip that Siringo learned much of Billy the Kid's early history, as Upson claimed to have known Billy from childhood. Unfortunately, most of Upson's information was grossly inaccurate and became the foundation of the Billy the Kid legend. Billy's daring outlawry and violent death caused Siringo to regard the Kid almost as one would a cult figure, despite the brevity of his involvement with the youthful gunman. His intense interest and fascination with the Billy the Kid would never waver and would remain with him throughout his life.[13]

When the time came for Siringo to appear in Mesilla for Coghlan's trial, it appeared that his trip had been in vain. Coghlan's attorney advised him to plead guilty to the charge of butchering stolen cattle rather than submitting to a trial. Instead of going to the penitentiary, as Siringo had hoped, Coghlan walked out of court after paying a $250 fine and court costs.

Siringo did not hurry to return to the LX Ranch. He dallied about Las Cruces, where a pretty girl from a well-to-do Mexican family caught his eye. He considered staking out a government claim for a homestead and then seeking the young lady's hand in marriage. After examining some land in Dog Canyon, he continued on to Tularosa. By then, his ardor having cooled some, he changed his mind about settling down. At Lincoln, Charlie laid over a few days to visit with Pat Garrett and his deputy, John W. Poe, and the saga of Billy's last days was retold. After a final stop at White Oaks to visit with friends, Siringo finally arrived at the LX Ranch in the Texas Panhandle, after an absence of eight months, and after having ridden horseback some three thousand miles.[14]

Charlie Siringo probably did not realize it when he returned to the LX Ranch, but the seeds of his destiny were now firmly planted. Since going to work for David T. Beals as an LX cowboy, Siringo had made the acquaintance of a young but soon-to-become notorious outlaw; he had led a posse of "fighting cowboys" to secure the return of stolen cattle; he had met Pat Garrett, who would win recognition as the slayer of Billy the Kid; he had confronted and appeared in court against a man who dealt in rustled beef; and he had managed to foil as assassination attempt on his life. At one time Siringo thought he had found his métier in being a cowboy and, apart from his other skills acquired later, he would always consider himself as such. Yet, he had experienced a new kind of adventure with thrills and challenges that were far removed from the prosaic duties he had known as a cowboy on the open range.

He might have been aware that the days of the open range were nearing an end, and in anticipation of it he could see that his own days as a wild and carefree cowpuncher were also numbered. Yet it is clear, from his later writings, that Siringo considered his New Mexico experience as merely an exciting diversion. He failed to recognize that it was pointing him away from the cowboy life, toward a profession associated with law enforcement. Siringo resumed his cowboy duties and continued working for the LX company until an unpredictable series of incidents began to manifest new directions in his life.

The first in this chain of events occurred in the fall of 1883 when David Beals purchased a farm two miles south of Caldwell, Kansas, on which to winter the LX cow ponies. At that time Charlie had been riding with his outfit in the western part of the Indian Territory gathering lost LX steers. They did not finish their work until the last part of November, when they arrived with their herd in Caldwell. When Beals told Siringo he was putting him in charge of the horse farm south of town, Charlie promptly bought some town lots and contracted for the building of a new frame residence. He then took leave long enough to return by train to Texas to get his mother, who was living on Cash's Creek near Matagorda Bay. He arrived back in Caldwell with his mother just a few days before Christmas. Siringo then took charge of the LX horse farm and, in his words, "put in a pleasant winter."

The second incident, which brought him closer to the end of his cowboy days, began on March 1, 1884, when he received a letter from Mr. Beals in Boston ordering him to take his crew of cowboys and cow ponies back to the LX Ranch in the Texas Panhandle. That night, after receiving his orders, Siringo attended church with Miss May Beals, a niece of David T. Beals. When church was over, she introduced him to her pretty little fifteen-year-old black-eyed chum, Mamie Lloyd. Charlie said he was "a sure-enough locoed cowboy—up to my ears in love," but he went to work with "a brave heart and [his] face lined with brass." He said it took plenty of brass to win the young beauty who was the only daughter of H. Clay Lloyd of Shelbyville, Illinois. Six days later, he and Mamie were married in the Phillips Hotel in Wellington, Kansas.

Three days after his wedding Siringo started for the Texas Panhandle, in charge of twenty-five cowboys, 100 cow ponies, and six mess wagons. By September 1 he was back in Caldwell with 800 fat steers. Beals ordered him to return at once to bring another herd, but Siringo, after obediently starting out, changed his mind, as he did not want to leave his young wife, who was pregnant. "I hated to quit the LX out-fit," Siringo would later write, "as Mr. David T. Beals was the best man I had ever worked for. He was an honest, broad-gauge cattle man." [15]

With his wife and mother to support and having given up his em-ployment as a cowboy, Siringo put on the suspenders of a merchant. He opened up a tobacco store featuring Oklahoma Boomer Cigars and not long afterward expanded his enterprise to include an "ice cream and oyster parlor." Siringo did well as a merchant and soon had five clerks and attendants in his employ. He was a believer in advertising and ran regular ads in the local paper. One of his advertisements in the *Caldwell Journal* offered the public "a good lunch, with a hot cup of coffee—none of your weak jim-crow stuff, but genuine cowpuncher coffee that will almost stand alone—thrown in." For a year and a half, from the fall of 1884 to the spring of 1886, Charlie and Mamie lived in Caldwell while Charlie pursued his career as a storekeeper. On Febru-ary 28, 1885, a daughter was born to Charlie and Mamie. They named her Viola. [16]

Siringo must have realized that an era in his life had been com-pleted, for it was about this time that he began writing his autobiogra-phy, *A Texas Cowboy or, Fifteen Years on the Hurricane Deck of a Spanish Pony*. The book was published in the fall of 1885, and the small edition was soon sold out by subscription. Because *A Texas Cowboy* had been an immediate success, Siringo wanted to get out a larger, second printing of the book. The following spring he gave up merchandising and moved his family to Chicago, where he could see to the publication of a second edition of *A Texas Cowboy*. This was the third link in the chain of incidents bridging Siringo's transition from his first profession of being a cowboy to his second, that of being a detective. On May 4, 1886, the Haymarket bomb explosion occurred, the final circumstance that thrust Siringo into a new career as a detec-tive with Pinkerton's National Detective Agency. That October the agency ordered Siringo to Denver, and Charlie moved Mamie and Viola to the city that would be his home base throughout his years as a Pinkerton detective. [17]

2 / LEARNING THE TRADE, WITH SUCCESSES AND SORROWS

SIRINGO's disillusionment with the Pinkertons began almost the moment William A. Pinkerton told him his credentials were satisfactory and that he could begin his training as an operative. Pinkerton told Charlie what his weekly salary would be, to begin with, and that he could expect raises as his work justified it. Then, almost as an aside, he added, "although there is more money in the business than the salary." [1] At the time Siringo thought it best not to question his employer as to what he meant.

He was not long in finding out. After the anarchist case he was sent to Cincinnati, Ohio, to work for a European nation against an Irish organization. On this assignment, Siringo said, he learned "some new lessons in grafting, but, as I benefited by this graft, I had no kick coming."

> I had charged regular rates for hotel and drinking expenses, but on returning to Chicago Assistant Superintendent McGinn had me make new expense bills, as he said the client was wealthy and it was the custom of the agency to allow their operatives to over-charge, so as to make extra money, thereby swelling the regular weekly salary paid by the agency. In this way, they could keep good men in their employ without paying a high salary. I remarked that it did not look right. He replied that if I remained in the business I would have to do it, as it would not be fair to other operatives who might be working on the same case for me to put in smaller bills than they did. I made out the new bills and doubled the hotel and drinking expenses. Of course, this added extra greenbacks for the lining of my own pockets. [2]

Siringo later admitted that during his years with the agency his salary was raised several times, yet his overcharges against clients added up to more than his salary. Charlie was glad when W. A. Pinkerton ordered him to move to Denver, Colorado, where he was to work out of a newly established office under the direction of superintendent Eams. Pinkerton expected the Denver branch would have a lot of cattle and ranch work requiring the expertise of a cowboy detective to handle it.

Charlie, with his small family, boarded a Pullman sleeper in late October and headed west to his new assignment. Their first quarters in Denver were in the home of superintendent Eams and his family. Ignoring the appearance of ingratitude, Siringo would later claim that by sharing Eams's roof he was able to learn "many new lessons in the crooked deals of the agency." Eams had been an assistant superintendent in Chicago for years and was a trusted fixture in the Pinkerton organization. As such, he had been allowed to pick his own operatives from those in Chicago who were to accompany him. Siringo was the only detective assigned to Denver who was not of Eams's choosing.[3]

In associating with these detectives, Siringo soon found out that Eams had made a good selection "when it came to genuine thieving toughs."

> But the king-bees of the "bunch" were "Doc" Williams and Pat Barry, the latter several years later being made chief of police of Portland, Oregon.
>
> This "Doc" Williams was one . . . who made false reports against the anarchists in Chicago. He was a once noted safe blower and was sent to an eastern penitentiary for safe blowing and robbery. He delighted in telling of how Mr. W. A. Pinkerton secured his pardon from the penitentiary in order to make him a trusted detective in his agency.
>
> "Doc" Williams and "Pat" Barry kept their trunks in the operatives' room full of stolen clothes, jewelry, etc. They would rob merchants while doing work for them. . . .
>
> These men gloried in telling of their many steals and other crimes committed in Chicago while employed by the agency. . . . Still one of the agency's favorite brags is that not since the establishment of the institution has one of their men been convicted of a crime.[4]

Siringo soon found a house into which he moved his family, having spent as little time as possible being the recipient of Eams's hospitality. While Mamie began anew the task of housekeeping during their first winter in Denver, Charlie spent his time doing what was called "city work." This included everything from working on divorce cases and shadowing millionaires, who he said "did not have the foresight to become clients of the big agency," to helping break up a gang of crooked streetcar conductors. These conductors had duplicate punches to ring in on the company, and each man was fraudulently making from ten to twenty dollars a day. Siringo did make short trips out into the mountains to work on a few criminal cases, but it was not until the early spring of 1887 that he was sent on his first cowboy operation.

In Archuleta County, in southwestern Colorado on the New Mexico border, a political dispute had gotten out of hand. The newspapers were calling it an uprising of anarchists, but according to Siringo "it was anarchy against anarchy, with the school of anarchy, my agency, as the third party." Archuleta County contained only seventy-five voters, mostly white, but the county government was controlled by the Archuletas, wealthy Hispanic sheepmen of Amargo, New Mexico, who sent their sheep herders into the county to vote on election day. This caused the Anglos to rebel, and, at the point of guns, they marched the five county commissioners out of Pagosa Springs, the county seat, and over the line into New Mexico. They were warned never to return, at the peril of their lives.[5]

In order to hold their offices by law, the county commissioners had to hold a meeting in the courthouse at Pagosa Springs within sixty days. One of the expelled officials went to Denver and hired Pinkerton's National Detective Agency to break up the insurgents and help restore the commissioners to office. Charlie Siringo was detailed to handle the assignment. In Durango, at the extreme southwestern part of Colorado, Siringo bought a horse and saddle and rode the sixty miles to Pagosa Springs. There, as a supposed Texas outlaw, he was to join the insurgents. The deposed commissioners, meanwhile, along with the county attorney and the county judge, arrived from Amargo, New Mexico, with sixty well-armed and mounted New Mexican warriors. The insurgents, with Siringo now one of them, numbered seventy-five; they met the New Mexicans at the bridge spanning the swiftly flowing San Juan River. A fight was avoided when the New

Mexicans withdrew a short distance and pitched camp in an abandoned government post.

Guards were kept on the bridge night and day for several days, and during this time Siringo managed to foil two assassination attempts against the New Mexican officials. His own life came very close to being put in jeopardy as he sneaked back and forth between the two camps. A truce was finally reached when the insurgents were promised an equal division of the political spoils. The county officials were then allowed to hold their meeting to satisfy the conditions of the law. Afterward, they departed for their homes in Amargo. With the case wrapped up, Siringo had only to appear and testify before a grand jury that was later convened in Durango. As a result, sixteen of the insurgent leaders were indicted for running the county officials out of the state and burning their property.[6]

On his return to Denver, Siringo was immediately dispatched to Mexico City to try to locate a Wells Fargo robber who had stolen $10,000 (a princely sum in those days) during a train wreck at La Junta, Colorado. Siringo found his man in Mexico City and trailed him to his home in Leavenworth, Kansas, where he was arrested and put behind bars. Siringo said later that he was kept "so busy and constantly on the jump" at the time that he never bothered to find out how many years in the penitentiary the subject of his chase received.

Siringo's next assignment took him to the White River country in western Colorado. After that he was assigned to a case in Wyoming. These were the first of many cases that would develop his skills and test his prowess as a cowboy detective. During the winter months Charlie returned to Denver, where his time was occupied doing "city work." He despised this part of his job because whenever he was in Denver he would be drawn into the schemes of graft and fraud against agency clients by superintendent Eams. On more than one occasion Siringo either refused to be a participant or was instrumental in protecting a would-be victim from violence at the hands of agency operatives.

One day Charlie overheard detectives Doc Williams and Pat Barry administering the third degree to someone in superintendent Eams's office. A frosted glass door separated the superintendent's private office from the operatives' room. Siringo watched through a peephole that had been made in the frosted glass to see what the rumpus was about. Through the peephole he saw a man being slugged by Pat Barry to make him confess to a robbery that Siringo knew Barry himself had committed. Siringo was so incensed that he drew his Colt .45 and burst into the room to order the beating to stop. He then "read the riot act" to superintendent Eams, telling him that he had seen detectives Pat Barry and Doc Williams commit the robbery that they were now trying to accuse an innocent victim of doing.

For the next few months Siringo had to keep his hand close to "old Colts 45" when in the presence of Williams and Barry, as both men had sworn to get even with him. On one occasion Pat Barry did attempt to draw his pistol on Siringo, but Charlie was faster and got the drop on Barry, making him lay down his gun. Siringo's fast action in behalf of an innocent man, and his exposure of two dishonest detectives, incurred both the wrath of superintendent Eams and his determination for revenge. Eams told Siringo that just as soon as he could get in touch with W. A. Pinkerton in Chicago, he was going to order him to be discharged in disgrace. Siringo continued with his duties and apparently nothing came of the incident. Later, Charlie learned from a Chicago colleague that Pinkerton ignored Eams's demand for his dismissal because he considered him too good a cowboy detective to be discharged for insubordination.[7]

Eventually, Eams's greed brought about his own downfall. According to Siringo, it was common practice to assign several cases to one operative and then charge each client the daily rate plus expenses. Siringo admitted to being assigned to as many as four cases at the same time and trying, or pretending to try, to work on them all. In this way Eams would charge clients for work never done, apparently enriching himself in the process. When W. A. Pinkerton discovered that Eams was pocketing some of these multiple assessments and not making proper records on the agency's books, he summarily fired Eams and the entire staff, including the bookkeeper and "lady stenographer." Charlie Siringo was the only man in the Denver office who was not discharged.

Pinkerton installed a new work force of detectives and office employees, and then assigned James McParland, the detective who had won fame for breaking up the Molly Maguires in Pennsylvania, to head the office as superintendent. Since the Mollies episode, McParland had worked on various private and government cases for the agency all over the country and in South America. Although his assignment as superintendent ended his active duty as a detective, many years of Pinkerton service still lay ahead of him until his retirement from the agency.

As for Siringo, who still disapproved of certain agency practices and tried to sidestep assignments not to his liking, he did get along well with his new superintendent. McParland's straightforward, no-nonsense, approach to crime fighting appealed to Siringo, and for the next twenty years he would serve as McParland's principal troubleshooter.[8]

In the spring of 1888 a message was cabled from New York to London setting in motion a chain of events that would lead to Siringo's assignment on a mine-salting case. The lord mayor of London had paid $190,000 for the Mudsill Silver Mine in Horseshoe Gulch, eight miles from Fairplay, in Park County, Colorado. Two mining experts had been hired by the British investor to make an on-site inspection of the mine before any money changed hands. When they reported seeing 30,000 tons of ore, worth thirty dollars a ton, the London official was convinced. Shortly thereafter, his New York agent, a Mr. McDermott, awarded a contract to the firm of Frazier & Chalmers for the construction of a mill on mine property to treat the ore. Later, when silver samples were accidentally found that were foreign to the class of ore indigenous to that mine, a fraud of immense proportions was suspected. When these findings were cabled to the English mine owner, he at once ordered an investigation.

McDermott, the New York mining expert, employed Pinkerton and urged the agency to assign its best detectives to the case. If fraud had occurred, McDermott hoped the agency might be able to recover most of his client's money. Both Pinkerton brothers assured McDermott that their best men would be put to work on it, especially since they had a personal interest in the case. William Chalmers, whose firm had been contracted to construct the mill at Mudsill, was the husband of the Pinkertons' sister, Joan. Since their brother-in-law was possibly an indirect victim of what looked like a gigantic fraud, the Pinkertons assured McDermott that they would leave no stone unturned in their investigation.[9]

The complete Mudsill file was forwarded to James McParland in Denver with orders to put his best operatives on the case. McParland summoned Siringo into his private office, gave him the Mudsill file to look over, and then explained the case in detail. He cautioned Charlie not to make any mistakes, as it could mean the cancellation of the Frazier & Chalmers mill contract. McParland emphasized the importance of this case to the Agency.

After a week in Fairplay making a secret investigation, Siringo ordered that work on the mill be stopped, as he was certain beyond doubt that the mine had been salted. Using the alias Charles T. Leon and pretending to be the dissolute son of a wealthy Texan, Siringo began cultivating the friendship of a man named Jack Allen. Charlie believed that Allen, or "Jacky" as he liked to be called, was somehow involved in the scheme to defraud the English investor. Jacky seemed to have plenty of money to spend and readily fell in with Charlie, who was now playing the role of a carefree spender. The two men began frequenting Fairplay's two dancehall saloons each night, dancing with the "free-and-easy" girls, and going on glorious drunks together. At the end of their revelry each night they would return to Jacky's room to sleep it off. Having gained Allen's confidence and aided by the lubrication of alcohol, Siringo was able to extract, bit by bit, information concerning Jacky's part in salting the Mudsill mine.

As the case wore into summer Siringo decided to bring Mamie and Viola out from Denver so that they could enjoy the cool mountain air. Through "Doc" Lockridge, a friend of Charlie's, who owned a mine near Alma, eight miles from Fairplay, Siringo arranged for Mamie to be introduced as Lockridge's niece visiting from Kansas. Mamie and Viola registered at the hotel in Alma where Lockridge was also a resident. Mamie agreed to call Lockridge "uncle" and pretend to be a widow who had lost her husband two years previously. In Fairplay, meanwhile, Charlie told Jacky that he had to ride over to Alma to visit an old friend who ran a saloon there. When Siringo reached Alma and entered the hotel parlor, Lockridge "introduced" Charlie to his "niece" and invited him to sit with them in the dining room. That evening, after everyone had retired, Siringo left his room and sneaked down the hall to the room where Mamie was staying. Then before dawn he sneaked back to his own room.

As Siringo's visits to Alma became more frequent, ladies in the hotel began to warn Mamie that the man paying her so much attention was one of the worst toughs and dancehall loafers in Fairplay. Mamie, however, ignored their warnings. Charlie knew that he was risking the exposure of his cover by these visits. Especially alarming was the likelihood of an error by little Viola. The child had been coached to call

Siringo "Mr. Leon," but there was always the possibility she would forget and call him "Papa," especially at the dining table during one of the communal meals. Once she did slip, but fortunately most of the diners had left the table, and the childish indiscretion went unnoticed.

Siringo spent eight months on the Mudsill case and managed to get away with the double life he was leading during the summer months. About four nights each week Siringo would carouse with Jacky and the dancehall girls, and the balance of the time he would be doing the tiptoe act and playing himself off as a respectable gentleman. During his association with Jacky Allen, the two men spent two weeks out in the mountains. This gave Charlie an opportunity to learn every detail about how the fraud was perpetrated, including the part played by Jacky's partners in the scheme. Finally, Jacky was arrested in Denver, where he made a full confession. The case was tried in the courts, and Pinkerton's British client eventually recovered $150,000 of his money. Jacky and his accomplices went to prison, and the Mudsill case set a legal precedent by which subsequent mine-salting cases were judged.[10]

For the next two years Siringo worked on a succession of cases, many involving considerable risk and danger. All the while his reputation as a detective and his stature within the agency continued to grow. Between assignments, however, Charlie found problems developing at home. His "girl wife," Mamie, had contracted a progressive illness which the doctors diagnosed as pleurisy. In late August, 1889, prior to embarking upon a new assignment that would take him to San Francisco, Charlie and Mamie broke up their housekeeping and sold their furniture. Mamie's health was failing badly, and her doctors had decided that an operation was necessary to save her life. Clay Lloyd, Mamie's father, insisted that she be sent to Springfield, Missouri, so she could be operated on by his personal physician, who was one of the best in the state.

Siringo saw his wife and little girl off on an eastbound train, and then boarded a "flyer" for the West Coast. Ordinarily he would have been looking forward to this assignment since it was his first trip to California. Yet he was plagued with worry over Mamie's illness and the fact she had to undergo surgery without his presence to comfort her. By the spring of 1890 Charlie had completed a strenuous nine-month detective operation and was reunited with his family in Denver. Although Mamie had come through the operation successfully, the doctors held little hope for her recovery, as the disease had irreversibly affected both lungs. For the moment, at least, Charlie and Mamie were together once more; with little Viola, they made a happy family threesome. They rented a house, bought new furnishings, and started housekeeping again. Because of Mamie's illness, Charlie was not sent out on long and involved cases but remained in Denver for assignment to the less desirable city work.

By the time fall arrived Mamie's condition had worsened, and Charlie asked McParland if he could remain at home to be at his wife's bedside. Early that winter Mamie died in Charlie's arms as he held her at an open window to get fresh air. Mamie's suffering during her last days "had been something awful," and when death finally came, even her physician, Dr. Herman H. Martin, shed tears. Before Mamie died, her aunt Emma Lloyd Read came out from Anna, Illinois, to provide what comfort she could for her niece. After Mamie's death Charlie agreed to Emma's suggestion that little Viola should go to live with her and her husband, Will F. Read. The Reads had no children of their own, and Charlie had no way of caring for a little five-year-old girl. Emma Read assured Charlie that she and her husband would rear Viola as if she were their own child.

With the death of his wife, Mamie, the breaking up of his home, and the separation from his daughter, another period in Charlie Siringo's life had come to an end.[11]

PART II
PINKERTON'S COWBOY
DETECTIVE, 1891–1907

Oh, see the train go 'round the bend,
  Goodbye, my lover, goodbye;
She's loaded down with Pinkerton men,
  Goodbye, my lover, goodbye.

—from *A Cowboy Detective*

3 / THE ANCHETA
SHOOTING INCIDENT

I N early February, 1891, an assassination attempt against members of the territorial legislature occurred in the ancient capital city of Santa Fe, New Mexico. The crime would not only involve Siringo in a new and important assignment but, more significantly, it would mark another turning point in his life.

On the evening of February 5, several members of the judiciary committee were in conference in the law offices of Thomas B. Catron planning the next day's strategy. Catron was a member of the Territorial Council, or upper house of the legislature, and a senior member of the committee. His law office was located in the glass-front Griffin Building, which was situated on the northeast corner of Washington and Palace avenues.

Inside, Joseph A. Ancheta, of Silver City, leaned against a window casing with his back to the street. Catron was behind a desk, facing Ancheta, with a pile of law books and legal papers in front of him. Elias S. Stover, of Albuquerque, a former territorial governor, and Pedro Perea, of Bernalillo, stood near the center of the room with T. B. Mills, of Las Vegas, off to one side. As the hour approached half-past eight, two men on horseback crunched through the snow until positioned directly in front of the well-lighted office on the Washington Avenue side. One of the riders aimed a shotgun and his companion a rifle at the men inside the office. Almost simultaneously, shots rang out, sending a charge of buckshot into the neck and left shoulder of J. A. Ancheta, while the rifle shot passed near the heads of Perea and Stover. Part of the buckshot lodged in the stack of legal papers and law books piled on Catron's desk.

Catron escaped injury, but Ancheta nearly died from the severity of his wounds. Although several people saw the gunmen, who were only thirty feet from the window when they fired, both assailants made good their escape. A hastily assembled posse, led by city marshal John Gray, trailed the two men about seven miles south along the Old Pecos Road. When Gray and his men returned emptyhanded, their only clues were that the left forefoot of one of the horses made a peculiar impression in the snow, as if there were only half a shoe, and the other horse was unshod.[1]

The next day, an emotionally charged legislature enacted a bill authorizing the governor to offer a reward of $10,000 for the apprehension of the assailants and another $10,000 to spend toward effecting their capture. Governor L. B. Prince immediately sent a telegram to employ Pinkerton's National Detective Agency in the case and asked that a detective be sent who could speak the Spanish language. Prince agreed to Pinkerton's terms of eight dollars per day for an operative and payment of all expenses. After a hurried consultation between W. A. Pinkerton in Chicago and James McParland in Denver, Charlie Siringo was detailed to the case. Siringo had not only proven himself to be an able troubleshooter but, more importantly to this operation, he was the only detective available who possessed a limited understanding of Spanish.

Within a week of the shooting Siringo was in Santa Fe and, using the name of Charles T. Leon, met with Governor Prince and Solicitor General Edward L. Bartlett in what would become a six-month-long cloak-and-dagger investigation. Secret night meetings were held in Prince's home on Palace Avenue, messages were sent by mail rather than by telegraph, and fictitious names were employed, all to maintain the secrecy of the investigation.[2]

From the beginning it was generally believed that the shots that wounded Ancheta were intended for Catron, who was a member of the "Santa Fe ring" and a prominent Republican in New Mexico politics. The Democrats were then in power in Santa Fe and their leader, Francisco Chavez, was county sheriff and a Masterworkman in the local lodge of the Knights of Labor. The White Caps, a lawless Hispanic organization considered to be allied with the Knights of Labor and whose members were mainly Democrats or of populist persuasion, were thought to be responsible for the crime. The White Caps marched in bands, placing white hoods on themselves and their mounts, spreading terror by murdering stock men and cutting fences.[3]

At the suggestion of Prince, Bartlett, and Catron, who were acting as a committee to oversee the investigation, Siringo began making plans to go to Las Vegas, a White Cap stronghold. There could be no doubt, the committee told him, that members of this lawless gang were the guilty ones and that possibly the whole organization was involved in the plot. He was instructed to work on the White Caps and, if possible, join their order. During the last election the White Caps had carried San Miguel County, Las Vegas being the county seat and had elected one of its leaders, Pablo Herrera, to the territorial legislature. Herrera had just finished serving a sentence in the penitentiary in Santa Fe, and Siringo resolved to win the friendship of this ex-convict in order to use him to become initiated into the White Caps.

Since Sheriff Chavez was also known to be a member of the White Caps, Siringo began spending money freely with him, and soon the two became fast friends. One night, as they were making the rounds in the "hurrah" section of Santa Fe, they ran into Pablo Herrera with several of his followers. Chavez introduced Siringo, and the combined group proceeded to celebrate. A few days later the legislature adjourned and, by invitation from Herrera, Charlie accompanied the lawmaker on the train to Las Vegas. After their arrival, Pablo introduced Siringo to all of his White Cap friends, including his two brothers, Judge José and Nicanor Herrera. Charlie thought Nicanor was a "fine looking specimen of the Mexican race." He also noted, but with his usual studied air of personal indifference, that Nicanor's "fierce determined expression . . . portended evil for his enemies."

As the days passed into weeks, Charlie and Pablo became inseparable. Siringo's expense accounts, which were forwarded monthly to Governor Prince, revealed frequent entertainment of White Cap leaders with the purchase of food, cigars, and rounds of drinks. Although Siringo was obliged to consume much bad liquor, he also managed to eat many fine meals in the company of "swell society" at the posh Montezuma Hotel, a noted resort and spa six miles from Las Vegas at Hot Springs.

Because of his engaging manner and his close friendship with Herrera, Siringo was initiated into the White Caps secret society despite his inability to handle Spanish fluently. By the end of April, after two months of investigation, Siringo returned to Santa Fe and reported to the governor that the White Caps were a separate organization from the Knights of Labor and that the two groups were not allied, as had been suspected. In fact, Siringo was convinced that the White Caps had nothing to do with the assassination attempt on February 5, although he still believed that Sheriff Chavez was "at the bottom of it and that Catron . . . [was] the man aimed at."[4]

While Siringo was still in Las Vegas, Governor Prince received a report from John Gray, who had been conducting his own investigation. Marshal Gray had backtracked the escape route and had interrogated a number of individuals who had seen two men whose horses' hoofprints fit the description of those of the assailants. Gray was able to identify the riders as Victoriano and Felipe Garcia, two brothers from Ojo de Vaca, or Cow Springs, a primitive village in the mountains southeast of Santa Fe. Gray's report was promptly relayed to Siringo, who then took up the trail to Cow Springs.

Charlie found the Garcias, and not long afterward he found their horses, including the one that left an unusual hoof mark. He cultivated the Garcia brothers' friendship and even was invited to stay in the home of another of their brothers. About a dozen Mexican families with small farms and ranches lived in and about the village of Cow Springs. Among them, Siringo found one man who admitted to being a White Cap. All the rest, to his surprise, professed to be Republicans![5]

During his stay in Cow Springs, Siringo was called upon to help bury a Mexican woman who had died of smallpox. He had taken the disease nine years before and, having survived, considered himself immune from taking it again. By the end of the week he became ill with a raging fever; he made his way to Lamy Junction, where he secured a room in the Harvey House and bought a bottle of Carter's Little Liver Pills, his favorite patent medicine remedy. He intended to return to Cow Springs the next day but, finding his condition had worsened, he instead boarded a train for Santa Fe. By the following afternoon he was obliged to summon a physician, and for the next few days a harrowing brush with death nearly put an end to his detective career.[6]

Governor Prince, meanwhile, had begun to complain to the Pinkerton Agency about what he felt were excessive expenses. Even before Siringo had finished his investigation of the White Caps in Las Vegas, Prince wrote superintendent McParland objecting to the operative's outlays and especially his expenditure of forty dollars for a horse and saddle. McParland replied that he regretted the high costs of the investigation but advised that before Siringo left the country, the horse and saddle would be sold and the governor's account credited by that amount.

Then on July 17 Governor Prince wrote McParland to complain about being billed eight dollars a day during the three weeks Siringo had been incapacitated by the smallpox. He asked that the detective agency adjust his bill accordingly. McParland replied that he was sorry but he could not take the same view, as Siringo had risked his life by following investigative leads and had thereby exposed himself to "that loathsome disease." He added that although Siringo's doctor and drug bills totaling fifty-one dollars had not been charged to the governor, he certainly felt that the agency was entitled to be paid for the operative's time and other expenses. McParland reminded the governor that during Siringo's illness he did not remain idle but continued to develop leads and contacts useful to the investigation, and at a time when "almost anyone else would have been thinking of taking a trip to another world."[7]

One week later Governor Prince abruptly notified McParland that he wished to discontinue the investigation, giving no reason for his decision. Siringo, meanwhile, following his recovery about the middle of June, had returned to Cow Springs and was continuing to sniff out information from the Garcia brothers. He elicited a partial confession from Victoriano Garcia, confirming his suspicions that both Victoriano and Felipe were the guilty parties. However, he was unsure of their motive, although he still believed that Thomas Catron had been their intended victim. Siringo laid the matter before Governor Prince and General Bartlett in a final meeting, advising that the Garcias be arrested. He felt the chances were favorable for a confession if the pair were jailed and made to think that all of their secrets were known. The governor thought otherwise, and nothing further was ever done. In 1893 the legislature rescinded the bill offering a reward, and the case was closed.[8]

Ending the investigation did not end the speculation surrounding the shooting of Senator Ancheta. In fact, several puzzling questions remained unresolved. Especially curious is why Governor Prince dismissed Pinkerton and called off the investigation. Obviously, he believed the agency was overcharging him and he especially disliked being billed for the time Siringo was ill with smallpox. That Siringo may have been padding his expenses to the agency, as was frequently practiced, is arguable. Out of $10,000 allocated for the investigation, $2,716, or slightly more than one-fourth, had been spent between February and July, and of that, $2,361 was paid to the Pinkerton agency. This amounts to nearly $400 a month, or $100 a week, not an inconsiderable sum in those days. However, Prince was wrong in his opposition to paying the agency for Siringo's time during which he had been incapacitated with a life-threatening illness incurred in the line of duty. In Prince's defense, however, it should be noted that his attitude toward a contractual obligation, involving one's labor, was typical of many in the nineteenth century who omitted the human factor from their equation of employer responsibility.[9]

Did Prince fire the Pinkertons because of what he believed were excessive expenses and unfair charges? Or, was the governor satisfied at that point that the Garcia brothers, who claimed to be Republicans, had perpetrated the attack, but feared that their arrest and prosecution would muddy the water for the party then out of power in Santa Fe? A modern writer has claimed that the investigation was halted because "the trail got too close to the powers that managed the Democratic Party." This seems an unlikely conclusion from the existing evidence.

Thomas Catron, who later became a U.S. senator from New Mexico, never desisted in his belief that he was the intended victim. Historian Ralph Emerson Twitchell concurred in the view that Catron was the target and that, although some of the White Cap members might have been involved or knew of the plot, the crime was the result of intense ill feeling between the followers of Francisco Chavez and his political rivals. Ironically, Sheriff Chavez, who was the prime suspect as the man behind the shooting, was himself assassinated less than a year after Siringo left Santa Fe. His murder, practically in front of the Guadalupe Church, set off a period of intense partisan bitterness, and Thomas Catron, who defended the accused murderers, continued to be deeply involved.[10]

When Siringo broke off the investigation, he was still convinced that Catron, and not Ancheta, had been the primary target of the Garcia brothers. Later, he changed his mind when he learned that Senator Ancheta and former governor Stover had been active in campaigning for a free public school bill. Ancheta's vote was felt to be so crucial, that when the bill was put to a vote, two of Ancheta's friends carried the wounded lawmaker into the council chamber on a stretcher so he could vote in favor of the bill's final passage.

Before the legislature passed the school bill on February 12, just one week after the assassination attempt, it had been widely but erroneously reported throughout the territory that the Catholic church was opposed to it. This was due to the presence of several priests on the House floor during the final days of the debate. Although the church had nothing to do with the shooting, Siringo was led to suspect that the Garcia brothers were religious extremists, and that Ancheta as well as Stover was an intended victim.

Albert Bacon Fall, who was then a member of the lower house and a supporter of the school bill, said that the strongest opposition came from Thomas Benton Catron! Fall maintained that Catron, one of the territory's largest landholders, tried to kill the bill with one crippling amendment after another, because he knew its passage would substantially increase his taxes. If Siringo's supposition concerning the Garcia brothers was correct, then it would appear highly unlikely that Catron was one of those meant to receive a bullet.

Governor Prince, who had access to all of these facts, may also have come to this conclusion. After all, no one was killed, and the exposure of possibly Republican individuals, whose motives were religious rather than political, might have been counterproductive. Siringo later admitted that he never was able to develop convicting evidence in the case, and the Ancheta shooting incident remains one of New Mexico's unsolved mysteries.[11]

Except for his almost fatal bout with smallpox, the months of investigation in and around Santa Fe had been a tonic for Siringo and had helped divert his mind from his personal sorrows. For Charlie, Santa Fe and the Southwest brought back a flood of memories of his years as an LX cowboy and his adventures in New Mexico during the days of Billy the Kid, of New Mexican mining towns and cow camps, and of old friends who had now put down roots in the territory. He liked the land and its people, and he decided that he wanted to put down roots there, too. "I hated to leave," he later wrote, "as I had found the climate of Santa Fe the finest that I had ever been in. The summers can't be beaten anywhere, and the winters are better than most places." Apparently, he tarried about Santa Fe for more than a month after closing his detective investigation.

Before returning to Denver, he located some public lands a short distance from the city and filed a homestead claim on 160 acres. Later, he filed a desert land claim on an additional 65 acres, and a homestead claim in his mother's name on an adjacent 140 acres. This gave him a total of 365 acres of land, which he named the Sunny Slope Ranch.

Throughout the ensuing decade and a half, until his resignation from the agency, Siringo would return to Santa Fe, between and during assignments, to visit his ranch and see to its improvements.

Upon his return to Denver, Charlie found he had accumulated a "fat little bank account." His eight-month sojourn in New Mexico had given him little opportunity to spend his own money, having had all of his expenses paid by the Territory of New Mexico. Despite his new-found affluence, his Denver homecoming was a bitter reminder that he was still alone, without a family.[12]

4 / FIGHTING
ANARCHISM
IN THE COEUR D'ALENE

FOLLOWING his return from New Mexico, Charlie was given a couple of weeks off before being assigned to his next case. The brief sabbatical was appropriate, in this instance, for he was about to embark on what would become his most difficult and hazardous assignment. McParland ordered Siringo into the Coeur d'Alene, a silver and lead mining district in Idaho's panhandle, to work for the newly formed Mine Owners' Protective Association, later simply referred to as the MOA, and to spy on the Coeur d'Alene Miners' Union, which was beginning to foment trouble.[1]

At first Siringo refused to go, saying his sympathies were with the labor organization and against the capitalists. However, McParland argued that the union leaders were a desperate lot of criminals like the Molly Maguires, and he proposed that Siringo accept the assignment conditionally. If, after infiltrating the union, he should decide that the mine owners were wrong, he could throw up the operation and return to Denver. Charlie agreed to McParland's proposal and soon found himself enmeshed in a labor dispute with literally explosive potential and far-ranging consequences.

Siringo arrived in Wallace, Idaho, the central town in the Coeur d'Alene region, in the fall of 1891, where he met with representatives of the MOA. He was cautioned about the difficulties under which he would have to operate and that the miners' union was on the lookout for detectives. He was well aware that two men had already been exposed and had left the country in fear for their lives.

The Coeur d'Alene mining district consisted of the supply towns of Wallace and Wardner Junction; the mines were centered about the villages and camps of Burke, Gem, Mullan, and Wardner. It was decided that Siringo would go to Gem, the toughest mining camp in the district, and send out reports on union activities. Only the superintendent of the Gem Mine, where he was to be employed as a shoveler, would know his identity.

When Siringo arrived in Gem, he found it to be a little town of about a thousand inhabitants, a couple of stores, and half a dozen saloons and gambling halls, which made it a lively place at night. The town was situated in a deep canyon, with wooded mountains on either side, and the Union Pacific Railway from Wallace to Burke ran through the center of its only street. At least half of the population were miners employed in the Helena & Frisco, Black Bear, and Gem mines.

Within two weeks after going to work Siringo became a member of the Gem Miners' Union, whose financial secretary, George A. Pettibone, was later to gain notoriety in the Western Federation of Miners.[2] Pettibone, whom Siringo described as a rabid anarchist, was the Gem representative on the miners' union Central Executive Committee, which was headquartered in Wallace. Siringo now had an opportunity to learn what the men thought and what they intended doing, and what he learned entirely changed his sympathies. In a letter to the MOA he wrote: "I find the leaders of the Coeur d'Alene unions to be, as a rule, a vicious, heartless gang of anarchists. Many of them were rocked in the cradle of anarchism at Butte City, Montana, while others are escaped outlaws and toughs from other states."

About two months after joining the union his ability to gather information was enhanced when he was elected recording secretary of the Gem branch. This was a useful position, as it gave Siringo access to all the books and records. "Seeing the character of the leaders," he said, left him with "no qualms of conscience as to revealing their schemes to my employers." The unions, he said, were being "run" by a number of dangerous anarchists who had completely duped the hardworking miners and were formulating demands to which the mine owners could not possibly agree. The focus of the demands, as might be expected, centered on wages.[3]

With the passage of the Sherman Silver Purchase Act of July, 1890, which raised the government's purchase commitment to 4 million ounces of silver a month, silver prices began an immediate upward climb. Not only was a new boom proclaimed, but many mines were reopened, and the mining labor movement was becoming a presence to be reckoned with. In the fall of 1890 the miners in the Coeur d'Alene began to organize independent unions modeled after those that had begun in the other mining regions of the West. On January 1, 1891, they strengthened their position by consolidating under a Central Executive Committee and began an offensive to establish a $3.50 minimum daily wage for all men underground. At that time the mine owners had not organized and, as the union took on the mines one at a time, many of the owners agreed to the minimum-wage demand. After all, most mines were showing handsome profits and paying substantial dividends. Not all owners readily agreed, but those who did not fell into line after brief strikes.

With the increased silver production, stimulated by higher prices, the government's purchase limit was soon exceeded, resulting in a collapse of the silver market. During the summer of 1891 the growing surplus caused a steep decline in the price of silver, and by the following summer it had fallen to a new low. Lead and copper prices also plummeted with silver, and, as prices fell, the mines' profitability fell as well. The Coeur d'Alene mine owners, those not already closed by the lagging economy, announced a rollback of wages for unskilled laborers to the previous level.[4]

Two classes of workers were employed in the mines: powder and drill men who prepared and set the explosives to knock the ore down into drifts; and shovelers, along with carmen, who followed the powder and drill men and who loaded the ore into cars for conveyance to hoists and elevation to the surface. Because of the exacting nature of their work, the powder and drill men were considered skilled labor and paid $3.50 a day for their services. The shovelers, or muckers, and carmen were regarded as unskilled labor and paid fifty cents a day less. With the fifty-cent-a-day cut in wages, labor agitators arrived from Butte, Montana, and began to stir up feelings of discontent among the muckers and carmen, claiming discrimination because they were not being paid the same as powder and drill men. Not only did the mine owners object to paying skilled and unskilled laborers the same rate of pay, the union's demand came at a time when any increase in production costs could force a closing of the mines.

Exacerbating the problem was a major financial panic, which began in 1892 and by the following year had swept the nation. It was one of the country's worst, for not only did it paralyze industry, but the silver, lead, and zinc markets failed, many banks closed their doors, and even the Northern Pacific, the Union Pacific, and other railroads went into receivers' hands. Although unemployment was becoming widespread throughout the country, the Coeur d'Alene union leaders paid no serious heed to this economic maelstrom.[5]

Not long after securing his post as recording secretary for the Gem Miners' union, Siringo was fired from his job as a mucker. The ruse of being a working miner had already served its purpose, so Siringo contrived his own discharge so that he would be denied work in other mines. He began shirking his duties and complaining, until his shift boss, a big taciturn Swede, summarily fired him. Charlie told his union fellows that he had an indulgent father in Texas who sent him money, and that he planned to stay on so he could work for the union cause. With his cover story established, he was then free to spend all of his time with his new-found friends who were union officials. He was also at liberty to mingle with the union miners in the camp's several saloons.

With the mounting discontent and continuing agitation, the miners finally struck, and their first action was against the scabs—men who remained loyal to or favored the owners' position. Feelings at once became very bitter as men were dragged from their beds at night and, after being marched up the canyon by a howling mob, were compelled to tramp through deep snow to Thompson's Falls, near the summit of the Bitterroot Mountains. Siringo said he helped trample the Constitution of the United States into the mud by helping the union gather up scabs to be run out of town. Sometimes, he said, weeping wives and children would beg for mercy as the scabs were marched through the street and "spat upon amidst the beating of pans and ringing of cowbells."

Other camps besides Gem were driving nonstrikers into Montana; people were forced out in the winter cold with little clothing and few supplies. Those in the unions who protested this inhuman treatment were subjected to the wrath of the union leaders and soon became silent. Later, the unions would provide press releases that were published in newspapers in Spokane, Washington, and in Anaconda and Butte, Montana, all sympathetic to the miners' union, describing how citizens' mass meetings had branded these men as undesirable and had run them out of the state. "I knew better," Siringo said, "but the general public didn't."[6]

Soon after the first uprising the men from the Burke union came to Gem where a joint meeting with the Gem lodge was held, and plans were laid for the flooding of certain mines. Siringo, in accordance with his duty as recording secretary, put these plans down in the minutes.

Later, Oliver Hughes, the president of the Gem union, ordered Siringo to cut this leaf out of the book in case it should fall into the hands of the MOA. Siringo dutifully cut out the page, as ordered, and straightaway mailed it to John A. Finch, owner of the Gem Mine and MOA secretary. Charlie had to hike four miles to Wallace after dark to mail it, as well as his other reports, because the postmaster at Gem and all of his assistants were staunch union men.

The strike dragged on through the winter, and Siringo continued his duties as recording secretary of his union. By the early spring of 1892 all of the mines in the Coeur d'Alene were closed down. Shortly after the closing of the mines a mass meeting between the unions and the mine owners was held in Wallace so both sides could air their views. The meeting brought no results, except that the miners' union Central Executive Committee decided it was time to declare war on the MOA. George Pettibone told Siringo that they had selected a secret crowd of the worst toughs in the union "to put the fear of Christ" into the hearts of the scabs; that if these men committed murder, the union would stick by them. No one outside the executive committee, of which Pettibone was a member, was to know who these men were, or who was financing them.[7]

The owners, meanwhile, were formulating plans of their own. According to Siringo, the next excitement came with the owners' decision to bring in laborers from other districts to work the mines. Several trainloads of workers from as far away as Michigan were brought into the Coeur d'Alene, including many immigrants from Poland, Austria, and Sweden who could speak no English and were unaware that the union considered them to be strike breakers. The strikers and their leaders regarded this action by the MOA as an attempt to destroy the union, and they intended to fight it at all costs. Arms were collected and distributed to union guards, who were ordered to seize the first trainload of scabs and send them back, or shoot them if the central committee desired it.

The mine owners, tipped off by Siringo, ordered the first train carrying 100 nonunion workers not to stop at Wallace, as the union expected, but to continue on to Burke, where the men detrained and were marched up the mountainside to a mine ironically named "the Union." Mine owner A. B. Campbell had already stored suppies in preparation for their arrival.

Several more trainloads of nonunion laborers were later imported and, since federal court injunctions sought by the MOA had by then been served on all union members, the strikers dared not openly attack the "blacklegs," as they were called. However, Siringo observed that the hundreds of pickets who met the trains used every possible means to frighten them. In spite of the armed guards provided by the owners to protect the nonunion miners, many of these scabs, caught alone at night, were set upon and beaten almost to death. Siringo said he learned some new lessons in human nature as he observed the fights and cruel acts by the union strikers on scabs for the next few months.

Meanwhile, George Pettibone, the central committee's secretary, had taken a fancy to Siringo and was revealing secrets to him he might not otherwise have learned. One of these secrets concerned the plot of a great uprising to take place in July throughout the Coeur d'Alene. If successful, the strikers intended to run the scabs and mine owners out of the country and take possession of the mines for the union workers. As on previous occasions, Siringo passed this information on to his employers.

In the spring, Siringo went into partnership with his landlady, Mrs. Kate Shipley, a woman with a small son. He bought a building with twelve furnished rooms, opened a store in the downstairs part, and gave Mrs. Shipley half the income for running the place. Siringo knew from information supplied by Pettibone that riots, instigated by the union's central committee, were likely to occur, so he had a board fence, sixteen feet high, built around the rear of his building to keep out prowlers. He loosened one of the boards at the bottom in case he needed to slip through and avoid being seen by having to go over the fence. It was a wise precaution.

Suddenly, Siringo's world began to cave in on him. A weekly newspaper called the *Barbarian*, run in the interest of the mine owners, published privileged information that could have come only from some member of the Gem union. Since Siringo was recording secretary and had charge of the books, the finger of suspicion was pointed in his direction. To resolve the matter, the secretary of the Butte City (Montana) union, under whose charter all of the Coeur d'Alene unions had been organized, came to Gem to find out how the leakage occurred. The man said his name was Tim O'Leary, but Siringo knew that his real name was Gabe Dallas, and he described him as "a one-eyed, two-legged, Irish hyena." Within a week Dallas had decided that Siringo was the culprit.

A special meeting of the Gem union was called and, prior to the meeting, a union man, who liked Siringo, warned him that he was suspected of being a traitor, as he had been seen mailing too many letters at Wallace. He told Charlie to "skip out" and not attend the special union meeting, as the chances were that he would be killed. Siringo assured the friend that he was innocent and that he would be a good soldier by sticking to his guns.

That night the large union hall was packed, as it was known that O'Leary (Dallas) would attempt to expose the spy who had given out union secrets. After Siringo had calmly read the minutes of the last meeting, Dallas made a speech proclaiming a traitor to be their midst and that he should not leave the meeting alive. Siringo was wearing "old Colts 45" in a "Wess Harding" [*sic*] shoulder holster beneath his coat, and concealed about his waist was his pearl-handle bowie knife. While Dallas was still speaking, Siringo began planning to kill as many as he could before he himself was killed.[8]

When Dallas finished his fiery speech, a ten-minute recess was called during which time Siringo's minute book was carefully examined. When a leaf was found to have been cut out of the book, Dallas angrily demanded an explanation. Siringo reminded the president, Oliver Hughes, that he had ordered the removal and destruction of the minutes contained on that page because it revealed union plans to flood the mines, information that could be damaging to the union should the book fall into the hands of the enemy. That Siringo might have given, and in fact did give, the incriminating page to the Mine Owners' Association apparently did not occur to anyone. After several anxious moments Hughes finally acknowledged the fact, and Siringo was temporarily safe from the wrath of Gabe Dallas and the union mob.

Siringo had no doubt that Dallas and his followers thought he would show his guilt during or after Dallas's blood-curdling speech and would make some excuse to the outer guard at the door during the recess so as to get out. Charlie said he was too "foxy" to try a break like that. Neither did he show guilt by his actions or looks, having mastered the art of deception while playing poker in cow camps on the range. Nevertheless, Siringo knew when he left the hall that henceforth he was a marked man. That night he slept with his loaded Winchester rifle and a sack of a hundred cartridges by his side. Two days later Mrs. Shipley called Charlie's attention to a man she had observed following him. Siringo knew the man to be "Black Jack" Griffin, a dynamiter who had been involved in one of his previous cases. When a friendly union man told him that Griffin was a member of the Mullan union, Siringo was certain that he had been recognized.[9]

By this time, law and order had ceased to exist in Gem, as well as in other mining towns in the Coeur d'Alene. On the Fourth of July, Siringo observed that American flags were shot full of holes and spat upon by the strikers. With rioting likely to erupt at any moment, the owners had the mines barricaded and guarded. The nonunion miners, or scabs, were fed at the mines and seldom ventured away from their quarters, but when they did, they were caught and cruelly beaten by strikers. Mine owners such as John Finch who came into Gem barely escaped being mobbed and were glad to get away with their hides intact.

On July 9 Siringo received a friendly warning not to attend the union meeting scheduled for that evening because he was "doomed to die the death of a traitor." This time guided by prudence, at the appointed hour Charlie handed his minute book to the guard at the door, along with a letter announcing that he was resigning from the union. In his letter of resignation Siringo continued to play his game of deception. He vehemently denied being a Pinkerton detective, saying that was "one of the lowest and most degrading professions that mortal man could follow." He was resigning, he said, because of the unjust attacks and suspicions against him, and he vowed that he would never "put foot in their union hall again." He then returned to his rooms to await events.[10]

Two hours later Siringo returned to the street and joined a group of Mullan miners, who did not recognize him as the "traitor" to the union cause. They told Charlie that the Homestead riots, which had occurred two days before, would be "child's play" compared to their approaching storm.[11] He also learned that a crowd of union miners were holding two scabs at Dutch Henry's saloon, getting them drunk, as they planned to kill them.

Siringo went to Dutch Henry's to warn the two nonunion miners of their danger, but before he could get near them he was attacked by a rabid anarchist and some twenty of his followers. Siringo held them off with his drawn pistol as he backed off toward his own quarters.

"Never mind, you traitor, we'll get you before morning!" their leader shouted.[12]

Once inside, Siringo picked up his Winchester and stowed the one hundred cartridges away in his pockets. He slipped out the back of the house and proceeded to the high board fence that surrounded the rear of his property. Although he spotted the shadowy figures of two men who had been posted to prevent his escape, Siringo decided to make a break anyway. He pulled aside the board he had purposely left loose and then crawled on his stomach, between fallen logs with heavy undergrowth, until he reached the swiftly flowing creek about a hundred yards distant. As he lowered himself into the water, he observed three more guards on the bridge fifty yards down from his position. Under the cover of darkness Charlie made his way across the creek and up the mountainside to the Gem Mine, where he found the superintendent, John Monihan, and a squad of armed guards. Monihan said he was expecting the rioting to start at any time, and he had 120 nonunion miners sleeping with their weapons beside them.

Siringo reported the plot against two of Monihan's miners in Dutch Henry's saloon, but he was too late. As they were talking, the town constable arrived with word that both men had been badly beaten and that one of them, near death, had been dragged to the bridge near the company office. After Monihan and two of his men carried the battered miner into the mill, Siringo volunteered to accompany one of the guards dispatched to Wallace to bring back Dr. W. S. Sims, a mine company physician. The mission was fraught with danger, as the two men had to get past armed union pickets in the darkness in order to reach Wallace. After locating the doctor, who returned to the mine with the guard, Siringo went on to report to John Finch, the secretary of the MOA. Finch told Siringo not to return to Gem as it would mean his death, but Charlie replied that his work there was not done. He knew that in any future court proceedings his value as a witness would depend on his eyewitness testimony.

Charlie boarded the train to return to Gem and, as luck would have it, ran into George Pettibone with a delegation of union officials accompanied by a Catholic priest. Siringo wondered what a priest was doing in such company. Pettibone angrily demanded to know why Siringo had a rifle with him and asserted that he could not return to Gem carrying it. "Can't I," Siringo replied. "You just watch me and see!"

When the train reached Gem, Charlie made his way to Mrs. Shipley's store without being molested, although he observed the town was seething with excitement. That night he slipped out to the Gem mill as he had before, expecting the riot would break out between midnight and dawn. When daylight came and everything remained quiet, Charlie returned to Mrs. Shipley's to find out what was happening. Although he made it to the store without incident, the woman was shocked by his audacity. She warned him that the outbreak was to start at any minute, and that he was marked to be killed since he was now definitely known to be a detective.

Precisely at 6:00 A.M. a shot was fired in front of the store, followed by a fusillade of shots echoing down the canyon. The rioting had begun! Once again Siringo attempted to slip out the back and return to the Gem mill, but now all of his escape routes were blocked by angry strikers. He knew that little time remained before the rioters would be at his door, so he sawed a hole in the floor of Mrs. Shipley's living room and lowered himself into the space provided by the foundation of the building. Mrs. Shipley then covered the hole with a carpet and a large trunk.

Siringo observed that his only means of escape was to crawl beneath the board sidewalk, which was raised about a foot or so above street level, although he was uncertain as to where it would lead him. Through a crack in the foundation wall he spotted his old enemy Dallas armed with a shotgun, and for a time he had him centered in his rifle sights. He was tempted to squeeze off a shot but realized that would expose his position, so decided against it. About this time he heard the sound and felt the shock of a tremendous explosion. Mrs. Shipley, some minutes later, called down to tell him that the Helena & Frisco mill had been blown up and that a mob of strikers was coming "to burn [him] at the stake as a traitor."

Within minutes, one-eyed Gabe Dallas, leading a mob of strikers, broke through the double doors of the store and threatened Mrs. Shipley if she did not reveal the detective's whereabouts. The plucky woman refused to be intimidated, but Siringo began to fear they would find the hole and set fire to the building in order to force him out. Dragging his rifle with him, he began to crawl beneath the board sidewalk, which was teeming with union miners who were searching for him. Some of the cracks in the boardwalk were wide enough that he knew he would be spotted if anyone should look down.

At one point, as he crawled beneath the boardwalk, his watch chain caught and tore loose from his clothing. On it was a three-dollar gold piece charm with his initials C.L.A. (for Charles Leon Allison, the alias he was using). He hated to lose it and, after discovering it missing, considered going back to hunt for it. While reflecting on the matter, he wondered if he was scared. "I had to smile at the thought, so I concluded to test the matter by spitting; but bless you, my mouth was so dry I couldn't spit anything but cotton, or what looked like cotton. I decided that it was a case of scared with a big S. I had always heard that when a person is badly frightened he can't spit; but this was the first time I ever saw it tested." [13]

After wriggling the length of three buildings, a distance that he said seemed like a mile, he came to a saloon with an open space leading under the building. He could see daylight streaming through another opening toward the rear, and he cautiously worked his way out into the open. Thirty feet away three men were standing guard. Because their attention was diverted to the tumult going on in the street, Siringo was able to slip past them. Still carrying his Winchester, he pretended to be a striker trying to get a shot at the scabs manning the Gem mine. Quickly, he moved some one hundred yards to a high railroad embankment. He knew he couldn't chance going up and over the embankment for fear of being shot at by both sides. So he entered a box culvert through which the fast-flowing waters of the creek passed under the embankment. A bullet whizzed past his ear as he was springing into the water, the only shot fired in his direction. After a strenuous struggle against the current, Siringo made his way through the culvert by grabbing the heavy cross timbers and hauling himself forward until he emerged on the far side. Two hundred yards still lay between him and the mill, and he faced the risk of being shot, once in the open, by both friend and foe.

Siringo sprinted the remaining distance and arrived at the Gem mill somehow unscathed from his ordeal. Shortly after his arrival a union messenger under a flag of truce brought a demand to surrender the mine and mill with the threat that otherwise the union would blow it up, as they had done the Frisco mill. Mine superintendent Monihan curtly refused, and before long strikers could be seen among the trees moving to the mine's upper works. As though he had not experienced enough danger for one day, Siringo took two men and proceeded up the mountain to cut and tie heavy poles across the tracks of the tramway. If the strikers attempted to blow up the Gem mill by sending an ore car down the tracks, fused and loaded with explosives, it would be derailed short of its goal by the barricade.

The owners, meanwhile, sent word to superintendent Monihan to surrender the mine and mill to the union for fear the continued resistance might result in further loss of life and the destruction of costly machinery. Siringo advised against a surrender, but Monihan replied that he had no choice. Charlie knew that his life was not worth a plugged nickel if he surrendered, so he and one of the guards escaped into the mountains and observed the strikers' activities from afar. On one occasion they slipped into Wallace, and Siringo was told that the union miners were still frantically searching for him.

On July 13 the governor of Idaho Territory declared martial law, and the secretary of war under President Benjamin Harrison ordered the commander at Fort Sherman, a garrison at Coeur d'Alene City, to proceed to Wallace and put an end to the violence. Other federal troops, dispatched from Montana on the day rioting had begun, were delayed because union men from Butte City and Coeur d'Alene had blown up the bridges. The troops arrived eventually, by following a circuitous route through Washington and Oregon. On July 14 Siringo's heart was gladdened as he observed, from his position of concealment, a thousand state and federal soldiers, under the command of Colonel William P. Carlin, march into the Coeur d'Alene. Altogether, six companies of the National Guard and twenty companies of U.S. Infantry were deployed to restore order.[14]

The next morning the sheriff and the justices of the peace were all discharged by the military commandant, and the mining company doctor, W. S. Sims, was appointed sheriff with Siringo appointed as a deputy. The *Spokane Review,* which had been sympathetic to the union, now gave its full support for the imposition of martial law. Calling the outbreak of lawlessness "indefensible," the paper summed up its position: "When armed bodies of men spurn the law and inaugurate a reign of terrorism, bloodshed and destruction, they forfeit the respect and sympathy of law-abiding people. No amount of specious pleading, no resort to quibbling and hair-splitting can make right such passionate deeds of violence."[15]

As a sheriff's deputy, Siringo actively assisted in the roundup of union leaders and others who had participated in the rioting and bloodshed. George Pettibone, Tom O'Brien, Joe Poynton, "Paddy" Burke, and other radical union officials were arrested and detained in a large stockade, or "bull pen" as Siringo called it. Pettibone, it was learned, had set the fuse to the explosives that blew up the Frisco mill, killing one man and maiming several others. Although injured himself by the repercussion of the blast Pettibone recovered to stand trial for his deeds. In all, six men had been killed, three on each side, with a dozen more wounded. Siringo appeared before the grand jury and provided detailed eyewitness testimony to secure the indictments against numerous union rioters. Later, in the trials held in Coeur d'Alene and Boise City, his testimony helped convict eighteen union leaders, including George Pettibone.[16]

By late fall, after an arduous year and two months, Siringo was able to close his operation in Idaho and return to Denver. He had begun the case with doubts and misgivings, as he had considered himself a strong union sympathizer. However, once he saw the direction toward disruptive violence being taken by the union leaders, he swung to the side of the mine owners. Although he condemned the brutal beatings the strikers inflicted on the hapless scabs and deplored the intimidating threats made against union miners sympathetic to the cause of the owners, he found no fault with the owners' importation of nonunion labor.

To Siringo, the union leaders had inflamed the miners by choosing a beguiling issue, that is, proclaiming the wage roll-back to be unjust discrimination against those who were unskilled, and, who incidentally, constituted the largest class of workers. Having aroused the majority of their members, the unions then presented demands which, Siringo believed, the mine owners could not possibly accept. Once he had decided that the union leaders were wrong, and were misleading the miners, he seemed indifferent to the actions taken by the mine owners. Sometimes, Siringo found the line separating right and wrong merged into that gray area where morality yields to prejudice, propaganda, and expediency. If Siringo seemed at times to practice a kind of situation ethics, there was one position on which he never wavered or compromised. That was his staunch opposition to anarchy and its by product, terrorism, such as occurred in the Coeur d'Alene. As a law-and-order man, Charlie always came down on the side opposed to violence.[17]

Although Siringo still championed the cause of the working man, his experience with the anarchy and brutality of radical labor leaders had, for better or worse, prejudiced his views and made him cynical about the benefits of unionism for workers. Professionally, his assignment in the Coeur d'Alene had simply been another challenge in his detective career, although one charged with difficult and dangerous situations to overcome. In the end, the miners' union was defeated, and Siringo, for his part, won the acclaim of the MOA and new laurels from the Pinkerton brothers who confirmed him as their premier sleuth.

Even though Siringo's mission in the Coeur d'Alene was finished, the unrest and violence there would continue throughout the decade. From the ashes of the Coeur d'Alene Miners' Union would rise the Western Federation of Miners, which would dominate the mining labor movement for nearly thirty years. Its leaders, including one familiar name from the past, would propagandize the ideology of the class struggle while practicing a policy of violence, terrorism, and murder. Siringo would meet them again in the next century.[18]

5 / IN PURSUIT OF
ROMANCE,
NOSTALGIA, AND
THE WILD BUNCH

AFTER the Coeur d'Alene riot and roundup of union anarchists, Siringo persuaded Will F. Read and his wife to move out to Gem and join him in his business enterprise. The Reads, who were rearing Viola, sold their home in Anna, Illinois, and moved to Idaho on the strength of Siringo's advice. Emma Read's health was a factor in their decision to move, and Charlie had argued that the vigorous mountain air would be beneficial for her. Will Read bought out Mrs. Shipley's interest and became Siringo's partner. By this time all twelve of the furnished rooms in his building were rented. He also rented space adjoining the store for a barber shop. Charlie then went to Spokane where he found Miss Gertrude Hull, whom he hired to clerk in the store. He confessed that he had gone to Spokane specifically to "round-up" a female clerk, and that he had "roped in the prettiest girl" he could find.

With the Reads close at hand, Charlie had the pleasure of seeing his little daughter Viola again, although no one knew that she was his child. When the Coeur d'Alene operation ended, and Siringo was due to return to Denver, he turned over to the Reads all of his rights in Gem, including, he said, his "good-will interest in Miss . . . Hull." Of the $3,000 Siringo had invested in Gem, much of it saved since Mamie's death, he could now expect to receive $135 a month from the rent of his building and furnished rooms, besides a good profit from his half of the store.

As soon as he arrived back in Denver, he began spending the anticipated profits from his investment. He figured he could easily afford it since his income from Gem was in addition to his weekly salary. Unfortunately, his good times were short lived. In early January, 1893,

Emma Read sent Siringo a telegram advising him that his building and store had burned to the ground, and that her husband was in jail for shooting a union dynamiter merchant named Samuels!

It seems that while the building was burning, Will Read carried his wife's trunk containing her keepsakes across the street and placed it on Samuels's store porch, where it would be safe from the blaze. As Read was not liked by the union men because of his friendship with Siringo, Samuels emerged from his store and kicked the trunk out into the street. A fistfight ensued, with Read knocking Samuels through his own storefront, shattering the plate glass. Samuels grabbed a pistol and fired a couple of shots at Read, missing both times. Read went back into the burning building and got his double-barrel shotgun, loaded with buckshot, and proceeded to shoot Samuels's right arm off at the shoulder. Read knew he didn't stand a chance in a town full of union men, so he made his way to Wallace, where he surrendered to a "friendly" sheriff. Later, when a preliminary trial was held, Read was released and the charges against him were dropped.

Except for the meager protection of a $500 insurance policy, Siringo's $3,000 investment in Gem had gone up in smoke. Fortunately, neither the Reads nor Viola were injured, and Charlie used the insurance money to pay some debts in Idaho and to assist the Reads, who later joined him in Denver.[1]

Siringo resumed his duties with the agency and was assigned to cases that must have seemed routine compared with his experiences in the Coeur d'Alene. Yet, he would later declare that 1893 and 1894 were years in which he lived an exciting life. For about three months he worked in Denver posing as a wealthy mining man under the name of Charles LeRoy. The case involved a $25,000 mining suit, and Siringo's guise enabled him to eavesdrop on private discussions that proved beneficial to Pinkerton's client. Interesting work, perhaps, but certainly not as "exciting" as his Idaho adventures had been.

What *was* making Siringo's life exciting was that he had met and fallen in love with pretty, blue-eyed Lillie Thomas of Denver. They met in the late summer of 1893, and Siringo proposed to her on September 13, her twenty-first birthday. Even though he was seventeen years older, Lillie accepted his proposal, and two months later they were married. For a time they lived in Cheyenne, Wyoming, where Charlie had been sent by the agency to work for the Union Pacific Railroad. Lillie would later refer to this period as a "happy time" in her life.

LX Ranch manager W. C. ("Outlaw Bill") Moore,
who ordered Siringo to go to New Mexico to recover
cattle stolen by Billy the Kid (from *Riata and Spurs*).

Siringo's tobacco store and ice cream-oyster parlor in Caldwell, Kansas, ca. 1885 (from *Riata and Spurs*).

Siringo's first wife, Mamie Lloyd, and their daughter
Viola, 1889 (from *Riata and Spurs*).

Broadside announcing a "Great Mass-Meeting" of workingmen in Chicago's Haymarket on May 4, 1886. The bomb explosion and riot that ensued was the incident that caused Siringo to become a detective (from the author's collection).

Siringo in 1893, at the time of his marriage
to Lillie Thomas (courtesy Betty Siringo
Kent and Carol Siringo McFarland).

Siringo and his second wife, Lillie Thomas, and son Lee Roy
Siringo in Denver, Colorado, 1897 (courtesy Betty Siringo Kent).

As Siringo's involvement in cases of long duration often kept him away for weeks and sometimes months, Lillie began to wonder if her marriage actually was happy. In the spring of 1895 McParland sent Siringo to Alaska to find the robbers of $10,000 in gold from the Treadwell mill. On this case he was gone from Denver for six months. Next, he was off on an assignment south of the border, where he chased a robbery suspect from one end of Old Mexico to the other. No sooner had he returned to Denver from that operation when he was sent to Arizona to run down another fugitive.[2]

In 1896 Lillie bore Charlie a son whom they named William Lee Roy, and for a time their precarious marriage appeared to be all right again. Unfortunately, the advent of a child did not bind the partners together in harmony for long. Unsavory characters coming to their home and asking for Siringo by name or by one of his aliases caused Lillie to worry for her safety as well as that of her son. Charlie wanted her to move to his ranch in Santa Fe, but by then the relationship had soured, and she decided instead to join her parents, who were moving from Denver to southern California.[3] Years later, Siringo referred briefly to the marriage: "Lillie and I agreed to disagree because she wanted to live in Los Angeles, California, while I insisted on making the Rocky Mountains my home. Although the matrimonial knot was severed, we still remain good friends, and correspond with each other. She often sends me nice fruits from her California orchard."[4]

If the dissolution of Siringo's marriage to Lillie bothered him, the agency gave him little time to think about it. The peregrinating requirements of his work, as well as the challenges and hazards that went along with each assignment, afforded him little opportunity to dwell on personal matters. However, there was one personal concern Siringo did manage to keep in mind, and that was his Sunny Slope Ranch.

Since the Ancheta case, Charlie had revisited Santa Fe on several occasions to see about his ranch. He had selected a site a short distance north of the Arroyo Chamiso and constructed a small ranch house. It was a two-room adobe, and its location on a gently sloping hillside provided a panoramic view of the Sangre de Cristo Mountains. The ranch was Siringo's pride and joy, his future retirement home, and Lillie had spurned it as an alternative to separation and divorce. Admittedly, the rooms in Charlie's adobe ranch house were uncomfortably small and austere, a factor Lillie may have weighed in making her decision to leave. Still, the location of the ranch house in a beautiful setting could not be denied.[5]

In 1897 Siringo returned to the scene of his days as an LX cowboy in the Texas Panhandle to investigate a cattle swindling case. He arrived in Amarillo, Texas, by train, at three o'clock on Christmas morning during a heavy blizzard. Charlie found refuge in a saloon run by Jack Ryan, who was a cowboy friend from the old days. Other cowboys from Charlie's past were there, and an early Christmas celebration commenced. Then Ryan mentioned to Siringo that his old friend John Hollicott, the manager of the LX Ranch, was at a saloon across the street. Siringo ran over to the nearby saloon, where he found Hollicott dancing a jig and having "a rattling good time," as he called it. The Scottish-born Hollicott, a fine-looking six-footer, was so glad to see Siringo he almost choked the diminutive detective as he dragged him up to the bar to take a Christmas drink. Siringo had first met John Hollicott in Kiowa, Kansas, in 1876. At that time Hollicott was a cowboy with the Hunter and Evans cattle outfit, while Charlie recalled that he was just drifting around to give "his mustache a chance to grow."[6]

At daylight Hollicott's coachman hitched up a spirited team of mules, and the two celebrants started for the LX Ranch on the Canadian River twenty miles north to take Christmas dinner. The ride was bitterly cold, as the temperature was ten degrees below zero. Siringo and Hollicott endured the subfreezing weather by pulling the cork from the five-gallon jug several times before reaching the ranch.

By 10:00 A.M. they were thawing out before a roaring fire in the large stone fireplace Siringo had helped to build twenty years before. There was the hearthstone that he and Bill Moore had put into place. Thoughts of bygone days flew thick and fast, and the flames of the log fire seemed to be playing hide and seek with other bright blazes of long ago. Siringo wondered if his familiarity with the jug, while enduring the cold ride from Amarillo, might have had something to do with his imagination.

Hollicott introduced Charlie to the Garnett Lee family, who lived on the ranch, which included a "good-looking, black-eyed wife and . . . two beautiful young lady daughters." About two in the afternoon Christmas dinner was served on the same old table from which Billy the Kid and Siringo had eaten together twenty years before. Charlie Sprague and Johnny Bell, two former chums of Siringo, were on hand to partake of the Christmas dinner. After the turkey with all the trimmings was disposed of, they spent the afternoon recalling past adventures and sampling the contents of the jug.

That evening a dance that lasted into the wee hours was held. Siringo liked to dance, especially when pretty young ladies were present, but Hollicott, who was well into his cups, insisted on dragging Charlie off to reminisce about their early cowboy days. Toward daylight the dance broke up, and the coachman drove Hollicott and Siringo two miles to the mouth of Pitcher Creek, where Hollicott had his private home.

The two men retired together in the same bed, and Hollicott was soon fast asleep. As Charlie lay by the side of his old cowboy companion, he could not sleep for the many memories crowding his mind. He recalled the day when he and Mr. Bates had slept at that very spot and had chosen it as the headquarters camp for the future LX Ranch. It was the summer of 1877, and Deacon Bates, David T. Beals's partner, had brought Siringo along into this wild unsettled country to help select a cattle range for the company Beals had formed.

The country was then alive with buffalo and Indians. Across the river from the mouth of Pitcher Creek, only a mile, 300 half-naked and painted Apache Indians were encamped. He thought about how he and Bates had wondered at what moment their scalps might be lifted. Then his thoughts shifted to the range they had staked out, which was forty miles square, and about the grass that was fine with not a single cow-brute to eat it, until the arrival of the first LX herd they had brought from Dodge.

These memories of free-and-easy days kept tumbling about in Siringo's mind, until "finally my brain felt like scrambled eggs—a jumbled up mess of woolly buffalo, painted Indians, yelling cowboys, bucking broncos, long horn cattle, [a] fat turkey gobbler, two pretty girls and a big brown jug; then I fell asleep."[7]

The next morning Charlie asked Hollicott to take him back to Amarillo so that he could buy a horse and saddle for his journey to the Indian Territory. Hollicott would not hear of it and insisted that Charlie lay over another night so they could continue to "hark back," this being a favorite expression of his. Siringo explained that he was in a hurry to reach his destination, and that it would take him at least a day or two to buy a horse and saddle. Hollicott replied: "Now Charlie, don't mention horse and saddle to me again. When you get ready to go, the best horse on this ranch will be brought up to the door, saddled and ready to mount, and if that don't suit you, I'll send my team and coachman to take you wherever you want to go."[8]

Siringo remained, and the next morning a five-year-old brown horse, sixteen hands high and in every respect a model piece of horse-flesh, was brought to the door of the stone house at the headquarters ranch. The horse was Glen Alpine, Jr. Charlie remembered the sire, who was a four-mile running horse, and the grandsire on the dam's side was an expensive trotting stallion that Mr. Beals had shipped from Boston when the LX Ranch was first established. Siringo knew this was one gift horse whose mouth he could look into with confidence. On the horse's back was Johnny Bell's saddle.

After Charlie had mounted Glen Alpine, Jr., and bid everyone good-bye, including the two pretty Lee girls, Hollicott told him to never sell this horse, but to shoot him when he had no further use for "his horse-ship." Siringo promised that the horse would never be sold. As Charlie rode off to commence the investigation that had brought him to Texas in the first place, he reflected pleasurably on the preceding two days. His unexpected meeting with Hollicott and subsequent visit to the LX Ranch had stirred nostalgic recollections of his cowboy past. It had been a happy and memorable experience from the time he stepped off the train in Amarillo early Christmas morning to that very moment. Siringo knew that his LX years, with their varied memories, were inextricably woven into the fabric of his life. Yet, he must have also thought ahead to the time when memories of similar bucolic pleasures could be generated on his own Sunny Slope Ranch.

Siringo eventually completed his investigation in Texas and set out on Glen Alpine, Jr., for a 600-mile ride into New Mexico. In the mining camp of San Pedro, 100 miles or so north of White Oaks, Siringo located a young Texas cowboy nicknamed "Cunny," who figured in his far-ranging cattle fraud investigation. Since he wanted to keep a line on Cunny, in case he was ever needed as a witness, he hired the young cowboy to take charge of his Sunny Slope Ranch. He told him he needed a man to look after the place, and that he was fixing the ranch up to be a "hobby horse" he could ride in his old age. Cunny agreed to go to work for Charlie since Santa Fe was only forty miles north and he would not be too far away from his Mexican sweetheart. Still, Siringo said that it took two days of his "valuable time" to pull Cunny away from his girlfriend.

When they reached the ranch, Siringo left Glen Alpine, Jr., in the care of his new foreman and then boarded a train for his return to Denver. Charlie had already come to regard "Glen" as his "pet horse" and the stallion became the first of many pets to find a home on the Sunny Slope Ranch. Later, Glen was joined by a mare, Lulu Edson, another pet horse. True to his word to John Hollicott, Siringo never sold or disposed of Glen Alpine, Jr. The horse died, at age fifteen, after a life of retirement and ease on Siringo's high country ranch.

Over the next decade Siringo made many trips to Santa Fe to see about his ranch and his pets. The young cowboy Charlie hired as his first foreman was never called as a witness and worked on the Sunny Slope Ranch for two years before moving on to try his hand at mine exploration. After Cunny's departure, he employed other caretakers through the years to oversee the ranch during his absence.[9]

Toward the turn of the century the open range was almost gone. By then railroads bound the country from one end to the other with tracks of steel, and fast trains shortened the time it took to cross long distances. With the telephone and telegraph, communication between points had become almost instantaneous. Just when the Wild West seemed ready to bow to the inevitability of law and order, a large band of outlaws began a crime spree that ranged across several western states. The outburst was the last gasp of the cowboy-criminal-badman to ply his trade before civilization had him completely hemmed in.

This band of outlaws was called the Wild Bunch or the Hole-in-the-Wall gang, after one of their favorite hideaways in the rugged region that slashes across northern Wyoming. The gang's undisputed leader was George Leroy Parker, nicknamed "Butch Cassidy." The others included Harvey Logan ("Kid Curry"), Johnny Logan, Lonny Logan, "Flat-Nose" George Curry (no relation to Kid Curry), Harry Longbaugh (the "Sundance Kid"), Bill ("Will") Carver, O. C. Hanks ("Deaf Charlie"), Harry Tracy, Bob Lee (a cousin to the Logans), Elza Lay, and Ben Kilpatrick (the "Tall Texan"). The most notable female hangers-on to the gang were Laura Bullion and Etta Place. Beginning in 1897 and continuing into the twentieth century, the Wild Bunch robbed trains and banks in Colorado, Utah, Wyoming, Montana, and New Mexico. Moving quickly from one outlaw stronghold to another, the group resisted all efforts to capture of dislodge them.

In 1899 the tide began to turn when elements of the Wild Bunch robbed a Union Pacific train at Wilcox, Wyoming, and killed a sheriff while making their escape. The Union Pacific Railroad Company was a client of Pinkerton's National Detective Agency, and W. A. Pinkerton put an army of operatives in the field to pursue this notorious gang. Siringo was assigned to the Wild Bunch case in the early summer of 1899, shortly after W. A. Pinkerton had traveled to the Denver office to map out strategy.[10]

Not long after Pinkerton's conference in Denver, a stranger drifted into the Montana cattle town of Landusky and quickly gained the confidence of the outlaw community. He was a man of slight build, almost grizzled in appearance, with a sun-weathered face and pointed handlebar mustache. "He had piercing gray eyes and wore his six-shooters, draw-fighter style, the holster tied with rawhide to his side." He said his name was Charles L. Carter, an "old Mexican outlaw," who was on the run from a murder charge. Because he was an experienced cowboy and an expert horseman, as well as possessing a congenial manner at the bar, men liked and respected him at the first meeting.

> This remarkable stranger succeeded in joining the ranks of the Wild Bunch and so ingratiated himself into the Train Robbers' Inner Circle that he managed to learn all their secret codes and plans and then he vanished as mysteriously as he had come. He was Pinkerton operative Charles A. Siringo, of the Agency's Denver office, and this information he obtained, together with the secret codes he had learned, was soon in the hands of the gang's intended victims. The leakage of this information held up the plan of the gang for nearly a year.

This is an excerpt from the agency's file on the Wild Bunch and is only the tip of the iceberg concerning this long and involved case.[11] Working undercover with these outlaws was not the only hazard Siringo experienced. Soon after his arrival in Landusky he was in a stagecoach accident and was plunged into the icy waters of the Milk River. In June, Siringo was almost killed when a team of wild horses ran away with a buckboard and overturned with him in it. Charlie sustained head and back injuries and was laid up for three weeks recovering from the accident. Characteristically, he spent his convalescing time in gleaning information about Kid Curry and the other Logans, including the planned robbery of another Union Pacific train.

Siringo continued to pursue various gang members, dogging their trails over mountains, across deserts and swollen rivers, through blizzards, from Wyoming to Arkansas and back again. In all, he spent

four years in the saddle chasing the Wild Bunch and covered an estimated twenty-five thousand miles. The relentless pursuit by Siringo
and other Pinkerton detectives, as well as by civil authorities, gradually diminished and ultimately closed the outlaws' avenues of escape.
One by one, they were all captured or killed. In 1901 Butch Cassidy
and the Sundance Kid left the United States for South America, where
they continued their life of crime. In 1911 Bolivian troops allegedly
killed the pair in a shoot-out in the village of San Vicente. Whether
Butch and Sundance were actually killed, or whether they escaped and
somehow made their way back to the United States as legend has it,
the days of the Wild Bunch were ended.[12]

During his pursuit of members of the Hole-in-the-Wall gang, Siringo managed to pass through Santa Fe several times and see to his
ranch and his pets. He also visited the Reads, who had resettled in
Silver City, New Mexico, and his daughter Viola, who was a student at
the Territorial Normal College there. Viola was now practically grown,
a pretty young lady soon to graduate from college. Seeing his daughter
so mature must have been a shock to Siringo, and intensified his growing urge to settle down and change his lifestyle. More and more he
began thinking of Santa Fe and his Sunny Slope Ranch.[13]

In the winter of 1905–1906 Siringo was sent on an undercover assignment to Oregon, with headquarters at Prineville in the north central part of the state. Later he would write about meeting a pretty girl
who "woke up little Cupid so that he gave . . . [him] a dig or two in the
ribs with his dart." Charlie had to visit the girl's brother, who owned a
horse and cattle ranch up the Ochoco River, and this pretty miss with
"the cute little dimples in her cheeks" did the cooking for them.
Whether or not this was the same young lady, Siringo did meet a girl
by the name of Grace while on this case, whom he fell in love with.
When Charlie returned to Denver, he kept in touch with Grace, maintaining a correspondence with her for the next year and a half.[14]

Siringo's last assignment with the agency was a year's work acting
as bodyguard for James McParland, who was losing his eyesight, while
he gathered evidence throughout Idaho against the Western Federation
of Miners. While on this case, Siringo crossed paths once more with
George Pettibone, his old Coeur d'Alene miners' union running buddy.
Pettibone had become an influential member in the Western Federation of Miners, and he, along with William "Big Bill" Haywood and
Charles Moyer, both WFM leaders, were charged with plotting the

brutal murder of former Idaho governor Frank Steunenberg. During his term in office Steunenberg had incurred the wrath of the WFM by calling out the state militia to put down labor rioting. The trial gained nationwide attention and pitted Clarence Darrow, a brilliant Chicago trial lawyer, against William E. Borah, who was about to begin a thirty-three-year career in the U. S. Senate. Darrow was defending Big Bill Haywood, the initial union leader to stand trial, while Borah and James H. Hawley acted as attorneys for the prosecution. Throughout the seventy-eight days of grueling court action, Haywood alternated between reading Voltaire, Marx, and Engels and issuing inflammatory declarations "to the workers of America." [15]

During the trial the Pinkertons reassigned Siringo to act as bodyguard for Albert E. Horsley, alias Harry Orchard. Horsley was an admitted dynamiter and murderer who testified that he had been hired by the Western Federation of Miners to kill the Idaho ex-governor. [16] He had done so by blowing him up with a bomb he had placed in the governor's front gate. Especially important and, in fact, the key to the prosecution's case, was the confession of Steve Adams, who was Orchard's accomplice and a fellow union dynamiter. Darrow, however, through an uncle, persuaded Adams to repudiate his confession. It was a devastating blow to the state's case, and even McParland's persuasiveness failed to get Adams to change his mind.

McParland had elicited Orchard's confession, which, along with the supporting evidence in the hands of Borah, made a convincing case against Haywood and the other union leaders. Clarence Darrow, through the clever use of sarcasm and innuendo directed against McParland, attempted to cast doubt on the veracity of Orchard's confession. Then, with matchless hyperbole, Darrow painted a picture of brutal capital oppressing weak labor. It was one of the most famous of Darrow's speeches and required eleven hours for delivery. Borah's summation was not as lengthy but, with the preponderant weight of evidence on his side, he skillfully presented the state's case against the defendant.

Despite the oratorical brilliance of the opposing lawyers, it was Judge Fremont Wood's charge to the jury that had the most telling effect. Wood advised the jurors that he had no doubt that Orchard's testimony was true, but "a person cannot be convicted of a crime upon the testimony of an accomplice alone." The charge, in effect, sealed the outcome of the jury's deliberation, and a verdict of not guilty was handed down. As William A. Pinkerton remarked, Adams's repudiation of his confession "pulled the plug on the state's case." [17]

Soon after the trial Siringo received a tip that a group of angry citizens were planning to hang Haywood, Pettibone, and Moyer along with their attorney, Clarence Darrow. He passed the information on to his chief, James McParland; and McParland, in turn, advised Idaho governor Frank Gooding, who was staying at the same hotel. According to the informant, the jailor had been paid off, and a number of prominent citizens from around the state were coming by train to lead a lynch mob. Governor Gooding met the citizens' group at the railroad station and persuaded them not to commit such an act of lawlessness, saying that the state would be disgraced by it. The mob dispersed and the would-be lynching was averted. Although Siringo's prompt action in behalf of his opponents did not win him any plaudits from the trio of WFM leaders, it did make an impression on Clarence Darrow he would not forget. Haywood, Pettibone, and Moyer were set free. Ironically, Pettibone's fate had already been sealed. During his confinement in prison he had developed "stir disease," the prison name for consumption, from which he soon died. Orchard was tried the following year and sentenced to be hanged; later, his sentence was commuted to life imprisonment. [18]

As Siringo carried out his duties during the Haywood trial, his mind turned to other matters of a more personal interest. He thought about his Santa Fe ranch and about Grace, with whom he had been corresponding. He also thought about the book he planned to write relating his experiences as a Pinkerton detective. Twenty-one years of active service now lay behind him. He recalled how naive and innocent he had been when he first walked into W. A. Pinkerton's Chicago office in the wake of the Haymarket bomb explosion, and how soon the disillusionment of reality had shattered his noble and altruistic dreams. Notwithstanding the obstacles of conscience, Siringo had continued his pursuit of a professional career in law enforcement. He thought about his many years in the saddle, and the detective operations he could no longer count that had taken him to every state and territory in the American West. He had followed outlaw trails under every weather condition, from blazing sun to freezing blizzard. He had observed human nature at first hand and up close; and if his education had been accompanied by a growing cynicism, he never became bitter or lost his sense of humor. Nevertheless, he felt it was time to hang up his six-gun and embark on a more pastoral and serene lifestyle.

Upon his return to Denver, he wrote out his resignation from the agency. McParland tried to persuade him to stay on and take a position as superintendent of an agency branch office. Siringo replied that his years of schooling with the Pinkertons had taught him all he wished to know about the ways of the world, and he declined the offer.

Having finally severed his ties with the agency, Siringo boarded a train in Denver and headed for Oregon to meet Grace, who had accepted his proposal of marriage. It was late August, 1907, when Charlie and his new bride stepped off the train at Santa Fe. George Tweedy, Charlie's ranch foreman, was on hand at the station with a buckboard to meet the newlyweds. As the wheels of the conveyance clattered along Cerrillos Road, life must have seemed rosy to Siringo. At long last, he was ready to begin leading the "simple life" on his Sunny Slope Ranch.[19]

PART III
NEW MEXICO INTERLUDE, 1907–1922

I liked [Santa Fe] so well that . . . I secured a tract of land a short distance from . . . the city and christened it the Sunny Slope Ranch . . . a "hobby horse" [for me] to ride in my old age.

—from *A Cowboy Detective*

6 / THE "COWBOY DETECTIVE" CONTROVERSY

HARDLY more than a month had passed after Siringo's arrival in Santa Fe when he received an urgent letter from James McParland asking him to undertake a complicated cattle operation in South Dakota for the agency. When McParland's message arrived, Charlie was deep into leading the simple life for which he had been yearning. Although he enjoyed helping his foreman milk his fine blooded Jersey cows and care for the white Leghorn chickens and the homing pigeons, his restless nature had begun to chafe at the regimen of tranquility. He wired McParland his acceptance, kissed his bride good-bye, and boarded a train for the Badlands of South Dakota. A few months later he was back on his ranch, but only for a short time. The William J. Burns Detective Agency in Chicago persuaded him to go to Nevada to find out how miners were "high grading" ore from a gold mine near the state line.

Grace Siringo, meanwhile, was finding the Rocky Mountains of the desert southwest vastly different from those of the rugged Pacific northwest where she had grown up. Not only was the scenery different, the people and customs were different, too. Perhaps her transition could have been made less difficult if her husband had not left her alone much of the time. Before Charlie left for Nevada, Grace told him she wanted to go home to visit her parents. Siringo readily gave his consent for, after all, his bride of six months was considerably younger than he was and this was her first time away from home. Eight months later, when Siringo completed his assignment for the Burns Detective Agency, he returned to Santa Fe and the Sunny Slope Ranch. Grace, on the other hand, did not return from Oregon. As her absence became more extended, Siringo tried writing to her to persuade her to come back, but she refused. A year and a half later, when it became certain that she would never return, he sought a dissolution of the marriage, and on April 15, 1909, the New Mexico Territorial District Court granted the divorce.[1] Somewhat discouraged with matrimony after three trips to the altar, with death terminating one marriage and divorce the other two, Siringo now seemed resigned to a life without female companionship.

A year later, in 1910, the lure of action and adventure again beckoned when the Burns Agency sent him to Morenci, Arizona, to investigate the daylight robbery of the Gila Valley Bank. Harvey Logan, alias Kid Curry of the old Wild Bunch, was the prime suspect, and Siringo traced the fugitive to Alma, New Mexico, a tiny village near the Arizona border that was notorious as a hideout for outlaws. There the trail disappeared, leaving Siringo only his report to file and to return to his ranch and his pets at Santa Fe.[2]

Animals had always been an important part of Siringo's life (who can forget his faithful dog Ranger from *A Texas Cowboy*), and now that he was alone once more, his pets would continue to dominate as companions and as the focus of his affections. As would be expected, Charlie was particularly fond of horses, and his two favorites at that time were Rowdy and Patsy, both offspring stallions of Lulu Edson, an earlier favorite.[3] His special feeling for horses, perhaps even an empathy for them, went back for many years. In Part IV of his "Addenda" to *A Texas Cowboy*, the 1886 edition, he devoted ten pages to "The Cow-Pony and How He Is Abused on the Large Cattle Ranches." Siringo deplored brutal treatment and cruelty to horses wherever he witnessed it. In his addenda, Siringo's humanitarian sensitivity is clearly revealed, providing the leaven that distinguishes this essay as an example of his best and most vivid writing. As a device to convey his point, Siringo asks the reader to imagine himself as the horse, whom he then carries through a litany of abuses that are moving and even heart-rending.[4]

Throughout his life Siringo was kind and tender-hearted to animals, and his fondness was not limited to horses. In the fall of 1904, while working on a case in Wyoming, he bought a half-starved Russian wolfhound puppy from a rancher on the Laramie plains. The animal was so weak he had to carry it across his saddle, and because of its emaciated appearance he named the pup "Jimmie Longlegs." Upon reaching a creek, he spied a mudhen and shot it for Jimmie, but before he could defeather the bird, the dog made a grab for it and in a wink had consumed feathers, bill, feet, and all. Charlie then changed Jimmie's name to "Eat 'em Up Jake," or E.E.U.J. for short. Upon reaching Cheyenne, he crated the pup and shipped him Railway Express to Santa Fe to join his other pets. Mr. and Mrs. Ben C. Volk, who had charge of Siringo's ranch at that time, kept the dog so filled up that when Siringo next saw him, he had grown to be a beautiful specimen of the Russian wolfhound breed.[5]

Later Charlie acquired another wolfhound, a female named Klondike, to be a mate for E.E.U.J. Nothing gave him more pleasure than to saddle Rowdy or Patsy, then go for a gallop and watch Eat 'em Up Jake and Klondike chase jack rabbits and coyotes. Siringo and his wolfhounds became a familiar sight around Santa Fe, as almost daily he would ride into town on one of his horses accompanied by one or more of his dogs. One of Charlie's friends was J. F. "Jack" Collins, who owned a curio store in Santa Fe. (These emporiums are now referred to as Indian arts and crafts galleries.) Collins was a recipient of one of Charlie's wolfhound pups, and he thought nothing of allowing his dog to sleep on the expensive Navajo rugs in his shop. Siringo's Russian wolfhounds, an unusual breed for that time and place, were so admired that he sold or gave away over fifty of E.E.U.J.'s puppies.[6]

Another of Charlie's pets was "Miss Pussy-cat." She had been given to him when only a wee kitten by Charles Ivey, a saloon man in Fort Steel, Wyoming. Because Siringo was working undercover at the time pursuing members of the Wild Bunch and using the name Harry Blevins, Ivey did not recognize him. Yet Siringo remembered Ivey from the time they both had worked as cowboys together on the LX Ranch in Texas in 1877. Although he could not reveal his identity to Ivey, he accepted the kitten and took it back to his Santa Fe ranch as a sentimental token of this one-sided reunion.[7]

It was during these years as a New Mexico rancher, and between assignments as a free-lance detective, that Siringo wrote his second book, another autobiography, which related his experiences with the Pinkertons. Through the financial support of a close Santa Fe friend, Charlie contracted with the W. B. Conkey Company of Hammond, Indiana, to publish his manuscript. He had entitled it "Pinkerton's Cowboy Detective, A True Story of 22 Years with Pinkerton's National Detective Agency." His Santa Fe friend, and backer, was Alois B. Renehan, an attorney, writer, and Republican politician, whom Charlie had known since 1894. Renehan had agreed to pay the publishing costs of Siringo's book in return for a one-third interest in the profits. This was not the first time Renehan had subscribed to one of Siringo's projects to make money, nor would it be the last. Somehow, the ties of friendship between these two men, each different from the other in many ways, would remain close and steadfast throughout their lives.[8]

Alois B. Renehan was born on January 6, 1869, in Alexandria, Virginia, but grew up in New York City, where his father was an associate editor of the New York *Tribune* under Horace Greeley. Later he moved with his parents to Brooklyn, then to Philadelphia, and after that to Washington, D.C. Renehan began his higher education at St. Charles College in Maryland, where he studied for the priesthood. However, he gave up the idea of taking vows and began to pursue other interests. During the next few years he worked in the Washington-Georgetown area, first as a stenographer and bookkeeper, then as a French translator for the Department of Agriculture; later he managed a construction firm, during which time he began to study law; and finally, he turned his attention to real estate and insurance.

Dissatisfied with opportunities in the nation's capital, he decided to try his fortune in the Southwest and headed for New Mexico. He arrived in Santa Fe on September 10, 1892, armed with a letter of introduction to Governor L. B. Prince. His first position was that of a stenographer for Edward L. Bartlett. He was admitted to the New Mexico bar in 1894 but did not take up an active practice of law until the latter part of 1896.

Renehan had been a Democrat in his early days, but because of a firm belief in a strong protective tariff, he switched to the Republican Party and remained active in party affairs throughout his life. He served two terms as city attorney of Santa Fe, and later he was elected to the city council, on which he served two terms as its president. In time, he would be elected to both the lower house in the state legislature and the New Mexico state senate. Renehan's interests were wide ranging: he was a classical scholar, he was interested in history, and he composed poetry. His background of experience, along with his natural business acumen, enabled him to become successfully involved in banking, real estate, and insurance, but it would be as an attorney that he made his reputation. Al Renehan was just beginning what would become a long and brilliant legal career when he and Charlie Siringo met and became friends.[9]

By January, 1910, Siringo had finished his new autobiography and had put it in the hands of his publisher. While the Conkey Company was typesetting the manuscript, they began promoting the book with photo-pictorial posters, headlined in bold red letters, at various railway station newsstands.[10] When a Pinkerton operative noticed one of these posters and tried to purchase a copy of the book, he was told it had not yet been published. After reporting these facts to his superiors, the agency succeeded in securing the galley sheets from the Conkey Company. The Pinkertons hired attorney John A. Brown, of the Chicago firm of Kern & Brown, and on February 28, 1910, the Superior Court of Cook County, Illinois, issued a temporary injunction against both Siringo and the Conkey Company, enjoining them from "publishing, advertising, selling, or offering for sale or in any manner printing, circulating, or disposing of any copy or copies of said 'Pinkerton's Cowboy Detective.'"[11]

Siringo received a letter from the Conkey Company with word of the injunction before actually being served himself. Included with the letter was a clipping from one of the Chicago papers carrying a news item concerning the injunction:

> "Pinkerton's Cowboy Detective" will not be placed on the market . . . if William A. Pinkerton, head of Pinkerton's National Detective Agency, can prevent it. He filed a bill for an injunction . . . today to restrain the W. B. Conkey Company from publishing the book . . . [which] is the work of Charles A. Siringo, formerly employed by the Pinkerton Company. "Such stories ought not be published," said Mr. Pinkerton. "They are damaging to the young reader and mislead the public. Despite my firm conviction on this point, however, I probably would not have sought to interfere had not Siringo taken the liberty of using my name. That I will not stand."[12]

Siringo was furious when he learned of the injunction, and he turned immediately to Al Renehan for advice. Because the book did not breach any confidences nor reveal any agency secrets, Renehan counseled Charlie to write his former employer and, without being bellicose, try to reason with him in friendly, persuasive manner. Renehan thought such a letter, carefully phrased, might resolve the matter. On the other hand, he cautioned, if Siringo tried to apply pressure by using threats, then he might find himself against a stone wall. Charlie listened to his attorney's avuncular advice and agreed he would write a letter to W. A. Pinkerton.

He was still in high dudgeon when he left Renehan's office and headed west from the plaza down San Francisco Street. He turned south on Don Gaspar and quickly walked one block to Gregg's Peerless Hotel. Entering the lobby, he seated himself at a writing desk provided for hotel guests and proceeded to dash off a nine-page letter to William A. Pinkerton. Instead of heeding Renehan's caveat, he threw down the gauntlet: "If you don't call off your dogs of war and insist on stirring up a hornet's nest, I may be compelled to . . . add a chapter or two of truths which will not look good to you." He then went on for pages citing case after case he could have put in the book but did not, because such exposure would have given the agency a tawdry image.[13]

When finished, Siringo carried the letter back to Renehan's office to have it typed. This gave the attorney an opportunity to carefully edit out some of the more inflammatory expressions. Charlie's "dogs of war" was changed to "call off your dogs," and the "hornet's nest" remark was eliminated completely. Renehan virtually rewrote Siringo's letter and, in doing so, expanded on the care he had exercised in the crafting of his book. "There is not a secret betrayed," he wrote, "not a reflection on the agency made, not an exposure of reprehensible methods and . . . facts, such as I might have used . . . You will not deny that I was 'Pinkerton's cowboy detective.' You will not deny that my work was well done and as ethical as could be. I believe I am entitled to some consideration from you," the letter concluded.[14]

At this point Renehan was probably unaware and Charlie may have forgotten that he had signed a contract when he went to work for the agency stipulating that all information he received during the course of his work "should forever be kept secret . . . and never directly nor indirectly revealed except to the [agency] or a person authorized by the [agency] to receive the same."[15] If Siringo did remember signing such an agreement, he probably assumed that it only restricted him from revealing agency secrets or matters of a confidential nature, and this he had done. Thus, he bitterly resented Pinkerton's action against him, as he considered the injunction an unjust infringement of his rights.

Renehan, on Siringo's behalf, hired the Chicago law firm of Sheriff, Dent, Dobyns & Freeman, and Fletcher Dobyns was selected to defend the case. Siringo's deposition was taken in Santa Fe and submitted to a master in Chancery in the Superior Court of Cook County. The case dragged on for the next year and a half, with negotiations continuing between the two opposing attorneys. Finally, Alois Renehan took a train to Chicago and met with both Dobyns and Brown to see if the problems could not be ironed out. As a result of these meetings, William A. Pinkerton agreed not to object to publication of the book if the Pinkerton name was removed from the title and every place it appeared within the text. Also, he insisted that the names of the principals in the book had to be fictionalized.[16]

Pinkerton's conditions made Charlie's "tiger blood" boil, and at first he refused to consider them. Alois Renehan, on the other hand, Charlie's partner in the book, had already borne the expense of paying the Conkey Company to keep the type for the book set up, as well as the cost of attorneys' fees and travel expense to Chicago. It is easy to understand why his feelings about the book were not as dogmatic as Siringo's. Fletcher Dobyns wrote Charlie in the fall of 1911 to advise him that, unless he had the financial resources to fight the case for at least five years, he should accept the palliative Pinkerton had offered. According to Dobyns, Pinkerton had told his attorney that if the case went against them, he would fight it all the way to the Supreme Court.[17]

Siringo realized then that he had no choice but to accede to W. A. Pinkerton's terms, and he set about at once making the changes that would permit publication. All of the names in the book, with the exception of a few of Siringo's fellow operatives, were to be fictionalized with names both parties had agreed upon. The manuscript's title was changed from "Pinkerton's Cowboy Detective" to simply "A Cowboy Detective." After Siringo completed these modifications, the Conkey Company struck two sets of galleys and sent them to Brown for his review and approval. As he leafed through the galleys, the Pinkerton attorney observed a few penciled notations to cure several printing anomalies, but in addition he discovered that in several places Siringo has allowed the name "Pinkerton," as well as a number of other banned names, to slip by. Brown circled these names that were still set in type in both sets of galleys, and to the side penciled in the fictitious name replacements. He then returned one copy with the dual corrections to the publisher.[18]

With the Pinkertons now apparently satisfied and with Siringo's revised book in press, Judge Richard E. Burke heard the Pinkerton petition to make the temporary injunction permanent. On December 12, 1911, Burke signed the decree for a permanent injunction against Siringo's use of the Pinkerton name or revealing information about the agency. Siringo completed his preface to the finished volume on January 6, 1912.

> This story of twenty years of active service as a detective . . . has been delayed for a long time in coming from the press. The delay was due to the protests of the author's former employers. These protests were undoubtedly rightful, but it was considered . . . that no harm could come therefrom, for the reason that the identity of persons involved was not disclosed except in reference to past facts, matters that were done and over with. Now this difficulty has been overcome and the objections removed by the use of fictitious names in many places.[19]

By late January, 1912, two thousand copies of A Cowboy Detective, in cloth, were printed, and although the Pinkertons had allowed significant concessions, the issue as far as Siringo was concerned still was not settled. Somehow, there was an inconsistency with his public confession that his former employer's protests were "undoubtedly rightful." An indication of this inconsistency was the envelopes he had printed showing his return address as "Charles A. Siringo, Author of [and then in large bold type] 'Pinkerton's Cowboy Detective'/A True Story of 22 Years with Pinkerton's National Detective Agency/P.O. Box 322, Santa Fe, New Mexico." Then with a pen he drew a single thin line through the name "Pinkerton's" in the title and wrote the capital letter "A" out to the side, leaving no doubt as to the original title.

In addition, superintendent McParland's name, which was changed to McCartney in the text of A Cowboy Detective and accompanying illustration, remains McParland in the Table of Contents and in the headnote to Chapter XXI. Tim Corn, which was the fictional replacement for Tom Horn in the book, still appears as Horn three times on page 233. Even the Pinkerton name appears on page 362. Clearly, Brown had missed these in going over the galley proofs and had allowed them to slip by, apparently just as Siringo had hoped he might. If the appearance of these names was in fact the deliberate and contrived evasions of a determined author, the accomplishment was not regarded as a *quid pro quo* in Siringo's mind for what he had been put through. Yet, for the time being, he kept his true feelings in abeyance as he occupied himself with other endeavors.[20]

When Siringo was not out hustling his new book, or off on a detective assignment, he relished his role as a gentleman rancher, tending his stock, enjoying his pets, and entertaining visitors and guests. Around Santa Fe he was much admired for his expert horsemanship and old-style cowboy manner. Even in his later days, the way Charlie could dodge prairie dog holes while riding at a gallop was the marvel of his friends. Siringo loved the trappings of the West and felt happiest when he was on horseback, his mount adorned with a silver-decorated bridle and saddle, and with silver spurs on his star-topped boots. He always wore the eye-shading sombrero and frequently wrapped the ancien régime silk sash around his waist in the style of the early-day Mexican vaqueros.

When Charlie's daughter, Viola, visited the Sunny Slope Ranch after her graduation from college in Silver City, for two weeks she accompanied her father on daily horseback outings. Other regular visitors included Siringo's attorney friend Alois B. Renehan and his pretty wife, who would ride out to see Charlie and his pets. Friends arriving Sunday afternoons usually found Siringo and George Tweedy indulging in a favorite indoor diversion—taking turns gazing at slides of faraway places through an old stereopticon.[21]

In late December, 1912, Siringo was employed to do some investigative work on the Texas Gulf Coast. He eagerly accepted the assignment, for it meant a return to the land of his youth, where he could not only renew old friendships but sell copies of his new book. Although he discharged the duties of his investigation within the first two weeks, he prolonged his stay at his own expense. For two months he visited acquaintances from Bay City to Port Lavaca. In Palacios he stayed in the fine resort Hotel Palacios, managed by C. M. Rebou, and in Blessing he was the guest of John E. Pierce at his new hotel. He visited the old Rancho Grande headquarters and the nearby Deming's Bridge-Hawley Cemetery to see Shanghai Pierce's $10,000 bronze statue, which had been erected before his death. It stood forty feet high, and Siringo thought it was "as natural as life." Looking at the statue, Charlie imagined he could hear Shanghai's voice, "which could be heard nearly half a mile, even when he tried to whisper."

Siringo was warmly greeted everywhere he went and seemingly had no problem selling copies of A Cowboy Detective at a dollar apiece, which was fifty cents less than the usual retail price. He observed in a letter to Al Renehan "that the difference between $1.50 and $1.00 cuts quite a figure in selling a book." Apparently, he had encountered resistance in some people who felt that a dollar and half was too much to pay for a book. So he had lowered the price to a dollar in order to make the sales. He became convinced that he needed to get out a cheaper paperback edition to offer to those who declined to pay the higher price for the clothbound copies.[22]

During his stay on the Texas coastal plain he met and became enamored of an attractive older woman whose name was Ellen Partain, the widow of T. E. Partain. Charlie had known the Partains during the days he had worked for Shanghai Pierce on the Rancho Grande nearly forty years before. Obviously, he and Ellen had much in common to talk about.

With the beginning of spring Siringo had intended to retrace the old Chisholm Trail. He had even brought with him his dog, Eat 'em Up Jake, and his two pet saddle horses, Rowdy and Patsy. Instead, soon after the first of March, he loaded his pets on an Atchison, Topeka & Santa Fe boxcar and shipped them back to Santa Fe. His excuse was that the horses, being used to the insect-free high altitude of the Sunny Slope Ranch, were being driven wild by the biting flies at sea level.[23] In any event, with his animals out of the way, Charlie popped the question to Ellen, and she said "yes." A month later they were married in Arkansas.

Charlie returned to Santa Fe and the Sunny Slope Ranch with Ellen, but as had been the case with Grace, the ship of matrimony began to founder and sink after only a two-month cruise.[24] The small windows in Siringo's two-room adobe ranch house provided little natural light, and the darkness along with the cramped quarters may have been depressing to her. Whatever the reason, Ellen did not remain at the ranch for long. Siringo's divorce petition, filed in September, noted that his wife had become restless and dissatisfied and would go back to Texas for visits with her kin. Her excuse for leaving was that she had business interests in Texas and it was not right that her husband expected her to remain full time in Santa Fe. On June 24 she left for Dalhart, never to return. She did come back to Santa Fe briefly in August, but not to Siringo or the Sunny Slope Ranch. By October 16, 1913, the divorce became final. Although he never lost his eye for the ladies, Charlie had seen the elephant as far as marriage was concerned, and he would try no more.[25]

7 / TWO EVIL ISMS
AND OTHER MISVENTURES

FOLLOWING his return to Santa Fe and his divorce from Ellen, Siringo began to actively plan for the publication of a paperback edition of *A Cowboy Detective*. The first printing was nowhere near to being sold out, but Charlie believed that an edition in paper wrappers, selling at a cheaper price, would have wider appeal. Renehan held the stock of *A Cowboy Detective* books as security for the money he had invested, and Siringo was obliged to buy the clothbound copies as he needed them at the wholesale price of seventy-five cents each. However, Charlie has possession of the plates, and in 1914 he began negotiations with the Hill Binding Company in Chicago. The company agreed to produce 5,000 copies of *A Cowboy Detective* in paperback for $625, or twelve and a half cents per copy. After mortgaging his ranch to raise the money, he gave this Chicago firm the go-ahead to manufacture the books.[1]

The paper cover of this edition carried a portrait of Siringo that, beyond a doubt, was his most dashing likeness. It had been taken in Boise City, Idaho, in 1907 during the trial of Big Bill Haywood. In the picture Siringo is seated and wearing a suit with a narrow-brim western hat. A boutonniere graces his lapel, and a gaudy stickpin anchors the Windsor knot in his tie. In his left hand he is holding a cane with a carved head, and in his right hand, lying across his lap, is an engraved silver-plated Colt .45 six-shooter.[2] A trace of a smile can be discerned beneath his mustache, and his eyes, gazing off to the side, sparkle mischievously.

In addition to the portrait on the front cover, the book differed from the first printing in two other features. The title page bore the imprint "Santa Fe, New Mexico, 1914." But the important difference was in the title itself. On the front cover Siringo had added a subtitle: "Twenty-Two Years with Pinkerton's National Detective Agency."

Charlie seemed determined to tell his life story despite any restrictions or prohibitions. The Hill Binding Company, unaware of the injunction, printed the books and shipped 2,000 of them to Charlie in Santa Fe. The firm agreed to warehouse the remaining 3,000 copies until such time that Siringo needed them.

By the end of the year he had shipped, on consignment, nearly half of his stock to various newsstand distributors; 500 of the new paperbacks were shipped to Fred Harvey in Kansas City, 200 to the Union News in Saint Louis, and a like number to the same firm in Chicago. He also consigned 200 of the clothbound copies to the Rock Island News Service in Kansas City. The Pinkertons must have done a double take when this paperback of *A Cowboy Detective*, with their name prominently displayed in the subtitle, appeared on the newsstands. But if they did take notice, they did not take any action. Charlie had thumbed his nose at the agency, in a small but conspicuous manner, and the Pinkertons let him get away with it.[3]

Still, Siringo took little satisfaction from such potshots in defiance of the Pinkerton injunction. Privately, he had been seething ever since the agency forced him to modify his cowboy detective book, and what he really wanted was to extract his pound of flesh. Before the first printing of *A Cowboy Detective* was more than two years old, Siringo began writing a new book in which he gave vent to his anger, frustration, and bitterness. By late summer of 1914 he finished his manuscript and gave it to Al Renehan to look over. It was a scathing and tendentious exposé of his former employers entitled "Two Evil Isms, Pinkertonism and Anarchism, By a Cowboy Detective Who Knows, as He Spent Twenty-Two Years in the Inner Circle of Pinkerton's National Detective Agency."[4]

Renehan, after reading the manuscript, told a friend that he thought Charlie was "going wild." The book really did not have much to say about anarchism, and, in fact, later on some officials of the National Socialist Party offered to support its publication if Siringo would agree to delete certain portions unfavorable to their cause and also change the name in the title from "Anarchism" to "Capitalism." Siringo said he could not conscientiously do this but admitted that circumstances might drive him to do it.[5]

Toward the middle of October, Charlie handed the Pinkerton agent in Santa Fe a package addressed to the General Manager of Pinkerton's National Detective Agency in New York. When Wells Fargo Express delivered the package to the New York City office, it was opened and found to contain a seventy-eight-page typewritten manuscript of "Two Evil Isms," a penciled illustration for the front cover design, and a letter from Siringo:

Santa Fe, N.M. Oct. 17, 1914

General Manager
Pinkerton [*sic*] N. D. A.
New York, N.Y.

Dear Sir:—

I am sending you herewith a type-written manuscript, and the front cover illustration of a new book, "Two Evil Isms" which I expect to have published this fall.

As your agency caused me a cash loss of $2,000.00 by tying up my other book, "A Cowboy Detective," after it was ready for the press, I am anxious to get your *lawful* objections to this one, "Two Evil Isms" before it is set in type. If you will point out any objectionable features, which are not lawful, and for the *public good*, I will gladly cut them out, as it is my wish to stay within the law.

So please act promptly, as I am *wanted*, as a witness, in a big case in Canada, wherein your agency will be the Star Actor, and it is my wish to have this booklet on sale there, at 25¢ a copy; also at the San Diego and San Francisco Expositions. On account of that good man, during his life-time, Robt. A. Pinkerton, and his descendants, I dislike to act as a witness against your agency, but I need the money.

Please return this manuscript at your earliest convenience, as I may need it, in case my other copy goes astray enroute to the printer.

I shall leave here, to be gone a couple of months, the last part of next week, but you can address me here, P.O. Box 322, until further orders.

Very truly yours,
Charles A. Siringo[6]

The Pinkertons did not have to read far in Charlie's manuscript to find "objectionable features." Among other things, Siringo charged that the Pinkerton operatives bribed juries, corrupted police officers and public officials, fixed elections, kidnapped witnesses, and even caused the execution of innocent men. If that was not enough to inflame the Pinkertons, then the cover illustration accompanying the manuscript was like waving a red flag in front of an enraged bull. The drawing, in red and black, depicted Uncle Sam in a standing position with one leg and his upper body entwined by a large snake labeled "Pinkertonism." Another smaller snake, its head held down by Uncle Sam's boot and labeled "Anarchism," was wrapped around his other leg.

The New York office forwarded this material to John A. Brown, the Pinkerton attorney in Chicago. Brown immediately wrote Siringo, Renehan, and the W. B. Conkey Company that the publication of "Two Evil Isms" would be grounds for not only civil but criminal prosecution. Brown stated in his letters that the typescript contained considerable matter that had been suppressed in the "Cowboy Detective" case, and that it was "false, scandalous, malicious, and libelous." Brown told the Conkey Company that Siringo's notice "savors strongly of blackmail and an attempt on Siringo's part to have Pinkerton's National Detective Agency purchase his manuscript from him."[7]

Renehan and the Conkey Company had nothing to do with "Two Evil Isms" but were presumed to be guilty by association because of their part in the earlier book, *A Cowboy Detective*. Renehan replied to Brown's letter saying that he had no interest whatever in the alleged book. "I was interested in 'The Cowboy Detective' and still am," he added dryly, "to the extent of some thousands of dollars that I would like to get."[8]

Charlie was undaunted by Brown's threatening letters. He told Renehan he had found a man in Ohio who, for a one-third interest in the book, would advance the money to publish it. By December, 1914, Siringo was temporarily residing in Chicago, at 422 South Dearborn Street, in order to line up a printer to have the work done. He also took his manuscript to the law office of Clarence Darrow to get his opinion of it. Darrow was appreciative of Siringo's prompt action, following the trial of Big Bill Haywood in 1907, which may have saved him from an angry lynch mob. Repaying the favor with free legal advice, Darrow told Siringo that the worst penalty in Illinois for criminal libel would be a $500 fine and a year in jail. Charlie replied, "That wouldn't kill me."[9]

By December 17 he still had not secured the money needed to publish his book, so he turned once more to his friend Renehan to solicit his help. In a letter to the attorney he said he had heard from his man in Ohio who had written that he would not be able to send any money for at least two more months. Siringo told Renehan that he had replied saying he could not wait that long because it would delay publication of the book until at least the end of February.

Then came the pitch: "I think so much of the 'Two Evil Isms' as a money maker that I would risk everything I own to get it out." Then as a clincher, and to show Renehan that others shared his unbridled optimism, he said that William J. Burns, of the Burns Detective Agency, after reading the first chapter of the manuscript, told him he thought he could sell a million copies!

Siringo then asked Renehan to "see Mr. Martin—the man who has a year's option on my ranch for $5,000—and persuade him to close the deal *now*. I would sacrifice $1,000 of the purchase price. In other words he could have the place for $4,000." He also asked his lawyer friend to see if he could sell an eighty-one-front-foot lot on Cerrillos Road that he owned, saying he would take $300 for it.[10]

He wrote Renehan again on January 22: "Clarence Darrow is now reading 'Two Evil Isms' for the second time to note any libel points. He will return it Monday—then the plates will be made and it will go the printer and binder in the course of a couple of weeks."[11]

Renehan filed both of Charlie's letters and in his reply made no mention of "Two Evil Isms." What could he say that had not already been said? There was no man in Ohio! That is, such an individual seems to exist only within the pages of Siringo's letters. Renehan probably guessed as much, but it did not matter. He knew Charlie was not just tilting at windmills, but attempting to refight a war he had already lost. This was one scheme in which Renehan did not intend to participate.[12]

Why was Siringo so determined to produce a book, even without financial support, that carried with it the very real threat of a jail term? This and other perplexing questions, raised by the "Two Evil Isms" affair, begin with Siringo's letter of October 17 to the Pinkerton Agency's New York office, a letter that can only be described as bizarre. The very idea that the Pinkertons might critique his manuscript and return it to him, especially after the "Cowboy Detective" experience, is patently absurd. If Siringo knew that, and he probably did, and his motive was only to "stir up a hornet's nest," why did he divert his bombshell by sending it to New York? Why did he not just direct his package to Chicago, W. A. Pinkerton's headquarters, in the first place?

John Brown's conjecture that Siringo's notice to the agency "savors of blackmail" and that it was an attempt to induce the Pinkertons to purchase his manuscript from him may have been an accurate assessment. If that is true, then by sending the letter and manuscript to New York, instead of Chicago, under the thin disguise of making a seemingly innocent interrogative, Siringo could later deny a charge of blackmail.

After all of Siringo's difficulties over the publication of "Pinkerton's Cowboy Detective," it seems unlikely that he really intended to publish "Two Evil Isms," especially after Renehan had read the manuscript and advised him of the probable consequences. Perhaps he figured he would not have to publish it. He may have reasoned that the Pinkertons might want to avoid an unfavorable exposé, even from a book that would have to be illegally published and distributed, and therefore might offer to pay him for his manuscript in order to keep him quiet. His letter had even suggested an appropriate purchase price. If successful, the payoff would not only wipe out his debts incurred by the Pinkerton litigation but would be sweet revenge as well.

Once he realized the Pinkertons were not going to take the bait, he then felt he had no choice but to publish his book in defiance of their threats, and then take his chances. His big problem, of course, was money. Siringo knew that Al Renehan was not a prospect with his already heavy investment in *A Cowboy Detective*. So when Charlie headed to Chicago, he hoped he could find a backer there, or that H. M. Martin might soon close on his ranch, which he had put up for sale. None of these alternatives had come to pass, including his last-ditch plea, of sorts, to Al Renehan.[13]

With everything arranged for publication except the money to fund his project, Siringo turned in desperation to his daughter for help. Viola, following her graduation from the Territorial Normal College (now Western New Mexico University), had met and married Joseph W. Reid, a native of California who was ranching near Silver City. Later, the Reids moved to Prescott, Arizona, and it was there Siringo contacted his daughter.[14] Viola agreed to send her father some money, precisely how much is not known. To secure the loan, Siringo could only give her a third mortgage on his Sunny Slope Ranch. Alonzo Compton held a first mortgage as security for Siringo's note of $625, the money he had borrowed to publish the paperback edition of *A Cowboy Detective*. Siringo also owed H. S. Kaunne & Company of Santa Fe the amount of $2,272, secured by a second mortgage on his ranch.

Although the exact details of Siringo's arrangements with the printer are not known, a likely scenario can be constructed from the available evidence. Siringo was eager and anxious to get his book out, and with the promise of money from Viola, it appears he persuaded the Hill Binding Company to extend him a line of credit secured by the 3,000 paperback copies of *A Cowboy Detective* it was warehousing. Hill was then to print as many copies of "Two Evil Isms" as the credit would cover, and this would get Charlie started with a book for which he seemed to have boundless enthusiasm.[15]

By early March *Two Evil Isms* was on the newsstands in Chicago. When a Pinkerton operative saw the book, he purchased a copy and turned it over to his superior. It soon found its way into the hands of W. O. Watkins, an assistant to William A. Pinkerton. Watkins flooded the Chicago streets with agency employees checking newsstands and buying up copies of the book. An examination of *Two Evil Isms* offered no clues as to where it had been published, for the only address was Siringo's post office box number in Chicago. While operatives were detailed to an around-the-clock surveillance of Charlie's post office box, the Pinkertons through attorney Brown went to court charging Siringo with "rabid, open and flagrant violation of the injunction."[16]

When watching Siringo's post office box proved fruitless, the agency began sending out detectives to call on all of the printing establishments in Chicago. On March 24 the agency had its first break when an operative visited the Hill Binding Company on West Van Buren Street and asked to buy twenty-five copies of the "pamphlet" *Two Evil Isms*. An employee told the detective that the company had indeed bound the book but did not have any copies for sale. Further inquiry revealed the fact that the J. Thomas Printing Company had actually printed the books.[17]

That afternoon the agency sent another operative to the printing company, located at 621 Plymouth Court. The office manager admitted that his firm had printed between 1,000 and 1,100 copies but that he had none on hand to sell. While he was talking, the Pinkerton detective noticed an order lying on the manager's desk from the Hill Binding Company, dated February 15, requesting that the printer deliver the plates of *Two Evil Isms* to the driver for the Garfield Park Storage Company. The agency then directed operatives to the storage company on Madison Street, where they learned the plates had been deposited with two large boxes belonging to one Will F. Reed of Kingman, Arizona. A warehouse man, yielding to the persuasive detectives, opened one of the boxes to reveal the plates and the remaining published copies of *Two Evil Isms*.[18]

The next day the Pinkertons petitioned the court to have the Garfield Park Storage Company turn over to them all of the books and the plates registered under the name of Will F. Reed. Their petition maintained that "Reed" was a name Siringo was using as an alias. Five days later, on March 30, the storage comany was ordered to retain custody of this property until the further order of the court.[19]

Siringo knew that when he began distributing his books to Chicago bookstores and newsstand dealers, he was, in effect, throwing a ticking time bomb, and he wanted to sell as many copies as he could before the bomb went off. He did not have long to wait before that happened. When the *Day Book*, an ad-less Chicago daily newspaper, appeared with a two-page review describing the book as "a Big Squeal" on the Pinkertons, Charlie decided it was time to leave the city. That afternoon he boarded a train for Santa Fe, intending to return to Chicago when things cooled off.[20]

Not long after his arrival in Santa Fe, Siringo was dismayed to learn that the Pinkertons had exposed his storage hideaway and that the court had impounded his books. His Chicago attorney, Lawrence B. Jacobs, an associate of Clarence Darrow, went to see John Brown to find out what arrangements could be made to possibly get the books released. Brown, who was trying to smoke out Siringo, told Jacobs that if his client wanted his books, he would have to petition the court for them. Furthermore, Brown said, he would object to any petition's being filed unless Siringo appeared personally in court. Jacobs replied that he could scarcely advise Siringo to appear in court when he was already in contempt for violation of its decree and injunctional order.[21]

Having his plates and books impounded was not the only problem Siringo had to face. On April 17 a Sergeant Donnelly of the Chicago police department arrived in Santa Fe with a requisition, signed by Governor Dunne of Illinois, for the arrest and extradition of Siringo. It seems that four days earlier a Pinkerton employee had gone before a Chicago municipal court judge and sworn out a complaint charging Siringo with criminal libel against Pinkerton's National Detective Agency. Renehan began at once to prepare arguments in opposition to the extradition request. He was convinced that the libel charge had no merit and was only a device to get Siringo back to Chicago, where he could be tried on contempt-of-court charges for having violated the 1911 injunction.[22]

On Wednesday afternoon, April 21, Renehan met with Governor William C. McDonald and Attorney General Frank Clancy to argue for a denial of the extradition request. Renehan pointed out that the act of Congress under which the extradition was sought required that it must be accompanied by an indictment or by an affidavit made before a magistrate, and that neither of these criteria had been met.

Charlie, meanwhile, must have felt confident about the outcome of the extradition proceedings, for he rode horseback around Santa Fe joking to friends "Boys, they tell me I'm a fugitive from justice," adding that he had no intention of quitting the "the saddle for any Pullman upholstery." Siringo's confidence was largely due to the fact that W. C. McDonald, New Mexico's first state governor, was an old personal friend. Siringo and the governor had known each other since the winter of 1880–81 in White Oaks, New Mexico Territory, when McDonald, then a young surveyor, and Siringo, and LX cowboy, met and became friends.[23]

The next morning Attorney General Clancy handed the governor his own legal opinion on the extradition request. Not only did he concur with Renehan's arguments, he cited other failures to comply with the rules of practice adopted by the governors of the states, including Illinois, represented at a conference held in New York state in 1887. While Siringo awaited McDonald's decision, some of his bravado must have faded a bit. This was apparent when the governor summoned him into his office, for he asked him, "What are you worrying about?" Governor McDonald had made the decision not to extradite his old cowboy friend to Illinois. Charlie was all smiles as he left the governor's office, remarking to those assembled outside, "I guess I ain't going to Chicago." After a lifetime of close calls, Siringo had dodged still another bullet. But this time the contretemps were humiliating.[24]

Siringo was not only not going to Chicago, he was not going anywhere outside the boundaries of New Mexico. Most of his work as a private detective had come from outside the state, but now, as a consequence of his own misventures, he was virtually a prisoner confined within the invisible walls of his own state's borders. On May 20 he wrote his friend in Vermont, William E. Hawks: "As matters stand I dare not leave this state yet . . . I have had a chance to go on detective work to Kansas and also California but am afraid to leave . . . for fear the P's will get me back to Chicago, as I am not able to stand a fight there in the courts."

He also told Hawks that it looked doubtful that H. M. Martin, who had an option to buy his ranch, was going to do so. He added that before Martin could buy his ranch, he had to first sell his own property in Joplin, Missouri. "Hope he will succeed as I need the money to pay you that $200," he concluded.[25]

With the threat of extradition behind him, Siringo continued to ponder the confiscation of his *Two Evil Isms* books and plates, and his ever-enlarging financial plight. The Hill Binding Company had extended him credit for the wholesale value of the 3,000 copies of *A Cowboy Detective* they had in storage. Since they had produced these at a cost of $375, or twelve and a half cents each, they offered to allow him a credit of $275 for his books. For this amount they agreed to print 1,100 copies of *Two Evil Isms,* with the two-color cover, which represented a cost of twenty-five cents per copy.

Siringo agreed to this arrangement even though the books would be prepriced to sell at twenty-five cents, and he would be losing money on any copies he sold wholesale. He must have figured that he would recoup his losses when he received the money from Viola and was able to order a larger run of *Two Evil Isms* at a cheaper price per copy. Instead, he now found himself in contempt of court for violating the 1911 injunction; he was also deeply in debt, and the few books he had produced, along with the plates, were under lock and key by court order.[26]

Finally, on July 3, after brooding over what he perceived to be the injustice of it all, Siringo wrote John A. Brown. His letter to the Pinkerton attorney read in part:

> My dear Sir:
>   You and your clients may think that you have got me frightened, on account of me keeping so quiet lately, since you worked that big bluff on me.
>   Knowing that I have got truth and justice on my side, even though your clients are over-supplied with money, influence and power, I shall keep pushing ahead until the grave swallows me up. A little thing like a year in jail wouldn't give me "cold feet." It would only store up energy and give me a rest.
>   For the past two months I have been busy writing a new book

for an eastern publisher, who wrote to me to try and get out one that will suit them. I have only got two more chapters to write, then I shall put my mind on "Two Evil Isms," and mail out the 2000 postal cards like the one enclosed, which I have on hand. And by that time if you have not released my plates in Chicago, I shall get out a new set. The cover colored-plates I have here with me. In case I have to make new plates an extra chapter will be added to the book.[27]

Siringo went on to warn Brown that a former Pinkerton "high official," who had read *Two Evil Isms*, offered to furnish him with additional material he would use should be decide to get out new plates. He ended his letter by saying he hoped Brown would come out in the open and "fight square," either by releasing the plates or by having the court order them destroyed. Charlie seemed determined to bluff the Pinkertons despite the advice of his attorney Al Renehan. Even John Brown must have deduced that Siringo's threats "to make new plates" were hollow. If his letter did have any effect, it was to spur the agency to secure the legal advantage that now lay within its grasp.[28]

Soon after the arrival of Siringo's letter, the Pinkertons through attorney Brown went to court, and on July 16 a Cook County judge of the Illinois Superior Court ordered all unsold copies of *Two Evil Isms*, as well as the plates used for its printing, to be turned over to the Pinkerton detective agency. The Pinkertons were then free to order the destruction of the plates and the remaining copies of the book. Charlie's appeal for Brown to come out in the open and "fight square" was apparently realized. Although the outcome was disappointing to him, it probably was not unexpected.[29]

Despite the debacle of *Two Evil Isms*, the final ignominy was still to come. The Hill Binding Company continued to press Siringo for payment of the $275 he owed them, and in November of 1916 he did send them a check for fifty-six dollars to be applied to the debt. Not satisfied with what they considered to be only a token payment, the company struck a deal with Fred Harvey and sold his newsstand distributors all of the remaining paperback copies of *A Cowboy Detective* for less than eight cents a copy.[30]

Two Evil Isms had been inspired by Siringo's desire for revenge against the Pinkertons and then propelled by an array of motives, most probably questionable. After failing in what may have been a calculated scheme to extort money from the agency, Siringo then became caught up in the euphoria generated by his own stubborn pride and vengeful determination. He gullibly swallowed the exaggerated praises of self-serving individuals who stood to gain by bad Pinkerton publicity and was blind to the legal realities that made any potential for profit virtually impossible. Ignoring the advice of his own legal counselors, both in Santa Fe and Chicago, and in defiance of warnings from Pinkerton's attorney John Brown, Siringo nevertheless convinced himself that *Two Evil Isms* would become a runaway best seller. Instead, it became not only a prison-threatening personal embarrassment but, even worse, it was an egregious financial disaster.

8 / A LAST CHANCE
FOR ACTION

IN the early spring of 1916 Governor McDonald persuaded Siringo
to accept a position as ranger, with a commission as mounted
policeman, for the Cattle Sanitary Board of New Mexico. He was
to be assigned a seven-county area north of the state's southern bound-
ary with Texas, and headquartered in Carrizozo. The governor did not
have to exert much pressure before Charlie accepted the job. It was
one more opportunity for action and the out-of-door life, the fillip
upon which he had thrived for so many years. It also carried with it the
assurance of a steady income at a time when his finances were at a particularly low ebb. As a rancher and businessman, Charlie had proven
to be disappointingly unsuccessful. His Sunny Slope Ranch had not
been self-supporting, although he had attempted to make it so, even to
making daily rides into Santa Fe to sell fresh eggs. He had always been
a liberal spender, generous to a fault with others, and with an indifferent attitude toward financial responsibility. Thus, he had never developed a knack for making money, or for hanging on to it. Especially
disappointing in recent years were his books' shortcomings as money
makers. Both *A Cowboy Detective* and *Two Evil Isms* had turned into
costly abysmal failures.[1]

So, on March 1, Siringo started south mounted on Rowdy, with
Patsy carrying the pack and with Jumbo, his Russian wolfhound and
offspring of Eat 'em Up Jake, chasing jack rabbits on ahead. Near the
edge of Carrizozo, Governor McDonald had a ranch home at Carrizozo Springs, where he and Siringo held frequent meetings. McDonald
told Charlie that he wanted him to put an end to the cattle stealing that
had been going on in and around the large Block Ranch, which the
governor and his associates owned, and which lay along the northern
foothills of the Capitan Mountains. McDonald said that the cattle

thieves were living in the vicinity of Arabella and Palos Springs on the east side of the Capitans. He warned Siringo that the thieves were a tough lot and would try to run him out of the country, as they had done other law officers who tried to apprehend them while they were stealing Block cattle.[2]

During the next few months Siringo and his partner, Bill Owens, a man Charlie described as a "fighting son-of-a-gun," worked their seven-county district, giving special attention to the Block ranges in the Capitans. They found many of the wells in the Arabella neighborhood full of Block cattle hides, which were thrown in after the animals had been butchered. From one well alone seventy-five hides were counted. After recapturing nine head of stolen horses from a Mexican outlaw named Chon Romero and his son, Siringo arrested four of the Block cattle thieves. He brought his prisoners into Arabella and charged them before the justice of the peace court. This was a mistake, for the justice of the peace was allied with the outlaws. The father of one of the thieves acted as lawyer for the defense and literally ruled the court. Siringo was not allowed to present his evidence, and when it was over, the prisoners were freed and the court costs, amounting to twenty-five dollars, were charged to Siringo. The judge ordered the constable not to allow the ranger to leave until the costs were paid.[3]

As Charlie started toward the door, the constable reached for his pistol in an attempt to stop him, but Siringo's hand was already holding the handle of his six-shooter. Charlie was then sixty-one years old, but he was leathery tough, and his eyes still conveyed a determination that was not to be taken lightly. He ordered the constable to stand back, which he did—as Siringo later remarked, "thus preventing the floor from being smeared with blood." Outside the courtroom "Red" Dale, a Block cowboy, sat on his horse while holding the bridle reins of Siringo's mount. Keeping his eyes on the crowd that had followed him through the door, Siringo reached his horse, whereupon he drew his rifle from its scabbard and held it in his hands ready for action. After quickly mounting his horse, Siringo and his companion then headed west at a gallop. After a couple of miles Charlie sent Dale back by the wagon road to the Block roundup camp. Siringo then cut across the mountains nine miles to Governor McDonald's Arroyo Seco Ranch. There he rounded up the nine head of stolen horses he had captured from Romero and started them for the Block ranch twenty miles west.[4]

He was barely out of sight when the Arabella constable whom he had faced down and a deputy, both armed with rifles and a warrant for Siringo's arrest, rode up to the Arroyo Seco ranch house. The ranch manager told the constable that Siringo had left for Carrizozo in an automobile and pointed to the recent tracks made by a car that had been there earlier in the day. Believing that further pursuit on horseback would be futile, the disappointed officers returned to Arabella. Siringo, meanwhile, reached the Block ranch by nightfall and was given a swift automobile ride into Carrizozo. The next morning he swore out warrants for the four prisoners the Arabella judge had set free. Then he and Deputy Sheriff John Baird drove to Arabella, a distance of seventy-five miles, and arrested the four released prisoners. At their arraignment the prisoners were each put under $1,000 bond to appear at the next term of district court in Carrizozo.[5]

Siringo continued to work in the Arabella and Encinoso area until the thieving gang became quite docile. By the following spring he was able to shift his attention to the vicinity of the Ruidoso River in the Glencoe neighborhood. There he was among old friends, and he found enjoyment in life once more. It was, he said, like going back to his early cowboy life, "where everyone seemed like a father, mother, brother or sister." He attended a spring horse roundup on the Mescalero Indian Reservation and was incensed at the manner in which the Indians brutalized horses. "They don't have any more mercy for a wild bronco than for a rattlesnake," he said, "and they don't know the first principle of handling wild horses."

During the summer of 1917 Siringo operated entirely from the Ruidoso Canyon and was put up at the ranch of Bert Bonnell. Charlie had known Bert's father, Ed Bonnell, from the early days when he ran a lumber yard in White Oaks. Bert had married one of Frank Coe's pretty daughters, Sydney, whom Siringo said was "a peach as a singer, musician, and knowing how to make visitors feel at home." She must have done a good job because Charlie spent the whole summer with the Bonnells.

Sydney's sister, Helena Coe Lemay, said that if Siringo's presence disturbed Sydney she never showed it. In fact, she added, Sydney accepted him as if he were a member of their family. Not that Charlie did not earn his keep, for he helped with the roundup and the branding, and any of the weekly chores that needed to be done. On Sundays he enjoyed perching himself, along with other spectators, on the top rail of the picket corral and watching the younger cowboys ride the bucking broncos. Frank Coe's ranch was just below Bonnell's, and Charlie especially enjoyed those occasions when the Coe children, who were all musicians, would assemble in the Coe parlor for an evening's musical recital.[6]

As a salaried state police officer, Siringo was at last financially solvent, and, in some ways at least, he was making the most of it. When he rode up to the Frank Coe ranch in the summer of 1917, Helena Coe LeMay remembered that she could hardly talk for staring at Siringo's clothing and outfit. Charlie was wearing a "huge Stetson with a rattlesnakeskin band" and a neckerchief of brilliant red silk. She could see a blue chambray shirt beneath a leather vest that was fringed at the waist and pockets. His chaps, she said, "glittered with silver conchos and the holster of his pistol was of tooled leather and fastened with a massive silver buckle." His boots were mostly hidden by a huge *tapadero*, but she could see his spurs, which were silver with very small rowels.

Siringo was a picture of western sartorial splendor, and his horse was equally well outfitted. His tooled saddle was embellished with silver conchos and was obviously new because it creaked noisily as the horse moved about. She noticed that the bridle was also tooled and "had a fringe two inches wide on the brow." Beneath Siringo's saddle was a fine Navajo saddle blanket of red-and-black design on a white background. Helena Coe also observed that the pack on the lead horse was fastened securely with a diamond hitch, which only someone practiced in the art could tie.[7]

Frank Coe was a justice of the peace, and Siringo brought some of his cattle-stealing cases into Coe's court. Frank's brother, George Coe, had his home just a mile above Frank's, and both brothers had been involved with Billy the Kid during the bloody Lincoln County war. Although Siringo continued to pursue his duties as a New Mexico ranger it was his interest in Billy the Kid that made him tarry in the Ruidoso valley. A book on the Kid was taking shape in his mind, and he felt there was no better place than to be among old friends who had known Billy and who had been participants in many of the stirring events involving the young outlaw. George Coe took pride in the fact that he had lost a finger in the battle at Blazer's Mill, and it was near George Coe's ranch where John Henry Tunstall was killed by the Seven River warriors, an event that started the Lincoln County war. Siringo enjoyed himself immensely during this period as he visited Roswell, Capitan, Nogal, White Oaks, and Lincoln, where he found old friends galore could "hark back" with to the days of the open range.[8]

Siringo's duties as a ranger ended in 1918, when the Cattle Sanitary Board ran out of funds to pay its twelve officers scattered throughout the state. He packed his cowboy outfit and headed north toward Santa Fe and his Sunny Slope Ranch. During his employment as a New Mexico ranger he had engaged Joseph B. Hayward, a Santa Fe real estate agent, to look after his ranch and to secure a tenant for it. H. M. Martin, from Joplin, Missouri, who had been leasing the ranch and had doubled the size of the ranch house from two to four rooms, moved out and did not renew his lease. Times were hard, and although Hayward found several prospective tenants, including George Tweedy, who had worked for Siringo, Charlie was skeptical of most of them for fear they would not properly tend his orchard.[9] As if this were not enough, Hayward wrote Siringo that his windmill had collapsed and needed to be repaired. Siringo did not want to spend more money than necessary and asked Hayward to have it rebuilt on a thirty-foot tower, not to its original height of forty feet. Later, George Tweedy wrote him that the windmill fan blades had been smashed and were being held together with wire.[10]

These problems, as well as others, were awaiting Siringo when he returned to Santa Fe in 1918. His biggest problem, however, was the promissory note, in the amount of $625, he had given Alonzo Compton in 1914 to finance his paperback edition of *A Cowboy Detective*. Although he had managed to pay off a $300 note to Compton that he had incurred on his mother's 140 acres, he had not paid a dime against the principal or the interest of the larger note. Finally, in November of 1919, Compton filed a petition in district court for a judgment against Siringo for nonpayment of his note.[11]

These were dark times for Siringo, but he continued to believe that he could resolve his financial woes by writing and publishing books. During his employment with the New Mexico Cattle Sanitary Board, Siringo wrote Renehan concerning a publisher who had expressed an interest in buying the plates for *A Cowboy Detective* to produce an edition in paperback. Renehan replied that if he could just recover $1,700, which was the least amount he knew he had invested in the book, not to mention his time, he would be satisfied. Moreover, he said he would not claim any profit the book might make in the hope that Siringo could make a stake from it. Even this prospect went awry, for before Charlie could decide how much to ask for his plates, the publisher changed his mind because, he said, "war reading" was dominating public taste.[12]

After his return to Santa Fe in 1918, Siringo began to write once more. As in the past, his writing was autobiographical, but this time he was laying off the Pinkertons. By 1919 his book, entitled *A Lone Star Cowboy,* was completed and published in Santa Fe that year. The subtitle read, in part, "Being fifty years [*sic*] experience in the saddle as Cowboy, Detective and New Mexico Ranger, on every cow trail in the wooly [*sic*] old west." He stated in the preface that *A Lone Star Cowboy* was to take the place of *A Texas Cowboy,* on which the copyright had expired. Unfortunately, *A Lone Star Cowboy* lacked the spontaneous style and youthful exuberance of the earlier work.[13] That same year he published *The Song Companion of A Lone Star Cowboy* in an edition of 2,000 copies. This was an undistinguished forty-two-page booklet of cowboy songs that also bore the Santa Fe imprint.

Ever since his first book, *A Texas Cowboy,* Siringo's writing had mostly been a chronicle of his own personal experiences. Then in 1920, or shortly thereafter, he took a different turn: he began a novel with a female heroine. The story, he said, was about "manhood and womanhood in the early days of Texas and the West," and he entitled it "Prairie Flower, or Bronco Chiquita." The plot, according to Charlie, began in southwest Texas in 1845 and ended in western Colorado in 1883, when the cowgirl heroine, Bronco Chiquita, married a Yankee and lived happily ever after.[14]

Siringo had a lifelong fascination with women, as evidenced by his four marriages and numerous romantic encounters recorded in *A Texas Cowboy* and *A Cowboy Detective.* Given his natural inclination and drive to write, his creation of a female heroine was predictable. Although "Prairie Flower, or Bronco Chiquita" would remain something of a literary chimera, to Charlie his character had a reality that would eventually develop beyond the pages of his manuscript.[15]

Siringo was a true *romantic* who had only to glance at a pretty girl and Cupid would shoot his system full of darts. He admitted that he could never look into a pair of "don't pass me up" feminine eyes after he had been "whooping 'er up Liza Jane," because he usually asked the lady to marry him. Then when he sobered up, he had a hard time extricating himself from a fool situation. Yet if Charlie was lucky in love, and he certainly seems to have been, he proved to be equally unlucky in marriage.[16]

By this time Siringo had been obliged to vacate his ranch, which he had leased, and was living with the Matias Nagel family in Santa Fe. However, he still kept his horses at the ranch, where he retained access to them. Yet, when he returned to the Ruidoso canyon in 1920 to complete his Billy the Kid research, his appearance bespoke his impoverished financial condition. Gone were the fine western clothing and the horse with the elaborate equipage. Instead, he was poorly dressed, afoot, and carrying a bedroll and camp equipment on the back of a burro. Even the magnificent Russian wolfhound was gone, replaced by a pack of nondescript hounds. As in the past, he stayed at the Bonnells' ranch, which was a hospitable home that never turned anybody away. After a time he took his leave in order to visit other places of interest to him, including Corona, near Roswell, in his quest for material relating to Billy the Kid.[17]

With the exception of his attempt at writing a novel, Siringo had four principal themes he liked to write about: his youth and cowboy life on the open range; his experiences during twenty-two years as a Pinkerton detective; Billy the Kid, whom he had personally known; and the western bad men he had rubbed elbows with or knew about. By 1920, with the publication of his *History of "Billy the Kid,"* he had touched all four thematic bases. This, too, was a small paperback of 142 pages, which Siringo had printed in Santa Fe.[18]

Unfortunately, neither the publication of *A Lone Star Cowboy* and the booklet of cowboy songs nor of the *History of "Billy the Kid"* made so much as a dent in Siringo's indebtedness. There were still plenty of copies of the original clothbound *A Cowboy Detective* on hand, but the potential for sales around Santa Fe had been exhausted. On top of his other debts, Siringo owed the New Mexican Publishing Company $700 in printing costs. As security, the company was holding the type metal, plates, and remaining book stock of *A Lone Star Cowboy* and *History of "Billy the Kid."* Somehow, Charlie could not regenerate the éclat of his first book, *A Texas Cowboy.*[19]

PART IV
CALIFORNIA SUNSET, 1923–1928

> You ought to get in the [movie] game
> with your expert horsemanship, quick gun
> work, etc., etc. A lot of former cowboys have
> made good all right.
>
> —Dr. Henry F. Hoyt to Charlie Siringo,
> June 17, 1921

9 / HOLLYWOOD AND
WILLIAM S. HART

I N order to make ends meet Siringo had been obliged to dispose of his mother's 140 acres adjacent to his original homestead. Although he continued to lease his Sunny Slope Ranch, he was unable, or unwilling, to repay Alonzo Compton, who held the mortgage on it. Compton had gone to court in 1919 seeking a judgment against Siringo for failure to repay the $625 note. The case was continued for almost three years, but finally, in September, 1921, the court ordered Charlie to pay Compton $1,125.70, which was the amount of the note plus the accrued interest. In the meantime Siringo had lost interest in Santa Fe, especially since financial circumstances had forced him to move away from his ranch.[1]

In June, 1921, he returned to Lincoln County and was visiting friends in Carrizozo when he received a letter from a physician in Long Beach, California, that had been forwarded to him from Santa Fe. The physician was Dr. Henry F. Hoyt, who wrote Charlie to tell him he had just finished reading *A Lone Star Cowboy,* which a friend had loaned him. He commended the book and reminded Siringo that they once had worked together as cowboys on the LX Ranch in the Texas Panhandle in 1877.[2] Like Siringo, Hoyt had known Billy the Kid and had even been given a horse by the Kid. Charlie was delighted to hear from Hoyt. He wrote back, and in the exchange of letters that ensued a warm friendship was rekindled. In fact, Hoyt may have unwittingly played a part in influencing Siringo to think about moving to Hollywood and becoming involved with motion pictures.

By the 1920s the American film industry was solidly rooted in southern California, with Hollywood as its capital. For years film makers had been translating the nation's recent frontier experience into popular cinematic myth, creating a genre of movie morality plays that commonly came to be known as Westerns. Staged against majestically scenic backgrounds suggesting the dawn of creation, or at primitive frontier towns and outposts far from the reach of civilization, the Westerns told over and over again the story of a modern knight waging the fight of good against evil. Sometimes the hero in a Western was a scout in fringed buckskin, or a dashing cavalry officer, on occasion a rugged mountain man, and even at times the Indian, but none of these matched in prominence or popularity the cowboy as the archetypal symbol of the American West.[3]

Siringo was fascinated by this new entertainment medium and uncritically embraced these romanticized depictions of a historical period in which he had been an active participant. Ironically, he failed to realize that the screen myth of the cowboy as hero, which of course he found irresistibly appealing, was due in part to his own autobiographical contribution. The movies, with their powerful visual impact, offered a new and exciting dimension that fired Siringo's imagination. It was a logical extension of the efforts he had been employing to preserve, by printed word, the memories of his own frontier experience. Perhaps unconsciously, he recognized the movie Western as an effective vehicle through which the American saga of migration and settlement could be portrayed to a public anxious to learn of its pioneer heritage. As his writings reflect, Siringo was very much aware he had been a witness to portentous events and had played a part in helping to tame the West when it was wild.[4]

Even though motion pictures had not yet begun to talk, Siringo, like many Americans of the time, had become an avid moviegoer. He didn't seem to mind that these silent Westerns, heavy with melodrama, were badly skewed historically. His strong inclination toward sentimentality and romance caused him to overlook such flaws. Siringo's favorite actor was William S. Hart, a popular Western star recognizable by his square jaw and gimlet eyes. Although preceded on the film scene by Gilbert Anderson, later known as "Bronco Billy," who couldn't ride a horse, and by Tom Mix, who portrayed the cowboy as a hard-riding, straight-shooting, but glamorously dressed caricature, Hart brought a realism to his films that later was referred to as Hollywood's "Western tradition."

The early Westerns, which began with Edwin S. Porter's *The Great Train Robbery* in 1903, were for the most part two- and three-reel potboilers. With little thought given to accuracy of detail, these Westerns were inexpensively made, and their plots were usually incidental to the out-of-doors action. After a hiatus in which the Westerns had declined in popularity, Hart helped to bring about their revival with a series of films, the chief novelty of which was the carefully crafted stories he introduced. Hart's Westerns, which were keenly romantic, sentimental, and charged with melodrama, seemed to be poetic evocations of the Old West. Hart disliked the circus-comedy approach of Tom Mix and was a stickler for authenticity. His first film as a director-star was *The Passing of Two Gun Hicks,* a two-reeler. Other pictures followed, including *Hell's Hinges* (1916), *The Gun Fighter* (1917), *The Narrow Trail* (1918), *Wagon Tracks* (1919), and *Sand,* which was President Woodrow Wilson's favorite Hart film. In 1917, while Siringo was working as a ranger for the New Mexico Cattle Sanitary Board, the Cowboys' Reunion Association, meeting in Las Vegas, New Mexico, voted Hart, along with actor Dustin Farnum, the most popular cowboy in the world. By the end of the Great War, Hart had become one of the nation's most admired Western stars.[5]

When Siringo wrote the actor a fan letter, he received in return a friendly response in which Hart said he knew of Siringo from his writings and was, himself, an admirer of the old cowboy detective. Charlie was so pleased with Hart's praise of his books that he had the letter reproduced on the back of business cards to hand out as advertisements. He had sent one of these cards to Dr. Hoyt, who immediately replied:

> I note your letter from "Bill" Hart on the back of your card. He is the leader here among the old time "two gun men" and I never miss one of his shows. He is quite often in Long Beach and has appeared in person on the stage here. In fact, most all the movie stars and staretts [*sic*] visit our beach occasionally, and many of the plays have been made here. You ought to get in the game with your expert horsemanship, quick gun work, etc, etc. A lot of former cowboys have made good all right.[6]

The effect of Hoyt's suggestion on Siringo can only be surmised. However, on visits to Corona and later to Roswell, he told "Shorty" Adams of his interest in going to Hollywood to act in films. Even if Charlie realized that his likelihood of becoming a western actor at age sixty-six was remote, he still might have fancied himself as a screenplay writer. In fact, it was about this time that Charlie began writing his novel "Prairie Flower" with the female heroine Bronco Chiquita.[7]

That November, Siringo along with some friends went on a hunting expedition to the Jemez Mountains northwest of Santa Fe. By then most of his pets were gone, including Rowdy, his favorite stallion. There was still Patsy, but he was seventeen years old and "hog fat," hardly a choice for a long, strenuous ride into the high country. Charlie packed his rifle, along with his other gear, and rode out on Sailor Gray to join his companions. They forded the Rio Grande at Cochiti Indian Pueblo and headed into the mountains.[8] Siringo came back sick from this outing, from sleeping in the snow with only a blanket, and developed what was thought to be pleurisy. Whatever the exact nature of his illness, it eventually turned into a severe case of bronchitis from which he was never fully able to recover. By the following fall, his health had deteriorated so, that when the Compton judgment went against him, he began thinking seriously about moving to San Diego, California, to live with his daughter, Viola Reid, and granddaughter, Margaret May. Viola was concerned about her father's health and for some time had been urging him to make the move to the West Coast.[9]

Since resolution of his financial problems was virtually impossible, the Compton judgment became the straw that broke the camel's back. Siringo knew that even if he was able to pay the court-assessed sum of $1,125.70, he still had the H. S. Kaunne & Company next in line. They had been holding a second mortgage as security for his note in the amount of $2,272 plus interest since 1914. Besides these debts were the sums he owed to the New Mexican Publishing Company. His financial obligations had simply become insurmountable, so he decided that the only thing he could do was abandon his Sunny Slope Ranch.[10] Charlie still retained one last piece of property. It was 151 acres of a 320-acre tract he had acquired in 1916, and although it was not contiguous to the Sunny Slope Ranch, it was located nearby and to the south of the Arroyo Chamiso. It, too, had a lien against it in the amount of $2.50 an acre, but Charlie's neighbor, a rancher named Pankey, offered to buy the property for the amount of the mortgage and $75 cash. Siringo agreed to these terms as he said he was through with the land.[11]

Before making a move to the West Coast, Siringo began to worry that his old antagonists, the Pinkertons, might reinstate the libel charge against him and try to have him extradited from California to stand trial. Alois Renehan wrote to Fletcher Dobyns in Chicago concerning the matter and asked him to make a quiet investigation. Because Dobyns was being called away to Washington, D.C., when Renehan's letter arrived, the inquiry was turned over to Leland C. Welts, an associate in his office. Welts wrote Renehan that the records of the clerk of the Criminal Court showed that under the date of November 20, 1916, the court had ordered the case stricken off with leave to reinstate. This was the only case appearing on the docket for that date, and it had been stamped "disposed of." He concluded from this that the matter was practically dead and that it was only a very remote possibility that any further action would ever be taken on it—especially, he added, since the Pinkertons had secured relief through "other means," meaning the court's order that led to the destruction of the plates and the copies of *Two Evil Isms* that were found in storage.[12]

With these legal considerations out of the way, Charlie's most difficult task before leaving Santa Fe was the disposition of his remaining pets. He raffled off Sailor Gray for $100 but he refused an offer of $150 for Patsy, fearing that the horse might fall into cruel hands. Instead, he took Patsy into the woods and sorrowfully put him to sleep with his Colt .45.[13]

In late December, 1922, he bid Santa Fe farewell and boarded a train for San Diego. He laid over for a week in Douglas, Arizona, to spend Christmas and the New Year with another friend from his cowboy youth, Jim East and his wife.[14] By the time he arrived in San Diego, he was so sick he could hardly drag one foot after the other. However, thanks to the able care of Siringo's daughter, his health improved somewhat, and by April he was well enough to move to Los Angeles into quarters located at 1730 West 53rd Street. He wrote Al Renehan that he was amazed at how the city had grown since his last visit in 1898. Because his only means of livelihood was the sale of his books, he asked Renehan to have J. F. Collins, the Santa Fe curio dealer who had purchased some of his stock from the printer, send him fifty copies of *A Lone Star Cowboy* to fill orders he said he had pending.[15]

Sometime in October he visited Hollywood and renewed his friendship with George Townsend Cole, who was the youngest son of Captain Cornelius Cole (then 101 years old), a former U.S. senator from California. George Cole, known as "Jack" to his friends, was an attorney, artist, and writer whom Siringo had known from Santa Fe days. Soon after the turn of the century, artistic émigrés had begun gravitating to the Ancient City (as Santa Fe is known, since its founding in 1610 makes it the oldest capital city in the United States), and Siringo had occasion on one of Cole's visits to meet him and become friends. In February he received a letter from Mrs. Betty Rogers inviting him to their Beverly Hills home to meet her husband, Will. At the time Siringo had to decline because he was not feeling well, but he answered saying he would like to pay the Rogers family a visit in a month or so.[16]

During the next few months Siringo moved two more times to different Los Angeles locations. Then in May, 1924, Cole persuaded Charlie to move to 6057 Eleanor Avenue, which was a location near his own and right in the heart of Hollywood. Siringo's new landlord, Linder Stafford, was manager of The Eleanor, an apartment house owned by the Coles. Stafford, who lived next door, had built a cabin behind his house, and Charlie moved into it. Over the cabin door he placed a sign that read "Siringo's Den," and from his windows Siringo could enjoy Mrs. Stafford's flower garden, even in the winter. Charlie wrote Al Renehan that he was feeling better "since moving to . . . Hollywood, where I can see the Flappers pass by." [17]

A favorite hangout for aspiring cowboy movie stars was the Water Hole Saloon, only a few blocks away, at the corner of Cahuenga Avenue and Hollywood Boulevard. It was there that assistant film directors could usually round up cowboys whenever they were needed, and drivers would customarily stop to give them a ride to Universal or the Lasky ranch. Siringo often walked to the Water Hole, as he liked to see the movie cowboys and cowgirls with their silver-mounted spurs and high Stetson hats. Although such costumes evoked memories of his cowboy days, he confessed that "such high hats and girls wearing pants were not seen on the early-day ranges." [18]

He had been living on Eleanor Avenue only a few weeks when he was invited to attend a social gathering at the home of Henry Herbert Knibbs. Knibbs, whose friends called him "Harry," was a Canadian-born novelist and poet who had also been a frequent visitor to New Mexico and was acquainted with Siringo's attorney friend, Alois B. Renehan. Knibbs told Charlie that when he was a guest at the "Willows," Renehan's home in Santa Fe, he drank "a fluid which made his soul soar skyward." Siringo smiled and nodded politely, although his host's elegant and poetic expression, a euphemistic admission that he became inebriated, probably passed over his head. While attending Knibbs's party, Charlie was pleasantly surprised to meet a number of congenial old-timers of note.[19]

Los Angeles, by the second decade of the twentieth century, had become a mecca for aging westerners of various intellectual persuasions, and Charlie's presence there, through his friendship with Jack Cole and Harry Knibbs, gradually became known to most of them. Eugene Manlove Rhodes, another transplanted New Mexican, was living on Marmion Way in the heart of the Arroyo Seco. Nearby was anthropologist-historian Charles Fletcher Lummis in the fine stone house he had built for himself, with his Museum of the Southwest close at hand. James Willard Schultz, advocate of Indian rights and prolific writer about the Blackfoot tribe, also lived in the vicinity.

Siringo and Rhodes became better acquainted when they would meet at the home of western writer W. C. Tuttle, who was the son of a Montana sheriff. Tuttle was struck by the similar appearance of Siringo and Rhodes, even though Rhodes was fourteen years younger than Charlie. An informal group, which met from time to time at the University Club for discussions about the bygone West, included Will Rogers, Charles M. Russell, Henry Herbert Knibbs, James W. Schultz, and E. A. Brininstool. Charlie and Harry Knibbs were already becoming good friends, and in time Siringo would become friendly with the other members of this group.[20]

Charlie, meanwhile, was having trouble making enough money to pay his rent and buy food. He had left Santa Fe deeply in debt and with only a small amount of cash realized from the sale of his horse and a few personal possessions. Then Al Renehan wrote to tell him that his deal with Mr. Pankey had fallen through and that he had repossessed Siringo's 151 acres. Charlie replied that, if Renehan wanted the property and would be willing to pay off the mortgage of $2.50 an acre, he would sign the deed to the property over to him. Siringo said he thought the land would be a good investment at that price once the severe drought then affecting the state was over. Renehan must have thought so, too, for a month later he sent a deed to Charlie for his signature.[21]

Another of Siringo's problems was solved when George Cole agreed to pay off Siringo's $700 indebtedness to the New Mexican Publishing Company. In return, Cole took delivery of the remaining *A Lone Star Cowboy* and *History of "Billy the Kid"* books, as well as the plates, which the printing company had been holding as security. Even though his financial situation was still acute, Charlie now had ready access to two of his books, which would enable him to fill orders more easily.[22]

In July, 1924, Siringo experienced a bit of financial relief when he got his first movie part as an extra in *Nine Scars Make a Man*. His role was as an old cowboy, and it provided him with some much-needed "eatin' money." Because of Siringo's age and poor health, work of this nature was an exception, and his primary livelihood continued to be the small returns garnered from occasional sales of his books.[23]

In October, Charlie received a note from Edward L. Doheny asking him to come to his office for a visit. Doheny had been much in the news in recent years and had been at the center of the firestorm surrounding Albert Bacon Fall in the Teapot Dome scandal.[24] Doheny told Siringo how he and Fall had been friends since their early years in New Mexico Territory, and that Fall had worked for him in his gold mine in Kingston, Sierra County, New Mexico. Fall later studied law, became active in New Mexico politics, served in the U.S. Senate, and finally was appointed secretary of the interior in the administration of President Warren G. Harding. Doheny, during this period, had gone into the oil business and become a multi-millionaire. Siringo found Doheny to be "a fine old Irishman," and he thoroughly enjoyed reminiscing about the old days in New Mexico. When the two men parted, Doheny asked Siringo to inscribe copies of A Cowboy Detective and A Lone Star Cowboy and send them to his home at 8 Chester Place in Los Angeles.[25]

The national election was held in November, and incumbent President Calvin Coolidge was elected over his opponents, John W. Davis, the Democrat, and Progressive Robert M. LaFollette. The Democrats' hope that the oil stain from Teapot Dome would smear Coolidge was not realized. The president won with a plurality of some two and a half million popular votes over the combined total of his two opponents, and Siringo cast his ballot with the majority. In fact, Siringo, whose political expressions tended toward populism, had voted the straight Republican ticket! He wrote his Republican attorney friend, Alois Renehan, that he knew he was happy over the outcome of the election. He also told him that he had completed the manuscript for a new book, to be entitled "Bad Man Cowboys of the Early West," and that he had submitted it to Yale University Press. His fears that they might "find it too tough, and bloody to suit them" were borne out, as the manuscript was ultimately rejected.[26]

On Easter Sunday, 1925, the Los Angeles Times ran a feature article on Siringo that he said brought him a "lot of misery, as well as pleasure." If the misery he alluded to was the visit to his Den by an old

Coeur d'Alene dynamiter, then the pleasure undoubtedly was the unexpected appearance of Western screen hero William S. Hart. Although Hart was still regarded as a movie personality, along with Fairbanks, Pickford, and Valentino, his career had passed its zenith and his popularity was beginning to fade. He had already retired twice from films because of his unwillingness to submit to studio demands that he conform to the more "streamlined" style of Tom Mix, or to revise his formula plots, which were becoming harder to sell to the movie-going public.[27]

In real life Hart was very much like the celluloid hero he portrayed on the screen. He was born on December 6, 1870, in Newburgh, New York, but grew up in Illinois, Iowa, Wisconsin, and Minnesota. His father, whom he described as a "white gold pioneer," was a traveling miller who searched for waterpower sites. During his youth Hart lived for a time in the Dakota Territory near the Sioux Reservation. The Indians fascinated him, and he learned to speak some Sioux and to converse in Indian sign language. He was intensely interested in the West and particularly in the cowboy, whom he carefully studied. While still in his teens, Hart learned to ride with a cowboy's ease and agility. Years later he developed an almost theological vision of the West in which history and romance were inseparable.

Hart left the West at age fifteen, intending to go to West Point. Instead, he became a successful actor on the legitimate stage. He turned to motion pictures in 1914, and it was as a film actor and director that he gained his greatest acclaim, especially in his Westerns. Hart's films achieved widespread popularity because they were animated by a spirit of romantic realism, in much the same way as the paintings of Charles M. Russell, whom Hart knew. Nevertheless, Hart insisted on imposing intensely sentimental, melodramatic, and sometimes even ridiculous plots, devoid of comic relief, in which the action was always secondary to the overstated story lines. Hart's films, like his stylized methods of acting, had become dated and were giving way at the box office to those of Buck Jones, Tom Mix, Hoot Gibson, and Jack Hoxie.

Hart was an unusual man who lived by a rigorous code that demanded fair play at all times. Adolph Zukor called him "one of the originals." It is said Hart divided all men into friends or enemies, with nothing in between, and all women were automatically ladies. He was a noble, sensitive, honest human being whose love of animals prompted him to fire anyone working for him who dared to abuse them. It is not difficult to understand why Charlie so admired the actor. Both men were incurable sentimentalists and romantics.[28]

Although Siringo and Hart had exchanged letters several years before, this was their first face-to-face meeting. A gentle rain was falling as Hart was ushered in, and he noticed that there were holes in the roof "large enough to throw cats through." He offered to have the roof fixed for Siringo before he caught his death of something. Charlie replied that he had already caught that four years ago, which was why he was leaving the leaks alone. He told Hart that the fresh, wet air allowed him to breathe better than if he had them covered up.[29] Hart then asked Charlie if he needed money to live on. "I told the big-hearted six-footer that I didn't need money bad enough to accept it now, but that the day might come when I would call on him. That the fact of his offering it to me was worth more than the money would be. He told me to call on him should I run short of cash to eat on. I have heard many good deeds done by big Bill Hart. There are only a few of his kind in the world."[30]

Less than a week later Hart paid Charlie another visit and brought him an inscribed copy of each of his books along with a quart bottle of seven-year-old wine from his ranch at Newhall. On the walls of Siringo's Den were hundreds of photographs, above which was a sign that read "Siringo's Rogue Gallery." As Hart read the sign above his own photograph, a smile flitted across that familiar hawklike face. Somewhat embarrassed, Siringo later wrote "that Hart was badly mistaken if he thought I was placing him in the rogue class. If there is one person in the whole world who has not a drop of rogue blood in his veins, that man is Bill Hart."[31]

The same *Times* article put Charlie in touch with Dr. A. M. Pelton, a physician who fifty years before had ridden twenty-five miles in the night to cut a bullet out of Siringo's knee. Dr. Pelton, who was then eighty years of age and quite wealthy, invited Charlie to dinner at his Hollywood home. Siringo thought it was not only "one of the finest homes in Hollywood . . . [but] it is the finest home I ever set foot into." Pelton asked Charlie to be one of his pallbearers should he die first, but if Siringo was the first to go, then he said "he would help dump him back into mother earth, while his wife and daughters did the flower act." Although he did not say so to the doctor, Charlie later mused that he would rather have the flowers now while still able to smell them.[32]

Not long after his visit with the Peltons, his wish to smell flowers was realized when Mrs. Eva Fenyes brought Charlie an armful of roses and other flowers. Drawn to Siringo's Den by the *Times* article, Mrs. Fenyes was a wealthy Pasadena lady who used to spend her summers in Santa Fe. Alois Renehan described her as "a splendid, kind, sympathetic woman with a great deal of intellectual capacity in various directions."[33]

Siringo wrote Renehan that Mrs. Will M. Tipton, another former Santa Fean, was bringing him her copies of the Santa Fe *New Mexican,* thus enabling him to keep track of Renehan's "Elephant stunts" he had pulled off with the New Mexico state legislature. In the same letter Charlie had sent a check for $4.50 ordering six copies of *A Cowboy Detective.* Renehan returned the check, saying that he felt Siringo needed the $4.50 more than either he or the bank receiver did. Besides, he continued, the books were his since he had taken up the note, and he was therefore at liberty to help him out on his own account. "I know that both of us lost a great deal of money on that publication," he concluded, "but that is water gone over the wheel."[34]

In August, through the generosity of Bill Hart, Siringo was employed for seven weeks as a consultant on the William S. Hart picture *Tumbleweeds.* United Artists, with some fanfare, had earlier announced that Hart was returning to the screen to star in an epic film about the opening of the Cherokee Strip in 1889. Barbara Bedford was signed to play the leading lady in this saga based on a Hal Evarts's story for the *Saturday Evening Post.* Hundreds of extras were employed, as well as horses, riders, wagons, and even a man on a high-wheeled bicycle, to dramatize the great land rush from southern Kansas into Oklahoma Territory. Hart told Charlie that he wanted him "to give his director some pointers," and to work as an extra. Siringo was given small parts in the film, in which he appears walking through a barroom scene and in the town celebration beating a drum. He wrote Renehan that the "work in the play was easy and the money earned proved a God-send."[35]

Of all of the Hart films, *Tumbleweeds* has been described as being imbued with more "dust-choked, wind-blown atmosphere" than any other. Even a set was built to depict Caldwell, Kansas, in the 1880s, which was near the time Siringo had been a resident of that frontier cattle town. *Tumbleweeds* looked like the kind of picture a cowboy might have made and, although he had nothing to do with the screenplay, Siringo may have contributed to the film's authentic western flavor by his presence as an advisor. Since Hart had a financial interest in the film, and perhaps because of it, *Tumbleweeds* did not compromise the actor's patented formula for making Westerns, although he did ameliorate some heavy-handed touches with moments of bright comedy.

The movie, which was produced at a cost of $302,000, an enormous sum for its time, was the most expensive of all Hart films. It was well received upon its initial showing in New York and generally enjoyed good reviews. It later became acclaimed for its superb photography and spectacular cinematic effects. The land-rush sequences, filmed on a vast scale at La Agoura Rancho some forty miles from Hollywood, are as visually dramatic and compelling as anything ever mounted for a Western film. Despite the melodrama Hart injected into it, as William Goetzmann observed, the film "was in keeping with the new wave of Westerns . . . that celebrated American history as myth and a grand national saga." Film historian Kevin Brownlow, with a somewhat different but succinctly candid perspective, described *Tumbleweeds* as "eight reels . . . [of] exquisitely shot hokum." [36]

United Artists disliked the film and wanted Hart to cut it down to five reels. When he refused, the studio deliberately mismanaged distribution by booking *Tumbleweeds* into minor theaters and second-run houses. Hart estimated that he lost $50,000 on his investment in the picture and $100,000 in potential revenues. The actor sued and won, proving that his contract stipulated that the firm was to make every effort to realize a commercial profit through the film's distribution. His victory gave him satisfaction only in principle, for on appeal the case dragged through the courts for the next quarter-century before United Artists was finally ordered to pay the judgment plus accrued interest. [37]

Hart's return to the screen had been a bitter and costly experience for him. He was discouraged by the changing trend in Westerns, and at age fifty-five felt it was time to step aside. After a meteoric film career that had spanned barely more than a decade, Hart once again retired from motion pictures, this time for good. *Tumbleweeds*, in many ways, was William S. Hart's greatest film. It was also his last. With Hart's retirement, Siringo's flirtation with the film industry also ended. [38]

10 / RIATA AND SPURS

I N February, 1926, Henry Herbert Knibbs told Siringo of Houghton Mifflin's interest in publishing some of his writings. The company had been Knibbs's publisher for a number of years, and he
had suggested they consider Siringo's life and adventures as a subject
for a book. Charlie wrote Ferris Greenslet, editor in chief, describing
his various books and including with his letter the manuscript of his
newest work, "Bad Man Cowboys of the Early West." He also sent to
the publisher, for the editors to study, copies of all of his books with
the exception of *A Texas Cowboy* and *Two Evil Isms.*[1]

Greenslet acknowledged Charlie's letter and "the package of books."
He thought the previous publication of *A Cowboy Detective* might
present some difficulty but said that they would study the whole situation and then offer some definite constructive suggestions. Siringo replied, saying that if they could not republish *A Cowboy Detective* in
its present form, then they might consider adding the best material
from *A Lone Star Cowboy* and make a larger volume called "A Longhorn Cowboy." The subtitle, he added, could read "Fifty Years in the
Saddle as Cowboy and Detective." He also suggested that John Hays
Hammond, who had written a laudatory article about him, be asked
to write an introduction.[2]

Assigned to the task of evaluating Siringo's work and helping to determine a format for a book was managing editor Ira Rich Kent. Kent
was somewhat disdainful of the project and suggested the house might
consider all of Siringo's books as a whole. Siringo's writings, he sniffed,
were the sort of material that finds its widest market in the hands of
the "train boy," and unless they are "freely edited," he felt the Houghton Mifflin imprint would look more or less out of place. Then casting
an eye toward profitability, he admitted that Siringo's books were interesting because they were "first hand chronicles of adventure "told

with a slap-dash-bang that is full of thrill."[3] By March 17 a decision had been made as to how Siringo's book should be structured. An autobiographical form was decided upon; it would employ material that had been covered in *A Texas Cowboy*, *A Cowboy Detective*, and *A Lone Star Cowboy*. *History of "Billy the Kid"* was dismissed as being redundant since that material had been covered elsewhere, and the *Song Companion of A Lone Star Cowboy*, which Kent felt was of little consequence, was rejected out of hand. Judgment was reserved on the "Bad Man Cowboys" manuscript, and it was shelved for future consideration.[4]

Greenslet wrote Charlie that "four or five of us here had read all of his books, and with very enthusiastic interest." He noted that they had arrived quite independently at the same idea Siringo had suggested, that the best of his material be woven into one continuous narrative that would make a complete autobiography. The planned book would begin with the *Lone Star Cowboy* narrative, carrying it on to the end of page 225, then insert material from *A Cowboy Detective* to continue the story through twenty-two years up through 1907, and then conclude with material from *A Lone Star Cowboy* from page 234 to the end. Although Greenslet admitted that this plan would result in a book "too large for comfortable publication," he suggested Siringo do it that way, putting in everything he considered desirable. Then the editors would "make final suggestions as to further omissions or inclusions." This last, no doubt, was a polite yet subtle way of keeping the door open for judicious editing as the manuscript came in hand.[5]

From the beginning, Kent perceived the possibility of trouble with the Pinkertons. In a memo to Ferris Greenslet he noted that Siringo's difficulty with the Pinkerton Agency was apparently no longer an obstacle. However, he warned that before publishing Siringo's book, the firm should launch a definite inquiry and seek answers to "our satisfaction." Apparently Kent's advice was simply filed, along with his memo, as Houghton Mifflin records reveal no further inquiry's having been made.[6]

Charlie wrote Al Renehan to tell him of Houghton Mifflin's offer to republish material from *A Cowboy Detective* and to ask him for his approval since the attorney still owned a one-third interest in the book. Renehan replied that his deal with the publisher was all right, and that he planned to be in Boston shortly after April 9 and he would see Greenslet and give him any authority they might want in order to use material from *A Cowboy Detective*. Renehan also told Charlie he was sending him the twenty-five copies of *A Cowboy Detective* he had asked for and that he could pay him for the books "if it is ever convenient for you."[7]

By the middle of April, Charlie had nine chapters completed, and he had decided on a title: "Riata and Spurs." The idea in using that title, he told his publisher, was to get just as far away as possible from the old titles, *A Cowboy Detective* and *A Lone Star Cowboy*. He added: "Of course, if you can pick a better title, do so. But should you use my choice . . . I would suggest that over the name 'Riata,' a miniature picture of a coiled rawhide rope be placed—as a few readers would not know the meaning of riata. Then over the name, 'Spurs,' put a pair of cowboy spurs buckled together by the spur straps."[8]

Before the month had ended, however, Siringo was beginning to have second thoughts about his choice for a title. In a letter accompanying additional chapters of manuscript, he wrote: "I enclose two more chapters of my new book, 'Riata and Spurs,' or 'Pistol and Spurs,' or 'Riata and Pistol,' whichever (you think) will make the best title." Wisely, Houghton Mifflin thought Charlie's first choice for a title was the best.[9]

In May, Harry Knibbs hosted a party honoring Siringo, as well as Mr. and Mrs. Will James and the Charles M. Russells. The Russells, who were building Trail's End, a mansion in Pasadena, told Charlie they would come by in their chauffeur-driven Lincoln automobile to take him to the affair. Siringo used the occasion to ask Russell if he would illustrate his new book, but the artist declined, saying he did not have the time. This proved to be a prophetic understatement, because Russell died suddenly five months later, on October 24, 1926.[10] Will James was Siringo's second choice to do the illustrations for "Riata and Spurs," but he, too, declined because his contract with Charles Scribner's Sons excluded his doing any illustrating for other publishers. Unknown to Siringo at this point, Houghton Mifflin had already decided to use photographs rather than going to the expense of paying an illustrator.[11]

By the first week in May enough of Siringo's new manuscript had been received and read to cause Ira Rich Kent to comment that "it seems fairly clear" some editorial attention would be required in order to improve it. He observed that better paragraphing alone would make a substantial difference, but that a cut in the catalogue of names and the day-by-day journal of unimportant events was also desirable. Although the naming of persons and places gave the story an air of authenticity, he thought Siringo was overdoing it.[12]

The next few weeks Siringo occupied his time in writing the remaining chapters of "Riata and Spurs." His preoccupation with his writing must have caused him to neglect his correspondence, for on June 27 Alois Renehan wrote William S. Hart in Hollywood to inquire about Siringo. He told Hart he had written Charlie "several very important letters" but had not received a reply. Renehan's letter to Hart arrived in Hollywood about the same time as the actor, who had just returned from attending ceremonies in Montana commemorating the fiftieth anniversary of the Battle of the Little Big Horn. Hart at once forwarded Renehan's letter to Charlie, who then wrote in reply to his attorney friend.[13] Toward the end of the month, with the end of his manuscript in sight, Charlie broke from his writing task long enough to attend a "Santa Fe picnic," which had been put on by homesick Santa Feans and others who were aficionados of the Ancient City. Charlie wrote Renehan that he had been in attendance and had seen old faces galore.[14]

On July 29 Siringo finished his manuscript and sent it to Boston along with a selection of photographs he thought appropriate for the book. Nearly a month later, after making a complete review of it, Houghton Mifflin wrote Siringo suggesting minor changes and offered him a contract covering the book's publication. Charlie replied, complaisantly accepting all of their suggestions and expressing willingness to sign their contract. As to the matter of the introduction, he said that if John Hays Hammond would not furnish one, he was positive that the governor of Pennsylvania, Gifford Pinchot, would write it.[15] Governor Pinchot had visited Charlie the year before during a visit to Los Angeles, and the correspondence between the two men that had followed was warm and personal. They had known each other since 1907 when Siringo was detailed by the Pinkerton Agency to guard his superior, James McParland, and the admitted dynamiter Harry Orchard in Boise, Idaho. Pinchot at that time had been chief of the U.S. Forest Service.[16]

August turned into September, bringing with it a foggy spell that caused a worsening of Siringo's health, and for a week Charlie was mostly bedridden. He had been living at 6057 Eleanor Avenue for more than two years, but with his continuing sickness he began considering a move to Azusa, some fifteen miles east of Pasadena. He thought the higher, drier climate might help his throat and lung trouble. His son, Lee Roy, who with his wife and baby daughter lived in nearby Altadena, persuaded Siringo to move there nearer him, rather than to Azusa. Lee Roy located a comfortable three-room bungalow on a lot at 2095 Morton Avenue in Altadena that Charlie could have all to himself. Siringo was certain that Altadena's thousand-foot elevation would benefit his throat and bronchial condition. So early in November, he packed his few belongings and collection of relics and he left his Hollywood den, which by then had become well known.[17]

In Boston, meanwhile, Houghton Mifflin had received the contract that Siringo had signed and returned on September 22. Also received, to their dismay and consternation, was a letter Siringo had forwarded from Governor Pinchot. The governor had written Siringo saying he was delighted "that you used my name as you did in the letter to Houghton Mifflin Company, and I shall certainly make good if I am to write the foreword for your new book." John Hays Hammond was Kent's and Greenslet's first choice, since as a nationally known writer he would command wider public recognition than the governor of the state of Pennsylvania. However, the editors had not yet approached Hammond to write a foreword and had planned to ask Governor Pinchot, their second choice, in the event Hammond declined. Siringo's invitation to Pinchot now seemed to preclude any other consideration.[18]

With the return of the signed contract, Charlie had also written Ira Kent saying he was worried that if they fixed the retail price of his book higher than three dollars, the book would not enjoy good sales. He said his landlord, Linder Stafford, told him that if the book cost more than three dollars, he could not afford to buy it no matter how good it was. Kent replied that it was too early to tell what the retail price of the book would be, but that they would endeavor to keep it as close to three dollars as possible. He also said they had decided to invite Governor Pinchot to write the introduction for "Riata and Spurs."[19]

Shortly after his move to Altadena, Kent wrote Siringo to call his attention to the fact that he had not made any mention of the death of his wife Mamie, although he had spoken of their courtship and marriage. He said that a "definite statement of the time of Mrs. Siringo's death would tie up that part of your chronicle and make later . . . passages, referring to other women, a little less incongruous." Kent went on to criticize Siringo's manuscript for using so much space in enumerating episodes and exploits instead of using it to give more detail concerning the exploits themselves. This was a maddening characteristic of Charlie's writings, wherein he would allude to an important incident and then dismiss it with scant attention. He had done this in relating his part in the pursuit of the Kid Curry gang, and Kent wanted him to rewrite that part of the narrative to properly flesh it out.[20]

Three weeks later Charlie wrote Kent that he was rewriting the part detailing the Alaska trip, and his experiences of four years pursuing the Kid Curry "Wild Bunch." He promised to get these accounts delivered before the first of the year and perhaps as early as December 20. By mid-December Siringo had submitted sufficient additional material to enlarge upon two or three of his most important exploits. Kent replied on December 23 that these details of the more important operations were immensely interesting, and that one whole chapter was now given to the pursuit of the Curry gang. Then in a postscript he noted that he had come, "with some surprise," upon the mention of Siringo's son and second wife. He said he did not recall any earlier references to these persons appearing in the book, and he asked if he wished to make one. Siringo's reply was terse and inexplicable: "It is my wish that you cut out all mention of my second marriage and my son. Nothing in it to interest the general reader."

A week later, Siringo again wrote his publisher that he wanted no mention made of his second marriage, or that he had a son. "These facts," he explained, "would have no interest . . . as they are not connected with my work as a detective." Siringo had supplied what he felt was a sufficient explanation for this strange omission, although hardly a believable one. Had Charlie become angry with his son, perhaps feeling neglected by him, especially at Christmastime? Or, was there some other reason that he decided against including this vital bit of personal data in his autobiography? These are questions that are not known and probably never will be.[21]

On Christmas Day, Siringo finished the last page of his rewrite for "Riata and Spurs," and his niece in Venice, Mrs. Alice Apple, agreed to type the manuscript for him. Mrs. Apple finished typing the manuscript right after the New Year, and on January 3 Siringo had it air mailed special delivery to his publisher. Ira Kent, however, was anxious to delay no longer than necessary to get the completed manuscript to the printer, and he liberally cut the last chapter recounting Siringo's life after leaving the Pinkerton Agency. He wrote Charlie that they had already prepared the last chapter from material in hand and, on comparing the two versions, thought they should do well to stick to the original. Then he added that the references to Siringo's second wife and his son had been removed, as he had requested.[22]

With the final editing of "Riata and Spurs" nearly completed, Ira Kent dashed off a memorandum to Ferris Greenslet regarding Siringo's statement that his difficulty with the Pinkertons over the use of the Pinkerton name was no longer a problem. Kent said it was his understanding that Greenslet was entirely satisfied that no possible difficulty could arise from the use of actual names connected with the Pinkerton association, or the use of the name Pinkerton in the book. He said he had noted in the *Cowboy Detective* book that all of the names were fictitious, but Siringo changed them in "Riata and Spurs" to actual names in accordance with the position that there was no further objection to such use. He was aware, he said, that the Pinkerton name did not appear on either the cover of the book or on the title page. Moreover, in editing the manuscript, he said he had deliberately omitted the Pinkerton name except in a few instances where it was particularly relevant. In most cases, he continued, the agency is referred to as simply "the agency."[23]

If Ferris Greenslet did have any second thoughts or misgivings over Siringo's use of the Pinkerton name in "Riata and Spurs," he kept them to himself. In fact, Houghton Mifflin was already advertising *Riata and Spurs* in *Publishers' Weekly*.[24]

In late January a reunion of old-timers was held at Siringo's Den in Altadena. Present were artist-attorney Jack Cole, writer-artist Will James and his wife, reformed bank robber Emmett Dalton, wild West showman Major Gordon W. Lillie (better known as "Pawnee Bill"), Ed Phillips, Orie Oliver Robertson, Leonard Trainor, A. E. "Al" Hall, Frank Murphy, and Buffalo Bill show rider "Tex" Cooper. A number of photographs were taken with Charlie holding the Winchester rifle that wounded Billy the Kid slightly in the ribs, at the time he killed Sheriff Brady in Lincoln, New Mexico, in 1878. Siringo had not seen Pawnee Bill since the two had first met more than forty years before in Caldwell, Kansas.[25]

Then a curious exchange occurred. Major Lillie told those assembled of the tough time Siringo had as city marshal of Caldwell, and that he was present during the period when the two factions were warring each other. Lillie said that the mayor had persuaded Charlie to be the town marshal until he could find a suitable man to accept the position. This was after Henry Brown, the marshal, and his deputy, Ben Wheeler, had been "mobbed to death" in Medicine Lodge, a nearby town, for holding up the First National Bank there, and killing the bank president Wiley Payne and his cashier, George Geppert. Siringo acknowledged that he accepted the appointment with the understanding that he would not wear a star or a uniform. He said that during the two months he held the job he managed to avoid close calls by getting the drop with his "trusty Colt's pistol, or double barrel shotgun." Charlie confided that he had forgotten about being a town marshal until Pawnee Bill reminded him of it, and that he had not mentioned it in any of his writings.[26]

There was a good reason Siringo had never mentioned being a marshal in Caldwell, Kansas: it simply was not true! Mayor William Morris had appointed John Phillips marshal on May 5, 1884, just six days after the deaths of Henry Brown and Ben Wheeler. Phillips was an experienced lawman who had previously served as marshal in Caldwell. After his appointment Marshal Phillips selected Bedford B. Wood to serve as his assistant. The *Caldwell Journal,* May 8, 1884, which carried a report of the appointments, concluded by saying, "both are good men and will make splendid officers."

After a lapse of forty-two years, one can charitably forgive Pawnee Bill for being confused as to who was appointed to replace Brown and Wheeler. However, no such excuse can be tendered in Charlie's behalf. Until Lillie's "reminder," Siringo might have forgotten the Medicine Lodge incident and who had been appointed to serve as marshal, but he *knew* he had never been marshal of Caldwell, temporary or otherwise. Why Siringo acknowledged as fact what Lillie presumably recalled in error, thereby floating a colorful yet blatant lie, one can only attribute to an old man's craving for recognition and attention.[27]

Not long after this get-together, Siringo wrote George Horace Lorimer of the *Saturday Evening Post,* offering to sell the serial rights to *Riata and Spurs.* He then wrote Ferris Greenslet to enlist Houghton Mifflin's cooperation should the *Post* be interested. "The truth of the matter," he told Greenslet, "is [that] I need money badly, as I have not earned a dollar in the movies, or writing short stories for magazines." He asked Greenslet what the chances would be of receiving a few hundred dollars' advancement on royalties, should he fail to sell the serial rights to the *Saturday Evening Post.* Greenslet replied that he would write the editors of the *Post* and offer to send them proofs of *Riata and Spurs* should they want to see them within a couple of weeks. He went on to explain that because the book was scheduled for publication before the end of April, they could not delay its appearance much beyond that date. However, he did ask the *Post* editors to let them know whether or not they could use any of the articles in time to permit publication by spring. He told Siringo that if this plan did not go through, then perhaps an advance against royalty could be arranged.[28]

Charlie was working on the final proof corrections when Roger L. Scaife, general manager and member of the Houghton Mifflin board, and Harrison Leussler, the house's western representative, along with a Mr. Hood, paid him a visit and spent the afternoon. Siringo liked both Leussler and Scaife, remarking "that both men are live wires . . . and likeable men." The feeling must have been mutual, for both Scaife and Leussler went away enthusiastically devising clever ways to promote Siringo's book.[29]

On March 5 Charlie dispatched the last revised proofs air mail along with the admonishment: "Don't fail to dedicate the book to my friend, Alois B. Renehan of Santa Fe, New Mexico. I enclose the printed dedication so that no mistake will be made. Remember that Mr. Renehan owned a third interest in my *Cowboy Detective* book, and this dedication is all he gets out of the deal."[30]

Efforts to arrange with the *Saturday Evening Post* for the serial publication of any portion of *Riata and Spurs* were unsuccessful because of the magazine's prior publishing commitments. Greenslet then wrote Charlie and enclosed a check for $300 which he said represented the amount of royalty for the advance sales of the book. The check arrived at a propitious time, for Siringo was on the verge of becoming a pauper. In addition to his money problems, and despite his move to Altadena, Siringo's lung and throat condition had worsened, rendering him gaunt-eyed and hollow-cheeked.[31]

With the publication of *Riata and Spurs* just around the corner, Harrison Leussler hosted a party honoring Siringo at the Alexandria Hotel in Los Angeles. More than one hundred booksellers and authors were invited to the gala dinner, and a group of Charlie's old Santa Fe friends sent him a congratulatory telegram: "Speaking for all your old friends, we hope you will get what you deserve, which is the best wish any man could make for you."

Among the fifteen signers of the telegram was Eugene Manlove

Rhodes, who had recently moved back to New Mexico, former governor Miguel A. Otero, and Alois B. Renehan. On March 25, the night of the party, Charlie was a sick man, but nothing could have kept him away. He knew that all of his friends would be there and that an unusual program had been planned. So, despite the way he felt, he dressed to the nines, which meant wearing his now loose-fitting gray suit with a red sweet pea in the lapel along with a red bandanna kerchief tied around his neck.[32]

Flanking Siringo at the head table were William S. Hart and Harrison Leussler. Others sharing head table honors were Dr. Henry F. Hoyt, Charlie's old cowboy pal from LX Ranch days, Henry Herbert Knibbs, who had opened the Houghton Mifflin door to Siringo, writers James W. Schultz and W. C. Tuttle, and Sioux Indian Chief Luther Standing Bear, who had been a performer with Buffalo Bill's Wild West Show. Highlights of the evening were a talk by Bill Hart in the Sioux tongue, translated into English by Chief Standing Bear, and a demonstration of a sign language conversation between Siringo and Jim Schultz.[33] Estelle Lawton Lindsey, writing for the Los Angeles *Evening Express,* covered the banquet at the Alexandria Hotel. She wrote that when Siringo addressed the audience recounting his experiences with Billy the Kid,

> [He] told the story in a quiet, conversational voice, standing . . .
> with Bill Hart on one side of him and Chief Standing Bear on the
> other. It was his party, given in his honor by Harrison Leussler,
> western representative of the publishing firm which regards Siringo
> as the great literary find of this year . . . [Siringo] held in his hand
> a Winchester rifle that had wounded Billy the Kid in one of his
> gun battles with the peace officers. Suddenly, as he talked along,
> he whipped out with a speed that made everybody gasp, the pistol
> of the Kid, now the property and the favorite gun of Bill Hart.
> Siringo looks like a whisp beside the giant movie star, but when he
> glances up your heart stands still.[34]

The next day Charlie wrote Al Renehan: "I wish that you could have been with us . . . [as] our party passed off in fine shape last night." The banquet and the attendant publicity in the Los Angeles papers brought Siringo two very unexpected visitors. On March 31, Mrs. Will Rogers and the recently widowed Nancy Russell paid him a visit at his Den in Altadena. He told Betty Rogers that her husband's name was mentioned in the closing pages of *Riata and Spurs,* which seemed to please her. She promised to arrange for him to pay a visit to their Beverly Hills home that summer during the months Will would be there.[35]

Although the visit of these two ladies pleased Charlie greatly, it was a letter delivered to him on April 1 that combined with their visit to really elevate his spirits. The letter was from Will Rogers, written from Spokane, Washington, three days earlier. Will wrote:

Dear Charlie:

Somebody in some town gave me the proof sheets of your book and wanted to know what I think of it. What I think of it? I think the same of it as I do the first Cowboy Book I ever read: "Fifteen Years on the Hurricane Deck of a Spanish Pony." Why, that was the Cowboy's Bible when I was growing up.

I camped with a herd one night at the old L.X. Ranch, just north of Amarillo in '98 and they showed us an old forked tree where some Bronk had bucked you into. Why, that to us was like looking at the shrine of Shakespeare is to some of these "deep foreheads." Well, this one you have written now is just what that was then. Why, if you live to be a thousand years old, you couldn't write a bad book about the Cowboys. The stuff they did might be bad, but you could tell it so well it would almost sound respectable. My Lord! with Western stuff being written by Soda Jerkers and Manicure Girls, there must be millions who would like to read the straight facts if they could find the book that had them.

This is to tell the world that your *Riata and Spurs* is IT. I hope to see you this summer. Will be home all summer. Where is Gene Rhoades [*sic*]—and Dane Coolidge? I am heading across Montana next week, but I make towns every night to camp in.

I got your picture of you and Pawnee Bill. Use this about the book any way you want if it is any good to you, for I sure mean it.

Visited the old L.X. Ranch when in Amarillo lately. The corral is full of oil wells.

[signed] Will Rogers [36]

Charlie was ecstatic about Will Rogers's letter and immediately telegraphed a copy of it to his publisher. He told Bill Hart that Rogers's letter was "worth thousands of dollars to me and my new book, *Riata and Spurs* . . . and [has given] it a send-off that can't be beaten." The truth of the matter, however, is that Harrison Leussler had given Will Rogers the proof sheets of *Riata and Spurs* and had asked him to write an introduction, or foreword, for the book. An introductory essay by a noted celebrity with such name recognition would greatly augment the contribution of the lesser known Pennsylvania governor, Gifford Pinchot. Instead of declining, Rogers side-stepped the solicitation by dashing off a letter to Siringo laden with lavish praises for *Riata and Spurs.* It was not exactly what Houghton Mifflin had in mind, although the publisher was later able to use excerpts of Rogers's letter to good advantage on the dust jacket of Charlie's book. Houghton Mifflin remained discreetly silent and never told Siringo of its role in prompting the humorist's letter to him.[37]

Harrison Leussler's banquet at the Alexandria Hotel, along with other "puffs" for *Riata and Spurs,* was making Siringo a celebrity of sorts. The Los Angeles *Evening Express* featured a write-up about Charlie, his western experiences, and his forthcoming book, and the Cauldron Club of Pasadena invited him to be its guest of honor and give a talk on April 21. However, Charlie's health, which would seemingly be better one day, would then take a turn and worsen the next. By April 7 he felt he was at last on the mend, although he confided to Bill Hart that he was still very weak.[38] Seven days later found him again very ill. By the morning of the twenty-first he was able to write Ira Kent that "the big show is billed to come off at the Cauldron Club tonight at 6:30 P.M.," and that he planned to read them Will Rogers's letter. "Sick or not," he wrote, "I am going to be there with both feet."[39]

11 / THE PINKERTONS, AGAIN!

O
N April 22, 1927, *Riata and Spurs* made its debut. Ira Kent had written Charlie the day before that the book would appear with a good deal of display in the East, and that the booksellers of the West Coast were prepared to give it a good send-off. With justifiable pride, he wrote Siringo that he had taken a copy home the evening before and examined it "with a critical eye" since he had done most of the editing. That he was pleased with it, he said, seemed to be a good sign and a measure of his enthusiasm for the book. He concluded his letter encouragingly by saying that an early opportunity they would take up, once more, the "Bad Man Cowboys" manuscript. "If *Riata and Spurs* goes as we all believe it will," he wrote, "the way will . . . be paved for this second book."[1]

The sale of *Riata and Spurs* on the day of publication was approximately 3,500 copies. This not only fulfilled the publisher's expectations but indicated a good run for the book. The first major review was that of Owen P. White in the *New York Times* issue of May 3. White praised the book, saying that it was filled with good humor, and that it was more authentic than most because it was written by a man who knew the West as it was. Charlie was very pleased with White's review, saying "it sure . . . [was] a fine article."[2] Other favorable reviews followed in the succeeding weeks, including a review by William Rose Benét in the *Saturday Review of Literature,* and one by Walter Prescott Webb in the *Dallas Morning News.*[3] Not all of the reviews were without criticism however. B. W. Smith, Jr., writing in the *New York Post Literary Review,* thought Siringo should have gone into more detail and not tried to cram seventy-two years into 276 pages. He did admit that Siringo's story, told in his own way, left the reader with an unforgettable picture of the man.[4] Perhaps the best review was the one that appeared that July in the *Nation*. Its author was J. Frank Dobie, who wrote:

> The new book, *Riata and Spurs,* is a remarkably faithful and graphic history of perhaps the most representative cowboy now living—just a "fool cowboy" who never became a cowman, a "waddie" without cares or responsibilities, reckless, as tough as rawhide, as honest as daylight, as ingenious as an old saddle horse, as wise as the rattle-bearing serpent of the plains. . . . *Riata and Spurs* is not only a history of facts; it is a revelation of character, an interpretation of the psychology of the . . . old-time cowboy. It is saturated with humor. Above all, it is written without the least strain for effect or the least playing up of the most adventuresome and hazardous work that any American frontier has known.[5]

While Charlie was eagerly awaiting the arrival of the twelve "author's copies" Kent said they were sending, he received a letter and check from Roger L. Scaife in the amount of $787.50. This, added to the $300 advance check he had received some weeks earlier, represented the total royalty in advance of publication. "While our contract does not stipulate that this payment should be made at this time," Scaife wrote, "we are glad to send it, and hope that you will find it useful."[6]

When Charlie received his copies of *Riata and Spurs* on April 29, he wrote Ira Kent:

> To say that *Riata and Spurs* is a work of Art only half expresses it. My thanks go out to everyone who had a hand in making the book perfect, from the printer's "Devil," up to the "Heap big Chief" at the head of the firm. You, especialy [*sic*], deserve my praise for your sound judgment in making the book a model of perfection.[7]

Having praised everyone at Houghton Mifflin for "making the book perfect," he concluded:

> I only find two typographical errors: In the preface, third verse and third line, it states "Remember, *man,* the Alamo!" when it

should read *men*. At the bottom of the Gem, Idaho photo-cut it states "Jenny Nelson's hotel"—when it should be *Jerry* Nelson's hotel.[8]

Some days later Charlie discovered still another error in the book. The caption under the photo of the only specimen of Billy the Kid's handwriting described the document as a bill of sale for the purchase of a horse, whereas the horse was a gift to Dr. Hoyt from the young outlaw. When Siringo wrote Scaife to thank him for the royalty check, he mentioned the error and asked that it be corrected "should you publish another edition of *Riata and Spurs*."[9]

Ira Kent accepted Siringo's thanks in the same spirit Charlie had intended it. "You may be sure," he replied, "I am immensely pleased to have your compliment on the editorial work done in *Riata and Spurs* because, to tell the truth, I have done it pretty much by my own hand—something that I do not usually undertake. The two typographical errors we are noting and will change as opportunity offers. If that is all there are in the book we shall congratulate ourselves."[10] In spite of these minor typos, Siringo was very pleased with *Riata and Spurs*. In a letter addressed to the publishing firm, he sketched a hand, below which he wrote: "Here's my hand! Tell Mr. Scaife and Ferris Greenslet to shake!"[11]

Charlie's health, meanwhile, continued to deteriorate. Dr. Henry Hoyt, his old cowboy friend from LX Ranch days, proposed that Siringo close up his Den in Altadena and move to Long Beach, where he could administer diathermy treatments. Although Dr. Hoyt was cheerfully optimistic to Siringo concerning his physical condition, he privately confessed that he was very feeble and that it was doubtful that he ever would come back to any nearly normal condition. Concerning the "electrical" treatments he planned to give Charlie, he explained that formerly he had given the "Gland treatment" to build up elderly broken-downs, as originated by the famous Austrian physician, Dr. Eugene Steinach. But since Dr. Steinach had cabled him in 1924 to abandon this regimen in favor of "electrical diathermy," he said he seldom had occasion to administer the "Gland treatment" anymore.

[Now] I have a combination of diathermy to increase the internal body heat, put new life into the circulation of blood and lymph, and, as these cases are most always more or less anemic, I follow up the electricity with hypodermics of iron and phosphorus intra-muscularly. If there is any show on earth for one to come back, this combination will do it.[12]

On May 2, the day Siringo moved from Altadena to Long Beach, Alois Renehan wrote to tell him he had just returned from Florida where he had gone to recoup his health. He told Charlie that the Santa Fe *New Mexican* had recently reported that *Riata and Spurs* was out, and he wondered if that was the book Siringo had dedicated to him; "no copy has arrived yet," he wrote, "but if you did promise to send me one I am quite sure that the promise will be kept."

The *New Mexican*, he observed, had published the table of contents of *Riata and Spurs*. Then, in an apparently declarative statement but with enigmatic overtones that an attorney typically would make, he wrote: "from the article I gathered the impression that much of your book originally called 'A Pinkerton Detective' [sic] and afterwards changed into 'The Cowboy Detective' [sic] is the basis of your new work." In the light of his previous experience, one has to wonder if the wheels were not already turning in Renehan's mind. If his thoughts did portend the possibility of legal difficulties for Siringo, he kept them to himself.[13]

Charlie relocated his new Den in an apartment house at 905 Daisy Avenue in Long Beach. He wrote Bill Hart to give him his new address and told him that his Den was the first door to the right at the head of the stairs. Not far away was Dr. Hoyt's office at 310 Broadway in the new Hubbard Building. Siringo planned to spend the summer in Long Beach, where he could receive the diathermy, or "electrical treat-ments" as he called them, three times a week. Dr. Hoyt gave Charlie a thorough physical examination upon his arrival and found his heart and blood normal and no sign of tuberculosis. He did find him suffer-ing from bronchial and catarrh trouble, and he discovered that he showed a tendency toward diabetes from eating too much sugar. Char-lie admitted that he was "a fiend on sweets," so Hoyt ordered him to drastically cut down on his sugar intake.

When Bill Hart learned of Siringo's move, he chided him for relocat-ing on "Daisy" avenue. "You just can't stay away from the girls, can you?" he kidded. He lamented Siringo's having to quit Altadena, for sentimental reasons he said. "It seemed to be such a cute little cabin you had over there all to yourself."[14]

Barely a month after the publication of *Riata and Spurs,* a seemingly innocuous letter from one John A. Brown, attorney and counsellor, was delivered to J. D. Phillips at the Chicago office of Houghton Mifflin Company. When Phillips opened and read the letter, he found it contained a detailed account, by Brown, of Siringo's earlier attempts to use the Pinkerton name in print and the legal remedies his clients had secured to prevent him from doing so. In the letter Brown referred to *Riata and Spurs* as a story by "a so-called cowboy detective." He enclosed a copy of the decree that had been entered by the Superior Court of Cook County along with an admonition to compare the text of *Riata and Spurs* with the former publication "if there is any question in your mind regarding the details of the articles in the present volume violating the injunction." Brown concluded pontifically that the Agency owed a duty to its clients to protect their names and to preserve inviolate those matters which are within its own peculiar knowledge. "Hence our insistence that the book published by you must suppress these items." [15]

Phillips forwarded Brown's letter on to Boston where Ferris Greenslet, after studying it, composed what he considered was a reasoned reply. His message to Phillips read:

> Pinkerton Agency's original objection was to Siringo's title "Pinkerton's Cowboy Detective," material from which much revised forms less than half of our book. After injunction against Conkey title was changed to *Cowboy Detective* [sic] and fictitious name substituted for Pinkerton in text. In our edition name Pinkerton occurs only on pages 123 and four, 134, 217, 26, 49, and 63. See no legal ground for injunction. Suggest consulting Fletcher Dobbins [sic] . . . who handled previous case of Siringo. Author believed no objection remained . . . [Although] legally responsible in case of trouble . . . [he] is old and ill and case ought to be settled on the grounds of common sense. [16]

At 2:00 P.M. on May 31, about the time Ferris Greenslet's night letter was being dispatched to Chicago, Phillips shot off a direct wire to Greenslet that the Pinkertons were now threatening an injunction and damage suit unless Siringo's book was withdrawn from publication. At the same time he advised that he was forwarding the copy of the injunction against the previous publication, and he asked to be supplied with any additional information that might shed light on the dispute.[17]

At this point there seems to be a blank in the records, as it is not known if J. D. Phillips talked to or engaged Siringo's Chicago law firm of Dent, Dobyns & Freeman, as Greenslet suggested. Apparently there was an exchange of letters between Houghton Mifflin; Allan Pinkerton, principal of the agency; and Asher Rossetter, general manager of Pinkerton's New York City office. On June 21 attorney Brown sent Houghton Mifflin in Boston a telegram amounting to an ultimatum:

> Investigation shows complete violation of injunction order in use of my client's name and business secrets. Client demands that you stop all publication and sale of *Riata and Spurs* and instructs me in case of your refusal to institute proceedings to inforce injunction order heretofore issued. Please advise by wire your intention on this demand.
>
> John A. Brown[18]

Kent, meanwhile, was working within his editorial department trying in some way to salvage whatever he could of Siringo's detective experiences. On June 30 he wrote Asher Rossetter what he hoped was a conciliatory yet persuasive letter. He began with a word of thanks for the "very courteous attitude that you and Mr. Pinkerton have shown us." After explaining that the first half of the book dealing with the author's experiences as a cowboy "apparently contains nothing to which you object," Kent said they were considering enlarging it to take the place of material removed that contained his adventures as a detective.

With these preliminaries out of the way, he then began an almost unctuous recitation of Pinkerton achievements, such as their secret service work during the Civil War, the undercover operations of McParland among the Molly Maguires, the adventures recorded in Mr. Allan Pinkerton's books, and other episodes of "your very remarkable organization . . . [that] have become part of our national history." Kent then opined that the famous Moyer-Orchard-Pettibone business in the Coeur d'Alene, about which so much had been written, might be unobjectionable for mention in the book. He thought this was probably the most conspicuous as well as the most interesting example of what seems "a possible salvage." Having opened the door, Kent then added the Haymarket anarchist affair, which he said was so well-known that

he thought it too could be included without offense. He ended by saying they would be "glad to know your attitude about these historical
episodes which have reflected so much credit upon the agency." [19]

The Chicago office of Houghton Mifflin was making similar over-
tures to Pinkerton attorney John A. Brown. On June 23 Brown wired
B. H. Ticknor, Houghton Mifflin's Boston office manager, advising
him to personally go to New York at once so as to take the matter up
with the agency. Brown said that an agreement, if reached, would dispose of the issue but if not, he warned, court proceedings would follow. Ticknor did go to New York, and he carried with him a two-page
typed statement Siringo had provided nearly a year and a half earlier,
wherein he briefly detailed the publishing history of his *A Cowboy Detective* book and his rounds with the Pinkertons. Pinkerton's general
manager, Asher Rossetter, was unimpressed by Siringo's statement.
"No truth can be attached to his letter," he told Ticknor, as "this party
is totally unreliable in every particular." [20]

Charlie, at this point, was still blissfully unaware of the turmoil
going on within the various Houghton Mifflin Company offices. On
June 15 his good friend E. A. Brininstool came by for a visit and had
him autograph his copy of *Riata and Spurs*.[21] Brininstool invited Siringo to join him the next day at the Alexandria Hotel for lunch and a
reunion with another ex-Pinkerton man, Charles Smith. Smith was a
house detective at the Alexandria, but he had worked with Charlie on
several cases, including the dynamiting of the Independence Depot in
Cripple Creek, Colorado, during the miners' union strike in 1904. Accompanying Siringo to the Alexandria was a Miss Evelyn Ramey, an
attractive young woman Charlie referred to as his bodyguard, and
whom he had affectionately nicknamed "Bronco Chiquita" after the
heroine in his unpublished novel.[22]

Back in Boston, Ira Kent was awaiting word from the Pinkertons in
response to his letter of June 30 to Asher Rossetter. Then on July 12,
Frank Bruce of Houghton Mifflin's New York office notified Kent that
he had talked to Rossetter and was told that Kent's letter had been referred to Allan Pinkerton, and that he was awaiting his reply. He did
not have long to wait, for the next day Rossetter notified Bruce that
Pinkerton said "their position in regard to *Riata and Spurs* was fully
explained . . . and [that] the only thing they can do is . . . insist that
we . . . live up to the letter of the injunction which they obtained." [23]

While Frank Bruce was relaying Allan Pinkerton's last word to

Houghton Mifflin in Boston, Kent was typing out a letter to Siringo telling him for the first time of their trouble. Although the dispute had by then been in progress for more than a month and its magnitude pretty well defined, Kent's letter to Charlie was kind and considerate, as he spelled out their problems in an almost offhanded manner. "Our reprinting [sic] of *Riata and Spurs*," he wrote, "is, I am sorry to say, held up because of some exceptions taken by the Pinkerton Agency. I won't bother you with details until we see whether or not we are able to straighten the matter out. It goes back, of course, to the old injunction against you and the Conkey Company."[24]

Before Kent's letter had even reached Charlie, Kent received the Pinkerton ultimatum slamming the door on any conciliation whatsoever. Kent wrote Charlie again, this time in more detail and with no attempt to spare the old man from worry. In fact, he intimated that the blame was Siringo's in that the Pinkerton action was entirely unexpected. They had believed his statement, he continued, that there was no longer an obstacle to publication of the detective material. He told Siringo that if they were to continue publication of the book, it would be necessary to omit all the episodes of his detective experiences while an employee of the Pinkerton Agency. He added that this would make a very big hole in the book, as it virtually removes everything from page 120 on. As a way to make up for this loss, Kent suggested using some of the material from Charlie's "Bad Man Cowboys" manuscript. He told Siringo that if he had any other useful material on hand, to send it to them immediately. He petulantly ended his letter by saying they wanted to get out the revised edition just as quickly as possible "without wasting time asking for explanations now."[25]

On July 18, before the arrival of Kent's second letter, Charlie was the guest, along with Bill Hart, of Mr. and Mrs. Will Rogers. He spent the day at their Beverly Hills home and was given a drive to see Will's ranch in the Santa Monica hills. Although Charlie thought Will was a "live wire" (one of his favorite expressions), his perennial eye for the ladies caused him to "fall in love" with Betty Rogers and their fourteen-year-old daughter Mary. When Charlie showed Will the letter Kent had written to him on July 13, Rogers was incensed and said he was going to send Allan Pinkerton, who was a warm personal friend of his, a two-hundred-word telegram asking him to call off the injunction, as the worry to Siringo would probably put him in his grave. Rogers felt confident his telegram would have a positive effect and said he would ask Pinkerton to let him know the result of his decision by wire. Siringo was grateful for Rogers's help and support but privately doubted his message would have any effect.[26]

The next day Charlie received Kent's second letter, and he sat down immediately to pen a reply. He said it was his understanding that the injunction had been canceled in the Superior Court of Chicago according to court records. He suggested, rather than substituting other material, using fictitious names, as had been done in *A Cowboy Detective*. "If this plan does not meet with your favor," he wrote, "then an interesting book could be gotten up by using material from the 'Bad Man Cowboys' manuscript." He ended his letter with a reference to his continuing poor health. Plagued for the past five years by an illness that had sapped his strength and vitality, Siringo now seemed resigned to his fate. That "tiger blood," which in the past had made him such a determined adversary, was no longer boiling within his now frail and wasted body.[27]

It had been more than three months since Charlie had written Alois Renehan in Santa Fe. Now that he was engulfed with troubles, he dashed off an almost frantic letter to his attorney friend, saying "I am up against it good and strong." He told Renehan he had figured he would receive about $10,000 in royalties on *Riata and Spurs* but that now he would not get anything because of its being tied up. He said his health, which had not been very good, was now worse over worrying about "that damned Pinkerton injunction." Renehan replied that he was very sorry the Pinkertons were making trouble for him again, and that they had certainly been "dirty" to him. He said he could understand the nervous strain Charlie had been under, especially in his debilitated condition. Then, with a remark certainly not calculated to allay Siringo's distress, he said he was surprised the Pinkertons had not attempted to extradite him from California, where possibly he would not have a Governor Bill McDonald to stand between him and injustice.[28]

Just a day or so after receiving Kent's letter of July 15, Charles received a telegram from the editor asking his permission to allow wholesale substitutions of material from the "Bad Man Cowboys" manuscript to replace nearly all matter after the ninth chapter. Siringo wired his permission, his resignation concerning the affair apparent in his statement: "Use your own pleasure about *Riata and Spurs*."[29]

The same day Kent sent his telegram to Siringo, he wrote a lengthy letter to Asher Rossetter in New York to explain in detail the changes the publisher was planning to make in *Riata and Spurs*. In his letter he said they would remove from the title page, the table of contents, and the list of illustrations, the parts that referred to Siringo's experiences as a detective. Also, they were removing all of the text beginning with Chapter X, page 120, as well as removing three illustrations on pages 126 and 170. The only part of the text that would be retained in these later chapters, he said, would be the last eight pages, which had to do with the author's "declining years in California."

In order to fill the void thus left in the book, the editor said they planned to use some other material dealing with the author's life as a cowboy and his acquaintance with "various picturesque figures among the frontiersmen." Kent assured Rossetter that this new material contained no references to Siringo's detective experiences and, in fact, no allusion to his being a detective at all. He offered to supply the agency with proofs of the substitute material as soon as they had them ready. In the meantime, he concluded, they would "greatly appreciate an intimation" that their proposed revision of the book was in principle satisfactory to the agency.[30]

Rossetter's terse reply to Kent's letter containing the proposed changes in *Riata and Spurs* was a model of arrogant concision. "Our attorneys advise Mr. Pinkerton," he wrote, "there is nothing for the Agency to state on the point of further Siringo publications by your firm until the complete book is issued."[31]

The day before Charlie had wired his permission to substitute material from the "Bad Man Cowboys" manuscript, he had written a long letter to Ira Kent explaining why he thought it would be best to use fictitious names in the book, as was done in *A Cowboy Detective*. He argued that the material in his "Bad Man Cowboys" was not autobiographical and hence would result in a book that a big gap left in his life story.

Kent was off for a week when Siringo's letter arrived, and Ferris Greenslet made the reply. He told Siringo that Houghton Mifflin had held many interviews and exchanged considerable correspondence with the Pinkerton people, who had made it clear that it would not be satisfactory merely to use fictitious names in the new edition of *Riata and Spurs*. "Nothing will satisfy them except the exact observance of the injunction," he continued—"the omission of all information obtained by you while in their employ." Therefore, he said, they had no choice but to omit the last part of the book as it originally stood from page 120 on, substituting in its place material from the "new manuscript." He said this was already in progress, as the typesetting was now proceeding. Greenslet assured Charlie that Ira Kent had done the job of rearranging with great care and skill, and that he thought the book was now in many ways an even better book than before.[32]

Chromo lithograph frontispiece from the first edition of *A Texas Cowboy*. It did not appear in the second edition but was later used as the front cover of the butcher-boy editions (from the author's collection).

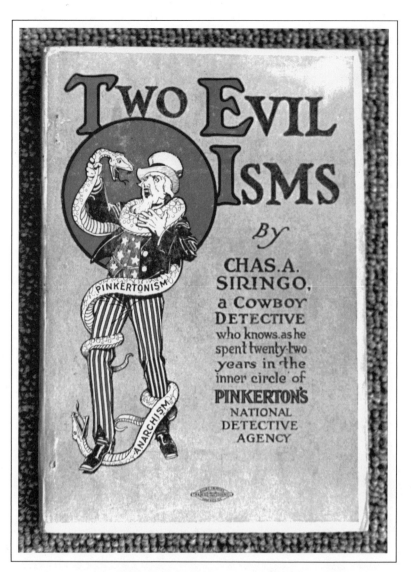

Copy of *Two Evil Isms* with the two-color pictorial front cover
(from the author's collection).

Siringo (*right*) and silent film star William S. Hart on the set of
Tumbleweeds in 1925 (from the author's collection).

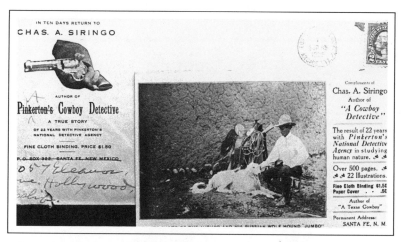

The envelope advertising *Pinkerton's Cowboy Detective* and a postcard advertising *A Cowboy Detective* (from the author's collection).

Old-timers, friends and colleagues of Siringo's through the years, gathered at Siringo's Den in Altadena, California, on January 30, 1927. Siringo is second from the left, kneeling and holding the gun. The group includes George T. ("Jack") Cole, Will James, Ed. Phillips, Orie Oliver Robertson, Emmett Dalton, Maj. Gordon W. ("Pawnee Bill") Lillie, "Tex" Cooper, Leonard Trainor, A. E. ("Al") Hall, and Frank Murphy (courtesy Carol Siringo McFarland).

Siringo, Evelyn ("Bronco Chiquita") Ramey, and
Charles Smith (house detective at the Alexandria
Hotel), photographed by E. A. Brininstool on June 16,
1927, on the roof of the Hotel Alexandria in Los
Angeles (from the author's collection).

12 / HUNTING RANGE
AND REST

URING the first week in August, Siringo made his third move
in as many months. When he left Altadena for Long Beach in
May, he had intended to stay for the summer so that he could
take Dr. Hoyt's electrical diathermy treatments. However, toward the
end of June Dr. Hoyt suddenly became very ill and abruptly left the
West Coast for his old home in Saint Paul, Minnesota. A week later
Siringo relocated his Den in Pasadena at 1477 North Fairoaks Avenue.[1] Less than a month after that, he moved from Pasadena to an
apartment at 1511 Grand Canal in Venice. He wrote Ferris Greenslet
that he was not feeling well and was moving to be near his niece, Mrs.
Alice Apple, should he become sick and need help.

He wrote his friend Bill Hart that he had moved to Venice, and he
hoped he would come and see him there. He told Hart that if he was
not in his apartment, he might be at his niece's home, which was the
first house north of the canal. He added that he also did some of his
loafing at her hot dog stand at 1802 Ocean Front. He enclosed a copy
of Ferris Greenslet's letter of July 26 with his letter to Hart, which he
said "explains itself as to my book *Riata and Spurs*."[2]

In early September, Kent wrote Siringo that the new edition of *Riata
and Spurs* was expected to appear quite soon. He commented that the
firm had had a great deal of trouble and labor in connection with it,
but that he hoped it would be all right now. Then on October 10 he
sent Charlie a copy of the revised edition. In an accompanying letter
Kent noted that the company had not made "very much fuss" about
the changes in the book, although they were substantial. As a result, he
felt certain the Pinkertons would have no reason for any objection, as
the editors had carefully removed any reference to Siringo's connection
with the agency.[3]

The new *Riata and Spurs* reached Charlie on Saturday, October 15, and he was very pleased with it. He wrote Kent that if the firm would let the public know of the changes in the book, it should become an especially good seller in Texas, Oklahoma, New Mexico, and Arizona, where he felt there was considerable interest in the lives of "those 'bad' cowboys."[4]

With the revised *Riata and Spurs* just off the press and barely in his hands, Charlie wasted no time in unveiling for his publisher his newest opus. It was his novel, which he had begun some six years earlier, entitled "Prairie Flower, Better Known as Bronco Chiquita." A screenplay writer who had read the manuscript told Siringo that as a history it had a wonderful basis for a motion picture plot but that it needed romance, especially if it was to have any value as a novel. Charlie then decided to rewrite it in proper "romantic" form. He told Kent that when the new *Riata and Spurs* arrived, he was all wrapped up in closing the third chapter of his revised novel.[5]

Siringo then asked Kent about his royalty, saying he was down to only seventy-five dollars and needed money to move to Tucson, Arizona, where the winter climate would be better for his throat trouble. He told the editor that if Houghton Mifflin had lost money by having a lot of "old *Riata and Spurs*" on hand, he felt he had shared in their loss by giving up his "Bad Man Cowboys" book, which he said had taken him two years to write.[6]

Ferris Greenslet, meanwhile, wrote Siringo on October 22 that he was sending him the first formal copyright statement covering the sales of *Riata and Spurs* to October 1. He said he knew Charlie would be disappointed because there was no check to accompany the statement. This was entirely due, he explained, to the unfortunate Pinkerton affair. According to his contract with Houghton Mifflin, Siringo could have been held liable for the costs, not only of all changes in the type and plates in excess of 20 percent of the cost, but also for any other legal and miscellaneous expenses incurred. However, Greenslet said that in view of all of the circumstances, the house would assume the costs arising from having to discard part of the edition already printed, of the presswork, paper, and binding in the part of the new edition necessary to replace it, lawyers' fees, and other incidentals arising out of the affair. Since this was a sum about equal to the cost of the changes in the plates, the publisher would divide between itself and Siringo the expenses incurred by what he described as "a legal flaw in the title to the property represented by the first edition of *Riata and Spurs*." Then, on a reassuring note, he told Siringo that, since the new edition was selling well, he was certain the small balance against the account would be speedily wiped out and that substantial royalties would be due at the next copyright accounting time—in six months![7]

A day or two later Ira Kent also wrote Charlie referring to Greenslet's letter and the absence of a royalty check. One item that Greenslet did not mention, he said, was the very substantial amount of editorial work that was required, and although it had had to be done during office hours, they had made no charge for it. He characterized the whole episode of the revision as a "laborious matter for some of us and an unpleasant one for us all." As to Siringo's historical novel, Kent, in what seemed to be a polite understatement, said that he could not help feeling a little hesitancy about it. "[This] is a difficult field," he told Charlie, "and I wonder if you would not spend your time to better advantage on historical writing instead of romance."[8]

One month after moving to the apartment at 2511 Grand Canal, Siringo moved again—this time to a room provided by his niece, who lived in the next block at 2417 Grand Canal. His health, which seemed to continually decline despite periods of slight improvement, was now aggravated by worry over his royalty loss. Greenslet's letter of October 22 was a tremendous blow to Siringo because of his growing financial distress. Charlie had written Bill Hart that he had expected to receive one dollar for each copy of *Riata and Spurs* sold, and that he was counting on this royalty in order to provide the necessities of life.[9]

He wrote Alois Renehan to find out if he stood any chance of being compensated for alleged plagiarisms committed by Walter Noble Burns in his book, *Saga of Billy the Kid*. Renehan replied that he had written Burns's publisher, Doubleday, Page & Company, and had sent them a copy of the "paralleled columns." He told Charlie he was sorry he was not only broken in health but broken in pocket, and to relieve the latter infirmity he said he was sending him a personal check for ten dollars.[10]

Frank Putnam, a young banker friend who visited Charlie from time to time, came by in November and drove Siringo for a visit with Charles Fletcher Lummis, and to see his fine unusual home.[11] Other than occasional excursions such as this, little occurred to occupy Siringo's time in the late fall of 1927. There was an exchange of letters between Siringo and Dale Warren of Houghton Mifflin's publicity department. Charlie had written an article about his association with journalist-poet Eugene Field and had submitted it to the *Chicago Daily News* for publication, since Chicago was the backdrop for the story. Although the *Daily News* declined to print the piece because of "pressing . . . space . . . demands," Ira Kent and Dale Warren thought the story "a wonder" and assured Siringo they would quote from it in their publicity notes.[12]

After unsuccessfully trying to get his publisher to print some postcards advertising *Riata and Spurs*, Charlie had 2,000 cards printed at his own expense. He sent fifty of the cards to Bill Hart and asked him to have Miss Cowen, his secretary, enclose a card with each letter Hart mailed out. Hart's reply, if there was one, is not recorded, so one can only speculate as to the actor's reaction to Siringo's request.[13]

For Siringo, Christmas of 1927 came on December 26 with the unexpected arrival of a check from his publisher in the amount of $200. Although it was still four months before the copyright accounting date, Ferris Greenslet said he was sending it "on the chance that it may meet your convenience . . . [and] with best wishes for Christmas and New Year's." Siringo immediately wrote to thank Greenslet for the check, saying it would "help shoo the wolf from my door until spring."[14]

Although Charlie was grateful for the money, he was very upset over some defective copies of *Riata and Spurs* he had recently received from Harrison Leussler in San Francisco. Out of twenty-two copies he had ordered, four contained scattered sheets from the first edition of *Riata and Spurs*. In his thank-you note for the Christmas check he told Ferris Greenslet he feared that hundreds of copies of the revised edition were ruined. Greenslet replied soothingly that they would be glad to exchange any defective copies returned to them. Somewhat pacified, Siringo acknowledged that they were probably not the only publisher to allow blunders to creep into their "mechanical department." Still, the thought that large companies, with all of their resources and know-how, could allow such deviations from perfection was baffling to him. "I cannot account for it," he lamented, "unless it is the Jazz Age in which we are living."[15]

Siringo continued to work on his novel "Prairie Flower," in spite of Kent's advice to the contrary, and near the end of February he completed the manuscript. Since Kent had not offered any encouragement, he sent it to his publisher but directed it to the attention of Ferris

Greenslet. Under separate cover he wrote Greenslet that "as fiction writing is something out of my line, I am not sure the story is written in a proper way. If it lacks fiction technique, it might be possible for you to have it whipped into shape so as to make a book of it . . . to be published in De Luxe style."

Less than a week later he wrote Greenslet again to convince him that the story "Prairie Flower" was historical. He said that many of the incidents mentioned, such as the fight over crossing the Royal Gorge by the Denver & Rio Grande Railroad and the Atchison, Topeka & Santa Fe Railway actually took place in 1878. Bat Masterson in Dodge City, he said, tried to hire him at ten dollars a day as one of his fighting cowboys on the side of the AT&SF but that he was working for the LX Ranch at the time and could not go. After verifying other incidents in his novel as historical fact, he assured the publisher that he could guarantee to sell one thousand copies if the book was published.[16]

In the meantime Siringo's livelihood depended entirely on the books he could personally sell. Harrison Leussler had agreed to help him by consigning copies of the revised edition of *Riata and Spurs,* and by March 1 Charlie had sold more than one hundred copies. In order to expand his market Siringo placed an advertisement in J. Marvin Hunter's *Frontier Times* magazine, which was published monthly at Bandera, Texas, and was widely subscribed to by those interested in firsthand accounts of frontier history. Hunter wrote Charlie thanking him for the ad and to compliment him for his "splendid book" *Riata and Spurs.* He told Siringo he felt his ad was "not strong enough," and he was going to expand on it, "for which there will be no [additional] charge. Your book ought to be in the hands of every old-timer," Hunter wrote, "and I am sure many of them will buy it when they learn of it."[17]

By the end of March, Charlie's novel had been evaluated and the manuscript was returned to him. Ira Kent said they had looked at it from every possible publishing angle. As a historical record, Kent said he found it immensely interesting, and that he had no doubt as to its accuracy, but they were "doubtful" about its story value when handled as a novel. He again advised Siringo that fiction writing is a difficult and exacting business and that he would do best to stick to the chronicles of fact and not try to compete with the novelist. With the manuscript Kent also returned a photograph Charlie had sent of Miss Evelyn Ramey, the real-life model of his heroine "Bronco Chiquita."[18]

Siringo, meanwhile, was energetically seeking a new outlet for his writing. About the time he had finished "Prairie Flower" and shipped it off to Boston, he wrote the publishers of *Cowboy Stories* and *Ace High* magazines, offering to run a department in *Cowboy Stories* called "Flashes from a Cowboy's Pen." Four years before, *Ace High* magazine had printed a story of Charlie's entitled "Prairie Fires," which won a first prize of twenty-five dollars, in gold, in their contest billed "My Most Thrilling Experience." It was this essay that gave Siringo the idea for writing "Flashes from a Cowboy's Pen." These "Flashes" would be short stories drawn from his many years of experience on the range and cattle trails, and would also include a generous commentary about outlaws he had known or knew about.

During the early months of correspondence with Houghton Mifflin as to what manner of book they would publish, Charlie had sent them several samples of his " Flashes from a Cowboy's Pen." Since this material was not used in either edition of *Riata and Spurs,* Charlie decided to seek another publisher for his product. Henry A. McComas, the editor of *Cowboy Stories* magazine, wrote Siringo on March 5 that they were very interested in his proposal and wanted to pursue it further.

Charlie was so elated after receiving McComas's letter that he wrote Ferris Greenslet to tell him to return the eight "Flashes" he had sent Ira Kent nearly two years before, as he intended to make a deal with *Cowboy Stories* magazine. Although McComas had only expressed an interest in Siringo's idea, Charlie's desperation for some measure of financial security caused him to be overly optimistic. "The deal with *Cowboy Stories* magazine," he confidently announced to Greenslet, "will tide me over for cash for a few years." Unfortunately, he failed to consider that the editor's "interest" might also carry a negative side, and, in fact, McComas declined Siringo's proposal.

Siringo accepted the rejection philosophically but continued to grind out more of his short-story episodes. Another plan was already formulating in his mind. Instead of trying to publish his "Flashes" serially in magazines, he decided it would be more advantageous to make a book from them. In a letter to William E. Hawks dated April 17 he said, "Mr. McComas did me a great favor in turning me down as a writer for *Cowboy Stories.* On giving the matter mature thought I can see where I would have done the same thing had I been editor of the magazine. The readers of the 'Flashes' would have considered them the ramblings of a deseased [*sic*] brain. A man never gets too old to learn. I can now, I believe, write a sensible book under the title of 'Flashes from a Cowboy's Pen.'"[19]

The winter spent with his niece in Venice was extremely severe for Charlie, as the damp ocean air aggravated his throat and bronchial condition. With the spring season at hand, his health began to improve, and by June he was well enough to leave Venice and move back to Eleanor Avenue in Hollywood, where he had started out more than a year and a half before. Thanks to his friend George Cole, he soon moved to the new Colehurst Apartments at the corner of Vine and Santa Monica Boulevard. The Colehurst, which was newly built by the Cole estate, was an ideal location for Charlie. He said it was "the finest arranged Apartment House I ever saw. It has every convenience. A man and wife cleans the two rooms every morning and changes the linen, etc." The Colehurst was equipped with a self-regulating elevator and consisted of four floors of apartments. Siringo's apartment was on the second floor. A drugstore, restaurant, newsstand, and barber shop occupied the first floor of the building. Best of all, the new apartment was conveniently situated for visits from his friends, including Jack Cole, Bill Hart, Harry Knibbs, Frank Putnam, and Evelyn Ramey.[20]

Bill Hart's office was nearby, just off the corner of Sunset and Cahuenga. When Hart stopped by to see Charlie at the Colehurst, he invited Siringo and Cole to visit his estate in Newhall the following Sunday. Cole drove Charlie to the actor's ranch, where the two men spent the afternoon. Later, Hart sent Charlie two autographed photos of himself, one to give to Cole. Since Siringo already had a photo that Hart had inscribed for him, he gave the other picture to Bronco Chiquita. Siringo's imagery was singularly inconsistent when it came to gender, and this was readily apparent a few days later when he wrote Hart to thank him. He told the actor that when he gave Bronco Chiquita the photo, she "was as tickled as a boy with his first pair of pants."[21]

Spring brought more than just an improvement in Siringo's health. To be sure, his body benefited by the small amount of weight he had put on, but a renascent outlook on life seemed to have renewed his spirits as well. Charlie traditionally sent greeting cards to his friends to commemorate the Christmas holiday season and the New Year, and for 1928 he planned to send out cards containing a sentiment of his own composition. He had a printer supply him with a quantity of cards on which the verse read:

> Greetings from a friend:
> Here's hoping your joys will be
> many and that you will work like
> Hellen B. Happy.
>
> > Sincerely yours,
> > Charles A. Siringo [22]

Siringo continued to busy himself by writing as well as by answering letters and visiting with friends. On July 6 he wrote E. A. Brininstool to give him his current address and to invite him over to see him. He told Brininstool that he was planning to go into downtown Los Angeles the following Tuesday, the tenth, and suggested a possible get-together. He said he was feeling much better since leaving Venice and returning to Hollywood. On July 12 he wrote Will Rogers, inviting him to come visit him at the Colehurst and telling him of the new book he was writing entitled "Flashes from a Cowboy's Pen."

By mid-July Charlie had completed thirty "Flashes," and he sent the one entitled "Prairie Fires" (which had won the award) to Houghton Mifflin, practically without comment except to assure the editors that the other "Flashes" were equally interesting. Then, mysteriously, he said he was working on a plan to recover his health and at the same time sell thousands of copies of *Riata and Spurs* in Arizona and Texas. "Will let you know of the plan later," he wrote. He never did, although he told Bill Hart he was going to write his publisher of his future plans to build "Siringo's Sweet Cabin Home on Wheels." Within a fortnight he had a reply from Houghton Mifflin Company. Diplomatic as always, the editors said that as soon as they received a little more of his manuscript, they would consider what had best be done with it in respect to publication. [23]

Viola Reid, Siringo's daughter by his first wife, had been living in San Diego when her father left New Mexico, but subsequently she and her daughter, Margaret May, had moved to San Francisco. Siringo's son by his second wife, William Lee Roy, was still living in nearby Altadena. It was Lee Roy who had been able to relocate his father in the comfortable bungalow in Altadena nearly two years before. Siringo's other granddaughter, Carol Siringo McFarland, remembered going with her father on occasion to visit Charlie. Siringo apparently did not have much patience with small children and appeared gruff and irascible to the little six-year-old girl. Lee Roy told his father that since he owned an eight-room house in Altadena, he would have two of the rooms fixed up for him to move into. Charlie was paid up on his rent in the Colehurst Apartments to August 1, but his son told him it would be another month after that before he could get his rooms ready for him. Siringo hoped the move back to Altadena would benefit his health. He knew that not having to pay any rent would benefit his pocketbook, and should he become ill, Lee Roy's wife could care for him.[24]

Charlie was feeling better than he had in months, and he seemed suffused with a new-found optimism. Then word reached Siringo that his friend and counselor of over thirty years, Alois B. Renehan, had died unexpectedly on April 20. Charlie was stunned by the news, and he wrote Stella Canny, Renehan's secretary, to convey his disbelief and grief. Miss Canny replied on July 17 concerning her employer's sudden demise. She said that Renehan had gone to Florida in March to finish out the winter. In every telegram and letter he sent back to his secretary and his partner, he said he was feeling better than he had for years. He traveled to Boston on business about the first of April and was returning home to Santa Fe when he was taken ill in Dayton, Ohio. He entered a hospital there, where he died ten days later.

The loss of his friend, who was fourteen years his junior, had a devastating effect on Siringo. Less than two weeks after learning of Renehan's death, Charlie went to Los Angeles and signed his last will and testament, which an attorney had drawn up for him.[25] Two days later he wrote his publisher to ask for a $200 advance on royalties, since his indebtedness created by the Pinkerton affair had by then been cleared. A week later a check accompanied by a pleasant note from Ferris Greenslet was on its way to Siringo.[26]

Although Houghton Mifflin had offered to consider his "Flashes from a Cowboy's Pen," Charlie now chose not to submit any additional material. Throughout his years of suffering from a persistent and debilitating illness, Siringo had always remained cheerfully optimistic, planning for the morrow with no doubt in his mind he would be there to carry on. The sudden shock of Al Renehan's death made Charlie acutely aware of his own mortality. He abruptly accepted as ineluctable the fact that his struggle to regain his health was a losing one. Unfinished projects no longer seemed important to him. He had run the race and the end of the course was in sight. He had stopped writing.

About the end of August or the beginning of September, Siringo moved in with his son at 999 Beverly Way in Altadena. His chronic bronchitis was not helped by the slight elevation in altitude, and on Sunday, September 30, his old cowboy friend and physician Dr. Henry Hoyt was called in to see him. Then, almost miraculously, he began feeling better and once more began to contemplate the rituals of living. On October 10 he wrote a cheery letter to his friend William E. Hawks telling him he had "fixed up a 'Den' at [his] son's home in Altadena— the town of Highbrows and Millionaires." He told Hawks that he might write some "short fact stories" for *McClure's* magazine in New York and to be on the watch for them.

It was not to be. Eight days later at 10:00 P.M. on Thursday, October 18, a sudden coronary brought death to the old cowpuncher and sleuth. He had lived seventy-three years, eight months, and eleven days. Although arteriosclerosis was officially listed as the cause of death, Dr. Hoyt ascribed Siringo's demise to a very severe chronic bronchitis of many years' duration that had gradually worn him out.[27]

The next morning Lee Roy sent a telegram to Houghton Mifflin advising the firm of his father's death. Roger L. Scaife, general manager, composed an immediate reply:

> We are just in receipt of a wire telling us of the sad news of the death of your father, our author. Will you please accept from us our very real sympathy for your loss? Our relations with your father as his publisher were always pleasant and satisfactory, and we realize with his passing goes a fine type of the old West.[28]

Services for Charlie Siringo were held quietly on Monday afternoon, October 22, with interment in Inglewood Cemetery. Those attending were mostly family members and close friends. E. A. Brininstool, Henry Herbert Knibbs, and George T. Cole were among the pallbearers. William S. Hart and Will Rogers were both in New York City when notified of Siringo's death. Unable to attend the funeral, they sent Lee Roy a telegram that read:

> Another American plainsman had taken the long trail. May flowers always grow over his grave.
>
> Will Rogers and Bill Hart[29]

PART V
RETROSPECTIVE

What is your life? For you are a mist that appears for a little time and then vanishes.

—James 4 : 14

13 / CHARLES A. SIRINGO:
AN APPRAISAL

CHARLES ANGELO SIRINGO now belonged to history.
Following Charlie's death the revised edition of *Riata and Spurs*
continued to enjoy good sales and was reprinted in 1931 under
the Houghton Mifflin Riverside Library imprint. Of the suppressed
first edition, publishing records show that 4,705 copies were sold before publication was stopped. Sixteen copies and the unbound sheets
for 1,500 copies remained in house and presumably were destroyed.
Yet the fact that nearly five thousand first-edition copies of *Riata and
Spurs* were published and distributed shatters the myth, perpetuated
through the years by antiquarian booksellers and bibliographers, that
the book is rare. Significantly, it is now about as difficult to procure a
copy of the first revised edition as it is the first edition.[1]

Of the two antagonists in this drama, the Pinkerton Agency and
Charlie Siringo, one of corporate formidability and national renown,
and the other formidable through an indomitable spirit and irrepres-
sible nature, neither emerges unblemished from the controversy that
divided them. In the beginning, when Charlie attempted to publish
"Pinkerton's Cowboy Detective," the Pinkerton Agency's objections
could be considered reasonable and valid. It had only been three years
since Siringo had resigned from Pinkerton service, and the agency
could justifiably argue for the privacy and protection of its clients and
the secrecy of details of its detective operations. Furthermore, he had
signed an agreement when he went to work for the Pinkerton firm not
to divulge or publish information obtained while an employee of the
agency. William A. Pinkerton's agreement to permit publication of *A
Cowboy Detective* with the exclusion only of the name "Pinkerton"
and the fictionalization of a few principals was a major concession,
especially for him. Even on this point, the mutually agreed-upon name

changes were thinly disguised and, in most instances, it was easy to discern true identity. The Pinkerton name was changed to Dickenson, for example; James McParland became James McCartney, and Tom Horn, one of the more notorious Pinkerton detectives, was changed to Tim Corn. As has been pointed out, both the names McParland and Tom Horn appear unchanged at least twice in the book.[2]

If the similarity of the fictional names to the real ones was not enough to tip off the individual's true identity, then their appearance in the book's accompanying photographs was a dead giveaway. The picture of "Jas. McCartney and the Author," facing page 514, is an example. The Pinkerton involvement in the Coeur d'Alene was widely known, as was their participation in the Haywood, Pettibone, Moyer affair. Both of these cases came under the supervision of James McParland, superintendent of the Pinkerton Denver office. This photo was from the Pinkerton files and was later reproduced in a book about the Pinkertons written with the agency's cooperation. That McCartney was in fact McParland could be readily seen from the photograph.[3]

The Pinkertons, while seeking an injunction to ensure their protection under a contractual agreement, still allowed Siringo wide leeway in the publication of *A Cowboy Detective*. The agency overlooked Charlie's violation of the injunction in 1914 when he reprinted a paperback edition of *A Cowboy Detective* and added the words to the front wrapper: "Twenty-Two Years with Pinkerton's National Detective Agency." It almost goes without saying that Siringo would not be inhibited by the imposition of a legal restraint. The catalyst in the affair was his publication of *Two Evil Isms, Pinkertonism and Anarchism,* which was an angry diatribe against the agency. From that point on, the Pinkerton Agency was not only Siringo's adversary but his implacable enemy.[4]

Siringo's self-righteous indignation in *Two Evil Isms,* wherein he charged the Pinkertons with abuses and corruption, represents a considerable shift from his earlier viewpoint. Although Charlie did not approve of the unethical practice of overcharging agency clients and may have been appalled by the corruption the agency sometimes sanctioned, his moral pragmatism—a kind of situation ethics—enabled him to ignore many of these practices. Siringo seemed to endorse the view that preserving the status quo was synonymous with maintaining law and order, and Charlie considered himself a law-and-order man.

Furthermore, he went along with the popular nineteenth-century belief that the attainment of worthy objectives was more important than the manner of their accomplishment; that is, the end justifies the means.

In *A Cowboy Detective*, after admitting that the Haymarket anarchists were convicted on insufficient evidence, he went on to say:

> A million dollars had been subscribed by the Citizens' League to stamp out anarchy in Chicago, and no doubt much of it was used to corrupt justice. Still, the hanging of the anarchists had a good effect and was worth a million dollars to society. Now, if the law-abiding people of the whole United States would contribute one hundred times one million dollars to stamp out anarchy and dynamiting, the coming generation would be saved much suffering and bloodshed, for we are surely playing with fire when we receive with open arms anarchists from foreign countries and pat them on the back for blowing up Russian and English Royalty.[5]

Three years later, after having been a victim himself of what he considered to be an injustice at the hands of the agency, he wrote in *Two Evil Isms:*

> It [the Haymarket trial] was to my mind a case of "money making the mare go" with the Pinkerton [*sic*] National Detective Agency using the whip. And, no doubt they feathered their dirty nest with a good share of the money, said to be one million dollars, put up by the Citizens' League of Chicago, to "stamp out anarchy."[6]

As to his earlier view that the conviction and execution "had a good effect" and therefore was justified, he seemed in *Two Evil Isms* to have shifted at least ninety degrees. "No doubt some of these anarchists deserved hanging, but for the life of me, I could not see the justice of the conviction, in the face of the evidence as I understood it."[7]

During Siringo's twenty-two years as a Pinkerton detective he maintained a discreet silence concerning agency methods and abuses, and he felt no compulsion to speak out against them. Only after W. A. Pinkerton forced Charlie to modify his "Pinkerton's Cowboy Detective" was his tiger blood aroused to the extent that he decided to make a public complaint against the agency. For his trouble, Siringo very nearly landed in jail after the debacle of *Two Evil Isms*. Years later

Charlie admitted that he had done "things" (his publication of *Two Evil Isms*) to William A. Pinkerton that made him his "bitter enemy" for the rest of his life. This statement is the only indication that Siringo may have felt some remorse, or misgivings, for his actions.

Siringo never did understand that the contract he signed when he went to work for the Pinkertons did anything more than exclude revelations of agency secrets and client-agency matters of a confidential nature. His own activities in pursuit of his duties were uniquely his, he believed, and he was not going to be denied what he thought was his right to exploit them. *Two Evil Isms* was the high point in Siringo's long dispute with the agency, and the court action it gave rise to confirmed and reinforced the Pinkertons' earlier legal initiative against him. On balance, Siringo was fortunate to have been able to evade W. A. Pinkerton's desire for revenge.[8]

Then, for more than ten years the "dogs of war" lay silent. In 1919 Siringo devoted only a few pages in *A Lone Star Cowboy* to his detective experiences, mentioning the Pinkerton name only three times. If the agency noticed, it probably felt the references too inconsequential to bother with.[9] The publication of *Riata and Spurs* eight years later was another matter. This was "Pinkerton's Cowboy Detective" all over again, disseminated nationally by a leading publishing firm. The Pinkertons wasted no time in threatening to come down hard on Houghton Mifflin Company. Allan Pinkerton, who had succeeded W. A. Pinkerton as principal of the agency, carried forward his late uncle's animus against Siringo for his volations of the injunction, and especially for what he considered was the scurrilous affront of *Two Evil Isms*.[10]

The Pinkerton Agency's big gun in the threatening battle was the 1911 injunction. The agency maintained that the injunction denied Siringo the right to reveal facts about Pinkerton clients, or details of detective operations, not to mention use of the Pinkerton name. It had been fifteen years since the publication of *A Cowboy Detective*, which meant that Siringo's detective experiences were anywhere from fifteen to forty-one years old. This was enough time that most, if not all, of his revelations involved happenings so well known as to render moot any need for secrecy. Of course, the Pinkertons were not really trying any longer to protect their clients or guard their own secrets, their attorney's protests to the contrary notwithstanding. They simply wanted satisfaction for Siringo's past imprudence and accusations against the agency. Had Ferris Greenslet understood the depth of these turbulent crosscurrents of bitterness, he might have realized that settling the case "on the grounds of common sense" was virtually impossible.[11]

The Pinkerton Agency, even as late as 1927, was still perceived as and in fact was a powerful organization, and Houghton Mifflin wanted to avoid going to court against it if possible. The publisher tried to save the first edition of *Riata and Spurs* through negotiation and conciliation. Failing that, the firm might have sought legal relief on the grounds that the agency had allowed an exception to the injunction with the publication of *A Cowboy Detective*. It could not argue that the facts revealed were for the most part in the public domain, because Siringo had contracted away his right to divulge these facts. Charlie, obviously, had not made that clear to Houghton Mifflin in the beginning.

All of the available evidence points to this as being the reason the publisher did not choose to go to court. Houghton Mifflin believed that Charlie had deceived them, either innocently or otherwise, by claiming title to a property that legally was not his to claim.[12] If this is true, then it is not hard to understand why the revised edition of *Riata and Spurs,* save for the words "Revised Edition" on the title page, contains no notice that different material had been substituted in eleven of the book's twenty chapters. Apparently, Houghton Mifflin considered the first edition of *Riata and Spurs* to be an aberration and wished to get it out of the way with as little fanfare as possible.[13]

Four years after the publication of *Riata and Spurs,* Richard Wilmer Rowan's *The Pinkertons, A Detective Dynasty* appeared, it being the first of several post-Siringo accounts of the Pinkertons written with the blessing and approval of the agency. In 336 pages of text Siringo is mentioned only once, and this in reference to his having written two books that Rowan described as highly critical of the agency. *A Cowboy Detective* and *Two Evil Isms* were the two books referred to, and only the latter criticized the agency. Rowan asserts that after twenty-two years' service as a Pinkerton detective, Siringo discovered the work he had been doing was something deserving of his contempt! Two decades later James D. Horan and Howard Swiggett coauthored *The Pinkerton Story,* a 366-page history of the agency in which Siringo's name appears just once, and then only in passing. In *Desperate Men: Revelations from the Sealed Pinkerton Files,* first published in 1949 and then revised and enlarged in 1962, Horan did mention Siringo briefly. Five years later Siringo fared better in Horan's *The Pin-kertons: The Detective Dynasty That Made History,* with his name appearing on three pages in connection with his exploits. Although Allan Pinkerton, namesake and grandson of the founder, died in 1930, the agency's bitterness toward Siringo has lasted nearly three-quarters of a century. Until very recently, it seemed that as far as the Pinkerton Agency was concerned, Siringo was a nonperson.[14]

The Pinkerton historians' silent treatment of Siringo, coupled with invidious remarks from high agency officials such as Asher Rossetter, tend to minimize and denigrate Siringo's role as a Pinkerton's detective. Such implications do not square with the facts. Siringo was highly esteemed during his years with the agency, by both Pinkerton brothers. Robert Pinkerton kept a photograph of Siringo on the wall of his New York office, and William Pinkerton told superintendent McParland that Siringo was as "tough as a pine knot." He said he never knew a man of Siringo's size who could "endure as much hardship as he does." When Flat Nose George Curry and Harvey Logan of the Wild Bunch began holding up trains of the Union Pacific Railroad, it was W. A. Pinkerton who ordered McParland to assign Siringo to the case. This suggests that Pinkerton placed considerable confidence in Siringo's ability to handle difficult assignments. John Hays Hammond, the Coeur d'Alene mine owner who employed Siringo in what was one of his most dangerous and terrifying Pinkerton operations, referred to him as "the most interesting, resourceful, and courageous detective I ever dealt with." It should suffice to say that Siringo's prowess and stature as a detective are too well established to be affected by Pinkerton writers' use of subtle recrimination and innuendo.[15]

The Pinkerton Agency's suppression of *Riata and Spurs* highlighted its ultimate triumph in its battles with Siringo, who was by then a broken old man trying to eke out a livelihood by writing stories and selling books. As it turned out, the withdrawal of the first edition of *Riata and Spurs* was essentially a Pyrrhic victory, for there was nothing in the book that did not reflect credit upon the agency and represent good publicity in its behalf. On the other hand, its truculence and intractableness in the matter only served to confirm and lend credence to Siringo's earlier charges of agency abuses and highhandedness.

Was Siringo simply a victim of a powerful, manipulative, and unfeeling organization? Or, does an examination of the Pinkerton affair instead suggest that Charlie might have been a self-promoting opportunist with crudely relativistic values? Whatever the truth, elements of which are probably embodied in both propositions, Siringo's image as an unequivocal figure remains untarnished. Especially impressive is the fact that he accomplished his life's work as a lawman without becoming a killer. For over forty years Siringo carried a six-shooter and had to draw it on many occasions, sometimes using his weapon as a club. Eugene Manlove Rhodes once compared himself to Siringo in the respect that, with every provocation and opportunity to become a killer, he relied instead on his nimble tongue and brain rather than the bullet.

When Siringo was asked in his old age if he had ever killed anybody, he replied that he did kill a fellow in the Indian Territory over a horse race, but "nobody knows anything about it," he added. Charlie admitted that he never wanted to be known as a killer, and he usually deprecated his part where a firefight was involved. When Siringo and Bill Owens, his partner employed by the New Mexico Cattle Sanitary Board, were in a fight with two thieves at Abo Pass, Owens fell with a shot through the chest. After he was down, Owens emptied his pistol into the thief who had shot him. Siringo minimized his own part in the shoot-out by simply concluding that "both of the thieves were killed." He once told Gene Rhodes that he deserved no credit for the bravery that was attributed to him because he was born without a sense of fear.

Whatever his other faults, Siringo did gain a reputation for sheer audacity in tight situations and fearless determination against unfavorable odds. In his later years he gloried in the revelations of his exploits and used them to polish his public image as an archetypal western lawman. In fact, his yearning in his old age for recognition and acclaim drove him at times to rather pathetic lengths. Like most notables, whose shortcomings and human frailties diminish their heroic image upon too close an inspection, Siringo is seen best at a respectful distance. There, he remains the rollicking frontier cowboy and longhorn trail driver, the determined and tenacious cowboy detective, and the admired example of a fiercely independent man of the West.[16]

In the historical scheme of things Siringo was never one of the movers and shakers. Frank Dobie called him "a fool cowboy" (a term Siringo used to describe himself) who never became a cowman. Even as a Pinkerton detective Charlie refused advancement, turning down several chances for promotion to superintendent. He said there was not "kick enough in office work." As a writer he burdened his prose with crude grammatical constructions, gauche interjections of "gentle reader" or "dear reader," and inconsistencies in spelling. His *History of "Billy the Kid"* and the revised edition of *Riata and Spurs,* which deal with "bad man cowboys," are frequently factually flawed, as Ramon Adams pointed out in several of his books.[17] Although *A Cowboy Detective* and the two editions of *Riata and Spurs* make interesting, even fascinating reading, it is Siringo's first book that establishes his efflorescence not only as a writer but as the quintessential cowboy. Indeed, it is Charlie's stylistic crudity, together with a youthful *joie de vivre,* that makes *A Texas Cowboy or, Fifteen Years on the Hurricane Deck of a Spanish Pony* so credible as a genuine, unvarnished cowboy narrative. It was the most widely read of Siringo's books and it is still celebrated for being the first cowboy autobiography. Perhaps of greater significance is that *A Texas Cowboy,* augmented to a degree by Siringo's later books, not only contributed to romanticizing the West but helped to create the myth of the American cowboy as a national folk hero.[18]

What makes Charlie Siringo such an intriguing character is the fact that he was an ordinary man moving among ordinary yet dangerously unpredictable people, and frequently under extraordinary and perilous conditions. Like the episodes of a Saturday matinee serial, with each installment different and exciting, Siringo's stories of his steely nerved exploits enabled readers to participate vicariously. But there is more to Siringo than just the drama of his life's adventures. There is a human quality and, more importantly, a humane quality that readers identify with.

William S. Hart, who made his fortune by helping to create the myth of the American West in his movies, once likened Charlie Siringo to Wyatt Earp.[19] Nothing could have been further from the truth. Writer Raymond Thorp, who knew both men, said they were as far apart as the poles. Thorp recalled that Earp's hands were those of a gambler, without even a casual callous to indicate his ever having toiled. Charlie's hands, by contrast, reflected his years of wrestling with steers. Two of his fingers were permanently bent from his being dragged by a horse. Earp had eyes that were "cold blue and mean," while Charlie's eyes were warm and brown, "the color of Idaho russet potatoes." He was always ready to "Whoop 'er up, Liza Jane," while Earp remained ever suspicious of each move anyone made. Thorp's judgment was that Earp preferred to resolve his suspicions by shooting to kill, whereas Charlie's method was to bend his pistol over an adversary's skull, thus affording him a chance to see flowers bloom again.[20]

Although Bill Hart knew and admired Wyatt Earp, it was the humane quality which Hart and Siringo perceived in each other that bonded their friendship. For example, when Siringo moved from Altadena to Long Beach so that he could take Dr. Hoyt's diathermy treatments, Hart wrote Charlie that he was worried about what had become of his pet cat. In his reply Siringo commended the actor for showing that "his heart was in the right place" because of his concern for "dumb animals." He told Hart not to worry as he had found Hollywood Tommy a good home with Bronco Chiquita.[21]

Eugene Rhodes visited Charlie shortly before the publication of *Riata and Spurs* to interview him for an article he planned to write for *Sunset Magazine*.[22] As he sat in Siringo's Den, he made notes of his subject's every move and mannerism. His impressions were later transcribed, as he had jotted them down, into his feature on Charlie. What emerges is a prose picture of Siringo that is sensitive and vivid. In so far as words can convey such an image, it offers a glimpse at the essence of the man.

He began by describing Charlie as "a youth of seventy-two . . . [with] faded brown eyes, but sharp eyes that never miss the slightest movement of any person or anything. Not nervous, but always alert. A thin face, brown like saddle leather; wind and sun have tanned that face beyond all changing. Most expressive hands; thumbs especially; thumbs which fill out and picture forth the story as he talks; a trigger finger that sticks out with every gesture. Fascinating forefinger. You can't take your eyes from it. Thin lipped; a mouth that would be hard if it were not for an occasional quirk of humor. Quite a frank smile and often a chuckle. Not a tall man; slender—yes, frail. You note this with a shock; listening, not once had you thought of him as a small man or as an old one. A small head, a boy's head. And he is a boy, full of mischief and keen fun. Looks right at you when you talk, but always notices what anyone else happens to be doing. Uses his right hand as he talks. Not flowery gestures, but helpful. Thrusts his idea home with that trigger finger. Small feet, corded throat . . . Carries a loaded cane; polished steer-horn tips on a steel rod; probably made for him in a penitentiary. Wears a small red silk handerchief, a low crowned Stetson, neat clothing and shoes; not boots. Straight back; does not stoop; head carried like a Chanticleer . . . Very gracious and polite to ladies. Quick to retort; shrewd wit—and a chuckle. Much more than 'a cowboy type.' An individual; not like anyone else you have ever known."[23]

Most of Siringo's life had been spent out-of-doors. He had characterized his youth as being "wolf wild and free as the wind." Thus his last years, spent for the most part in relative poverty, alone and sick in a big city, make his life story a bittersweet one. The kindnesses and charity of sympathetic friends, as well as the support of a remote but not uncaring publisher, lie in sharp contrast to the tensions and disappointment visited against him in retaliation by the Pinkertons.[24]

Finally, there is an incongruity if not a paradox in the story of Siringo's struggle against the vicissitudes of old age, illness, and financial adversity while at the same time he mingled with affluent friends and was lionized by celebrities of national renown. Siringo's dignity and pride in his independence are juxtaposed against an almost desperate urgency in his battle for survival. The varying efforts, both private and corporate, of those reaching out to fulfill some measure of social responsibility, not to mention the obligation children have to care for an aging parent, are clearly apparent. If nothing else, his last years provide an unspoken commentary on a twentieth-century society as yet uncertain, uneasy, and even unconcerned regarding the needs of the elderly and less fortunate.

Charles Peavy, in his study *Charles A. Siringo, A Texas Picaro,* commented on the irony that Siringo "should spend his last days in . . . Hollywood," and that the "open spaces he loved" were so far from "the asphalt and concrete canyons of Los Angeles."[25] Although Peavy's simile is more appropriate for either New York or Chicago than for Los Angeles in the twenties, the irony is well taken, but it even goes beyond that. Charlie had admired the verses of an old cowboy song by Charles Badger Clark, Jr., and he ended both *A Lone Star Cowboy* and *Riata and Spurs* by saying he hoped the words of the song would be carved on his tombstone. The verses read:

> 'Twas good to live when all the range
>   Without no fence or fuss,
> Belonged in partnership with God,
>   The Government and us.
> With skyline bounds from east to west,
>   With room to go and come,

I liked my fellow man the best
    When he was scattered some.
When my old soul hunts range and rest
    Beyond the last divide,
Just plant me on some strip of west
    That's sunny, lone and wide.
Let cattle rub my headstone round,
    And coyotes wail their kin,
Let hosses come and paw the mound,
    But don't you fence it in.[26]

The irony is that cattle, even if there were any, could not rub Charlie's headstone 'round because his grave was never marked. Neither do coyotes wail their kin, nor do "hosses" paw the mound, but the sounds of jet airliner traffic can be heard from nearby Los Angeles International Airport, and perhaps the shadows of their wings occasionally traverse his gravesite in Inglewood Park Cemetery. Siringo's monument, on the other hand, is more lasting than any words chiseled in stone. Clark's verses in *Riata and Spurs* have probably been read by far more people than would ever visit Charlie's grave and see them on a tombstone. After all, Siringo's books are in themselves the monument that forever establishes his place in the American frontier West.[27]

EPILOGUE

FOLLOWING their father's death, Lee Roy and Viola divided Charlie's meager possessions. Viola took most of her father's books, including a number of copies he had personally inscribed to Lee Roy. She also took a portrait of her father that he had inscribed to his mother, Bridgit, along with a carved center table he had owned. Lee Roy kept his father's cowboy hat and scarf, certain other mementos, including a few photographs, and all of his personal papers. The latter included his manuscript "Prairie Flower, Better Known as Bronco Chiquita" and the manuscript he had been working on immediately prior to his death ("Flashes from a Cowboy's Pen"). In 1935, after the death of his wife, Lee Roy moved away from Altadena. He rented his house but, because of its ample size, one room became a place in which he stored his father's papers and remaining memorabilia, along with some of his own personal possessions. Some time later he returned to find that the renters had cleaned out the room, burned its contents, and were using it as a playroom for their children.[1]

In late 1939 or early 1940, still in the midst of the Great Depression, Viola sold her father's books to Dawson's Book Shop in Los Angeles for what little cash they would bring. She even sold the carved center table and the portrait of her father that he had inscribed to her grandmother.[2]

Lee Roy and Viola, Siringo's only children, were never close. In fact, following Charlie's funeral, they went their separate ways, never to contact one another again. Viola, a multitalented woman, lived with her daughter, Margaret May, in many locations throughout California. Although Margaret did get married, the union was not a happy one, and she returned to live with her mother until Viola's death in 1960. Twelve years later, Margaret succumbed to cancer at the age of sixty-five. She left no children. Viola and Margaret are both interred in Inglewood Park Cemetery, but in a different area from where Charlie is buried. Lee Roy lived out his days in California and died of a heart attack at age fifty-nine, and within three days of the twenty-seventh anniversary of Charlie's death. Because he had fathered two daughters, Carol and Betty, and no sons, the Siringo name ended with him.[3]

Lillie Thomas Siringo, following her move to California and divorce from Charlie, married a widower named MacGuire. Lillie was a seamstress and milliner by trade, so she was always beautifully dressed. Because she was a pretty woman, with fair skin and violet-blue eyes, her husband, "Mr. Mac," was very jealous of her. In fact, he made her life so unbearable that eventually she divorced him. Later, she met a man named Jessie Thornton through her son Lee Roy. Thornton owned a livery stable and would invite Lee Roy to ride on the wagons with him. Lillie later said that she thought Thornton was the "prettiest man" she had ever seen. Thornton must have had similar feelings about Lillie, for the two were married in Ventura, California, on June 22, 1914. Lee Roy's oldest daughter, Carol, grew up listening to "Grandpa" Thornton's stories of his youth in Nebraska and his adventures as a cowboy in California. Betty, her younger sister, went to live with Lillie and Jessie Thornton after the death of her mother. Siringo remained on friendly terms with his ex-wife and her husband, even to the exchanging of gifts at Christmastime.[4]

Charlie's last wife, Ellen Partain, following her divorce from Siringo, married a man named Sapp. If she regarded her marriage to Siringo as a mistake, her choice of a successor was an even greater error—a fatal one in fact. While on a hunting trip, Ellen was killed by a gunshot at the hands of her husband. He said that the shooting was accidental, but friends of Ellen and others claim that he murdered her. As she specified in her will, she was buried alongside her son, Jimmy Partain, and her first husband, T. E. Partain, in the Hawley Cemetery (the old Deming's Bridge Cemetery) near Blessing, Texas.[5]

Miss Evelyn Ramey, Charlie's Bronco Chiquita, was twenty-two years old when Siringo died. Her father, William J. Ramey, who had lent Charlie money, was a maintenance employee for the city of Los Angeles. Except for the fact that she had a brother named Clyde, little else is known about her or the remaining course of her life. She never married, and she died in Los Angeles on Siringo's birthday, February 7, 1964.[6]

In Santa Fe, site of Siringo's retirement home, the city limits eventually grew to encompass much of Charlie's Sunny Slope Ranch, and a large residential area now surrounds his old ranch house. When Gene

Rhodes wrote his article on Siringo for *Sunset Magazine* in 1927, he said its purpose was to stimulate interest in *Riata and Spurs* and to take Santa Fe to task: "To make them see that one of Plutarch's men walked with them face to face. This was Siringo's home, his chosen place; yet every lonely ranch from Matamoros to the Coeur d'Alene knows more of him than Santa Fe, who was never aware of Siringo frail and shy and mild." Now, Rhodes would be pleased to note that Siringo Road connects what used to be Charlie's ranch with south St. Francis Drive. Within the vicinity of the ranch house are now Rancho Siringo Road, Rancho Siringo Drive, Rancho Siringo Lane, and Siringo Court. Charlie Siringo's connection with Santa Fe has not been forgotten.[7]

NOTES

Abbreviations Used in the Notes

CMNH Los Angeles County Museum of Natural History, Los Angeles, California

HLHU Houghton Library, Harvard University, Cambridge, Massachusetts

LMNM History Library, Museum of New Mexico, Santa Fe, New Mexico

NMSA New Mexico State Records Center and Archives, Santa Fe, New Mexico

TANM Territorial Archives of New Mexico, State Records Center and Archives, Santa Fe, New Mexico

Introduction

1. Charles A. Siringo, *Riata and Spurs, The Story of a Lifetime Spent in the Saddle as Cowboy and Detective*, 263. Photographs facing pages 258 and 264 show Siringo during this time to be holding his age quite well. See John Hays Hammond, "Strong Men of the Wild West," *Scribner's Magazine* 77 (Feb.– Mar., 1925): 122, for a description of Siringo in 1891. By comparison, he had changed very little after sixteen years. For a discussion of Siringo's third wife, Grace, see chaps. 5 and 6.

2. Siringo, *Riata and Spurs*, 120–26, 263; idem, *A Cowboy Detective: A True Story of Twenty-Two Years with a World Famous Detective Agency*, 21–24; idem, *Two Evil Isms, Pinkertonism and Anarchism: By a Cowboy Detective Who Knows, as He Spent Twenty-Two Years in the Inner Circle of Pinkerton's National Detective Agency* 1–5. For an excellent account of the Haymarket incident, see Henry David, *The History of the Haymarket Affair*.

3. Siringo, *Riata and Spurs*, 121–23, 126, 184–95; idem, *A Cowboy Detective*, 13–14, 15 (quotation), 24, 197–228, 507–508. A summary of Siringo's detective experiences can be found in Orlan Sawey, *Charles A. Siringo*, 96–130.

4. Siringo contracted with the M. Umbdenstock & Company in Chicago to publish 2,000 copies of *A Texas Cowboy*, half in cloth and half in paper

wrappers, a small number that accounts for the rarity today of the first edition. The first printing sold out within a month or two, and Siringo ordered the printing of 10,000 additional copies, again half in cloth and half in paper. In the second edition, which carries the publisher's imprint of "Siringo & Dobson," Siringo corrected the date of his birth from 1856 to 1855 and added thirty-one pages of "Addenda." One must presume that "Dobson" was a partner who provided Siringo with financial assistance. Siringo's original spelling in the title of both editions was "Cow Boy." (Future references to either the first or second edition of *A Texas Cowboy* will employ the modern spelling.) Before the second edition was exhausted, he sold his copyright, plates, and remaining book stock to the Rand McNally Company, which continued to publish the book until the copyright expired in 1914. Siringo estimated that during this twenty-eight-year period he was paid a royalty on approximately half a million copies. Publishing records, however, reveal the figure to be closer to half that number. After 1914 the J. S. Ogilvie Publishing Company brought out a cheap pulp edition and in a smaller format, which continued in print until 1926. Charles A. Siringo to Ira Rich Kent, Feb. 3, 1927, in the Siringo/Houghton Mifflin Company file, Houghton Library, Harvard University, Cambridge, Mass. (These records will hereafter be cited as HMC Records, HLHU.) Charles A. Siringo, *A Texas Cow Boy or, Fifteen Years on the Hurricane Deck of a Spanish Pony . . .* (1886), [iii], [13], [317]–47; J. Frank Dobie, "Bibliography of Siringo's Writings" in *A Texas Cowboy* (1950), xxxviii; John H. Jenkins, *Basic Texas Books: An Annotated Bibliography of Selected Works for a Research Library*, 492.

5. Siringo, *A Texas Cowboy* (1886), [13]–14; Matagorda County Records, 1860, p. 3, Eugene C. Barker Texas History Center, University of Texas, Austin, Tex.

6. Siringo, *A Texas Cowboy.*

7. J. Frank Dobie said of him: "No other cowboy ever talked about himself so much in print [but] few had more to talk about." Dobie, *Guide to Life and Literature of the Southwest*, 119.

8. Siringo admitted, years later, that it was his intention when he went to work as a Pinkerton detective to later write an account of his experiences. Siringo, *Two Evil Isms*, 107. Dobie, in his introduction to *A Texas Cowboy* (xxxi–xxxiii), briefly surveys Siringo's difficulties with the Pinkertons. Fuller accounts are found in Charles D. Peavy, *Charles A. Siringo, A Texas Picaro*, 12–24; idem, introduction to *Two Evil Isms, Pinkertonism and Anarchism* (1967), iii–xi; and Sawey, *Charles A. Siringo*, 86–95.

9. James D. Horan, *The Pinkertons: The Detective Dynasty That Made History*, vii–x, 25–36, 49, 52–61, 81–98, 238, 327, passim; James D. Horan and Howard Swiggett, *The Pinkerton Story*, 5–10, passim; Siringo, *A Cowboy Detective*, 16 (first quotation); idem, *Two Evil Isms*, 2 (second quotation). See also Richard Wilmer Rowan, *The Pinkertons, A Detective Dy-*

nasty, for an earlier historical account of this unusual law enforcement organization.

10. Horan, *The Pinkertons,* viii–x; Ray Ginger, *The Age of Excess: American Life from the End of Reconstruction to World War I,* 35–52, 79–80, 114–17, passim; John Chamberlain, *The Enterprising Americans: A Business History of the United States,* 140; Justin Kaplan, *Mr. Clemens and Mark Twain,* 158 (first and second quotations), 159–72; idem, *Mark Twain and His World,* 98–100, 125.

11. Ginger, *The Age of Excess,* 17, 56–61; Horan, *The Pinkertons,* 204–237, 329ff., 335–38; Richard Hofstadter, *Social Darwinism in American Thought,* 105; Robert E. Riegel, *America Moves West,* 590–93. For a thorough study of this famous episode of murder and violence involving an Irish secret society in the Pennsylvania coal fields in the 1870s, see Wayne G. Broehl, Jr., *The Molly Maguires,* 349–50, passim.

12. David, *The History of the Haymarket Affair,* 157ff., 182–206, 226, 330–31, 340–42, passim. The Haymarket was a long, oblong space enclosed by rather large buildings of the factory and warehouse type. The square was selected because a large gathering was anticipated, and it could accommodate some twenty thousand people. Parsons, a southerner and a professed socialist, had settled in Texas after the Civil War, where he edited the Waco *Spectator* and later was elected secretary of the Texas state Senate. He moved to Chicago in 1873 and in the succeeding years was nominated for various political offices on the socialistic labor tickets. Ibid., 198, 226. Ida M. Tarbell, *The Nationalization of Business, 1878–1898,* 160–61; Ginger, *The Age of Excess,* 57–59.

13. Siringo, *A Cowboy Detective,* 11–12, 16–17; idem, *Two Evil Isms,* 1–2; idem, *Riata and Spurs,* 120–21, 123–24.

14. Siringo, *Riata and Spurs,* 263 (first quotation); idem, *Two Evil Isms,* 3 (second quotation), 4 (third and fourth quotations), 5–8, passim. Siringo was directed to attend the Haymarket trial as an observer to watch for jury tampering by the defense.

15. Siringo, *Two Evil Isms,* 2–7; Ginger, *The Age of Excess,* 58–59; Horan, *The Pinkertons,* 256, 358; Hofstadter, *Social Darwinism in American Thought,* 68, 108, 201–202; David, *The History of the Haymarket Affair,* 221–22, 228, 353ff. Eight men were brought to trial for the bombing; all were convicted, and seven men were condemned to death. The sentences of two were commuted to life imprisonment, and a third committed suicide just hours before his scheduled execution. In 1893 Gov. John P. Altgeld pardoned the three remaining anarchists because he believed they had not been legally convicted and because the available evidence unmistakably showed that they were innocent of the crime for which they had been tried. Ibid., 227–28ff., 316, 487–94.

16. Siringo, *Two Evil Isms,* 2 (quotations), 4.

17. Ibid., 5.

18. Philip Taft, *Organized Labor in American History*, 154 (first quotation); Horan, *The Pinkertons*, 338 (second quotation), 329 (third quotation); Irving Bernstein, *Turbulent Years*, 432; Ginger, *The Age of Excess*, 124–25.

19. Siringo, *Two Evil Isms*, 4 (quotation); Horan, *The Pinkertons*, 355; Chamberlain, *The Enterprising Americans*, 165. As the nation received news of the battle at Homestead, there was widespread sympathy for the strikers, while Carnegie, the Pinkertons, and the McKinley Tariff Bill were editorially denounced in newspapers from coast to coast. An investigation by the House Judiciary Subcommittee sustained the legality of the Pinkerton participation at Homestead. Whether there was ample justification for the agency to have been there was another matter. Other strikes that summer, of railroad switchmen at Buffalo, of soft-coal miners in Tennessee, and silver miners in the Coeur D'Alene, helped discredit Harrison's administration. Yet it was the bloody events at Homestead that served to rally the Democrats in November and helped elect Grover Cleveland to the presidency. Ginger, *The Age of Excess*, 125–26; Horan, *The Pinkertons*, 350–58.

20. Siringo, *Two Evil Isms*, 35.

21. Pinkerton detectives pursued the Jesse James gang and the Younger brothers in Missouri and other Middle Border states, and the Renos in Indiana. When master thief Adam Worth stole a Gainsborough painting in 1876, the biggest haul in his thirty-five-year career, Pinkerton's men hounded him for over twenty years until the painting was recovered. The Pinkerton reputation for unrelenting pursuit and apprehension became so formidable that on several occasions thieves, after robbing banks that were agency clients, anonymously returned the loot upon learning they had violated Pinkerton protection. Horan, *The Pinkertons*, x, 160–79, 189–202, 303–16, 329.

22. Siringo, *A Cowboy Detective*, 22–23; Horan, *The Pinkertons*, 515. In brief, anarchists believed and taught that government was the instrument of capitalists to oppress the workers and that government, then, was an enemy to be overthrown. Although Albert Parsons was a native-born American, the presence in Chicago of so many European immigrants espousing the imported ideologies of communism, socialism, and anarchism explains to some extent the prejudices and fears harbored by Siringo and the Pinkertons. Clarence B. Carson, *Organized Against Whom? The Labor Movement in America*, 40; David, *The History of the Haymarket Affair*, 75–76; 142–43, 208–209, 341.

23. Horan, *The Pinkertons*, 515–16. Throughout this introduction I have leaned heavily on James D. Horan's excellent study, *The Pinkertons: The Detective Dynasty That Made History*, for the appraisal and assessment of Allan Pinkerton and his two sons. In defense of the detective agency founder, one of Pinkerton's biographers wrote: "He had come into contact with the more vicious side of the early labor combinations and apparently sincerely believed that Unions were hurting rather than helping the cause of the working man. His was not a mind for analyzing social problems but rather a genius for de-

tail, organization, and practical results." See Oliver W. Holmes, "Allan Pinkerton," *Dictionary of American Biography,* VII, 623.

24. Siringo, *Riata and Spurs,* 124 (quotation); Horan, *The Pinkertons,* x–xi, 49, 493, 515–16.

25. Dobie, introduction to *A Texas Cowboy,* xxxv; Sawey, *Charles A. Siringo,* 96; Kaplan, *Mr. Clemens and Mark Twain,* 197–98; idem, *Mark Twain and His World,* 108 (first three quotations); Siringo, *Two Evil Isms,* 108 (fourth and fifth quotations). Siringo said that one reason he refused advancement, and preferred to remain a detective, was because he could do as he pleased when out of sight of his superiors in office (*Two Evil Isms,* 76). Clemens viewed Victorian civility as a veneer masking widespread corruption in business and in government, coupled with a religious hypocrisy that condoned social customs and traditions that were cruel and unjust. These created horrors, he believed, were the result of adult conceptions of duty, honor, and conscience. Throughout the *Adventures of Huckleberry Finn* Clemens portrays Huck's strong sense of justice and innate humaneness (his sound heart) as being in collision with what he, Huck, perceives are the social and ethical standards of society (his "deformed conscience"). Kaplan, *Mark Twain and His World,* 108; idem, *Mr. Clemens and Mark Twain,* 198; Ginger, *The Age of Excess,* 147.

26. Horan, *The Pinkertons,* xi, 49 (quotation), 515–16.

27. Douglas Branch, *The Cowboy and His Interpreters,* 150 (first quotation); Samuel L. Clemens, *Following the Equator: A Journey Around the World,* 654 (second quotation); Kaplan, *Mark Twain and His World,* 166.

Chapter 1

1. Siringo, *A Cowboy Detective,* 13–16; idem, *Riata and Spurs,* 121–23.

2. Siringo, *Riata and Spurs,* 37 (first quotation), 36 (second quotation); idem, *A Cowboy Detective,* 315; Robert R. Dykstra, *The Cattle Towns,* 112–13. Nyle H. Miller and Joseph W. Snell, *Why the West Was Wild: A Contemporary Look at the Antics of Some Highly Publicized Kansas Cowtown Personalities,* 6–7, contains a description of Dodge City as recorded in the *Dodge City Times* of Sept. 1, 1877. See also Robert M. Wright, *Dodge City: The Cowboy Capital and the Great Southwest in the Days of the Wild Indian, the Buffalo, the Cowboy, Dance Halls and Bad Men,* 142–44, passim. By contrast, a contemporary editorial in the *Kingsley Graphic* referred to Dodge City as "The Beautiful Bibulous Babylon of the Frontier" (quoted in ibid., 144).

3. Robert K. DeArment, *Bat Masterson: The Man and the Legend,* 79–80; Siringo, *A Texas Cowboy,* 148; idem, *A Cowboy Detective,* 315–17; *A Lone Star Cowboy,* 63–64; *Riata and Spurs,* 36 (first two quotations), 37; Siringo to Raymond W. Thorp, Apr. 6, 1926, in Thorp [ed.], "'Old Colt's Forty-five': Letters of Charley [*sic*] Siringo," *Western Sportsman* 5 (July, 1940): 14 (third and fourth quotations); George G. Thompson, "Bat Masterson: The Dodge

City Years," *Fort Hays Kansas State College Studies* No. 1 (1943), 15. Siringo referred to Mason as "a town marshal" (*Riata and Spurs,* 36) whereas, according to Miller and Snell (*Why the West Was Wild,* 276), Mason had been appointed a policeman on May 12, 1877, by Mayor James H. "Dog" Kelly, and Lawrence E. Deger was the city marshal of Dodge.

4. Siringo, *A Cowboy Detective,* 317–18.

5. In 1892 Siringo was introduced to Masterson in superintendent McParland's office in Denver, and it was then that he learned of the intended ambush. Siringo, *A Cowboy Detective,* 317–18. During the summer of 1877 Masterson was undersheriff of Ford County serving under Sheriff Charles E. Bassett. Miller and Snell, *Why the West was Wild,* 323–24.

6. Siringo, *A Cowboy Detective,* 318; idem, *Riata and Spurs,* 37–41; idem, *A Lone Star Cowboy,* 64, 67. Siringo ran into Wess Adams five years later in 1882, in El Paso. Adams told Siringo he belonged to "Curly Bill's outlaw gang" and said that "they were making all kinds of money." Charlie declined Adams's invitation to join the gang and concluded by saying he had not heard of Adams since (*A Lone Star Cowboy,* 67).

7. Walter Prescott Webb, H. Bailey Carroll, and Eldon Stephen Branda, eds., "LX Ranch," in *The Handbook of Texas,* II, 1; Siringo, *Riata and Spurs,* 38–40, 41 (quotation); idem, *A Texas Cowboy,* 149–59; idem, *A Lone Star Cowboy,* 67–72.

8. Siringo, *Riata and Spurs,* 63–64; he gives a much briefer account in *A Texas Cowboy,* 175. The passage of forty-one years, no doubt, enabled the author to write from a different perspective. In his *History of "Billy the Kid": The True Life of the Most Daring Young Outlaw of the Age* (70) Siringo also recalled the name of John Middleton as another of the outlaws in the Kid's group at the LX Ranch during October and November, 1878.

9. Siringo, *History of "Billy the Kid",* 94–95; idem, *A Lone Star Cowboy,* 134; Leon C. Metz, *Pat Garrett: The Story of a Western Lawman,* 71; J. Evetts Haley, "Jim East, Trail Hand and Cowboy," *Panhandle Plains Historical Review* 4 (1931), 49–50. James H. East, interview with J. Evetts Haley, Sept. 27, 1927, on which part of Haley's article was drawn, in the archives, Panhandle Plains Historical Museum, Canyon, Tex. East claimed the party left the LX Ranch on Nov. 16; however, Cal Polk, who at seventeen was the youngest member of the posse, later wrote in a remarkable unpublished manuscript that they left the ranch on Nov. 22. Cal Polk manuscript, p. 51, copy in the archives, Panhandle Plains Historical Museum. See also Siringo, *A Texas Cowboy,* 198ff., and Sawey, *Charles A. Siringo,* 67–71, for a discussion of Frank Stewart's controversial role in Siringo's posse. The brief account here essentially follows that given by Siringo in *Riata and Spurs,* 75–77 (quotations).

10. Siringo, *Riata and Spurs,* 76; idem, *History of "Billy the Kid,"* 95; Haley, "Jim East," 50–51; James H. East interview, 3 (quotations); Siringo, *A Texas Cowboy,* 199 (quoting Bill Moore). Col. Jack Potter, an old-time trail-driver, author, and New Mexico legislator who was often critical of Siringo in

his writings, defended Siringo's decision *not* to accompany Garrett's posse: "I don't think Siringo had any fear, as it was a part of his instruction to go on to Fort Stanton [*sic*], and commence making investigation of cattle being sold and slaughtered [there]." Col. Jack Potter to Orlan Sawey, Oct. 16, 1947, original letter in the author's collection.

11. Siringo, *History of "Billy the Kid"*, 96–108; idem, *A Texas Cowboy*, 215–53; idem, *Riata and Spurs*, 77–92; Haley, "Jim East," 51–61; Metz, *Pat Garrett*, 72ff., 162 (quotation). John Hollicott was selected by the LX Company to replace W. C. Moore as ranch manager (*Riata and Spurs*, 92).

12. Siringo, *A Lone Star Cowboy*, 193–202; idem, *History of "Billy the Kid"*, 108–33; idem, *Riata and Spurs*, 104–10; Metz, *Pat Garrett*, 87–88, 91–117.

13. Siringo, *A Texas Cowboy*, 225–66; idem, *A Lone Star Cowboy*, 167–69, 172ff.; idem, *Riata and Spurs*, 93–94, 96–101. Perhaps Siringo was fascinated with Billy the Kid because he felt his and the Kid's life were similar in many ways. Sawey, supporting this view, compiled a list of striking parallels that are more than coincidental. "Both were orphaned early, both had stepfathers, both had Irish mothers, and both were 'on their own' early in life . . . Siringo was hotheaded as . . . [was] the Kid and as free with his knife. In his years as a detective Siringo many times used as an alias the name 'Lee Roy,' which appeared in an early dime novel as the Kid's name. Later Siringo named his son Lee Roy. Even stranger is the fact that the two men looked alike. Several times Siringo was mistaken for the Kid" (Sawey, *Charles A. Siringo*, 65).

14. Siringo, *A Texas Cowboy*, 285–308; idem, *Riata and Spurs*, 102–104, 110.

15. Douglas Branch, *The Cowboy and His Interpreters*, 112; Siringo, *A Lone Star Cowboy*, 210–12; idem, *Riata and Spurs*, 75 (first quotation), 111–15 (second, third, and fifth quotations); idem, *A Texas Cowboy*, 309–10, 314–15 (fourth quotation).

16. Siringo, *A Texas Cowboy*, 316; idem, *A Lone Star Cowboy*, 211ff., 225; idem, *Riata and Spurs*, 116 (first quotation), 118; advertisement in the *Caldwell Journal*, Feb. 19, 1885, quoted in J. Frank Dobie, "Charlie Siringo, Writer and Man," introduction to *A Texas Cowboy*, xxix (second quotation). Viola's birthdate is given on her death certificate, which is dated July 31, 1960, Los Angeles, in the State Registrar of Vital Statistics, Sacramento, Calif. Siringo never revealed the birthdate of his daughter in any of his autobiographies, and perhaps for a compelling reason. For Viola's birth to have occurred on Feb. 28, conception could not have taken place earlier than late May or early June of the preceding year. Soon after his arrival at the LX Ranch (near the end of March), Siringo, by his own accounts, was sent on an extended roundup from which he did not return to the Panhandle headquarters until July 1. Clearly, he had to have made a side trip to Caldwell, Kansas, probably in late May, that ranch manager John Hollicott was unaware of. See *A Texas Cowboy*, 314–15; *A Lone Star Cowboy*, 213–14; and *Riata and Spurs*, 114.

17. Siringo, *A Cowboy Detective*, 24; idem, *A Lone Star Cowboy*, 225; idem, *Riata and Spurs*, 120–26; Siringo to Kent, Feb. 3, 1927, HMC Records, HLHU. An advertisement in the *Caldwell Journal* on Oct. 8, 1885, announced that "the book [*A Texas Cowboy*] is now in press and will be sold only by subscription. Price $1.00. Address the publishers, M. Umbdenstock & Co., 134 Madison Street, Chicago, Illinois. For an agency, write to the author at Caldwell, Kansas." Those writing in to become agents were supplied with receipt booklets wherein advance sales could be recorded. One such booklet, complete and unused, is in the author's collection. See Dobie, "Charlie Siringo, Writer and Man," xxx (citing quotation from the *Caldwell Journal*).

Chapter 2

1. Siringo, *Two Evil Isms*, 8.

2. Ibid.

3. Ibid., 9 (quotation), 10. In both *A Cowboy Detective* (24) and *Riata and Spurs* (126) Siringo simply says that they were glad when fall came and Pinkerton ordered him to move to Denver.

4. Siringo, *Two Evil Isms*, 10.

5. Ibid., 11 (quotations); idem, *A Cowboy Detective*, 24; idem, *Riata and Spurs*, 127.

6. Siringo, *A Cowboy Detective*, 25–33; idem, *Two Evil Isms*, 11–12; idem, *Riata and Spurs*, 127–28.

7. Siringo, *A Cowboy Detective*, 33–38 (first two quotations), 39ff.; idem, *Two Evil Isms*, 11–18 (remaining quotations); idem, *Riata and Spurs*, 128–34.

8. Siringo, *Two Evil Isms*, 20–21 (quotations); Broehl, *The Molly Maguires*, 354.

9. Siringo, *A Cowboy Detective*, 69–70, 74–76; Horan, *The Pinkertons*, 244–45. Joan Pinkerton was a twin sister to brother Robert and the only daughter of Allan Pinkerton. Joan had married "young Chalmers" over the strenuous objections of her father who was a fanatical believer in phrenology. According to the determinations of this pseudoscience, Chalmers did not have the necessary brain power to amount to anything more than a store clerk, and Pinkerton believed that Chalmers would surely fail his daughter as a husband. Despite these imagined handicaps, William Chalmers went on to become one of the foremost industrialists in the Midwest. Ibid., 244, 322.

10. Siringo, *A Cowboy Detective*, 75–85; idem, *Riata and Spurs*, 136–39.

11. Siringo, *A Cowboy Detective*, 12 (first quotation), 92 (second quotation), 93ff., 114, 116 (third quotation); idem, *Riata and Spurs*, 142ff., 137, 151, 153; idem, *A Lone Star Cowboy*, 213.

Chapter 3

1. The *Daily New Mexican* (Santa Fe), of Friday, Feb. 6, 1891, carried a full account of the shooting and the events that followed; Siringo, *A Cowboy Detective*, 115–17; idem, *Two Evil Isms*, 31–32; idem, *Riata and Spurs*, 153–54; William A. Keleher, *The Fabulous Frontier: Twelve New Mexico Items*, 113–14; Ralph Emerson Twitchell, *Leading Facts of New Mexican History*, II, 509–10, 509 n.428; idem, *Old Santa Fe: The Story of New Mexico's Ancient Capital*, 417–18. See also Walter John Donlon, "LeBaron Bradford Prince, Chief Justice and Governor of New Mexico Territory 1879–1893" (Ph.D. dissertation, University of New Mexico, 1967), 250–57 for an account of this incident.

2. Council Bill 122 of the Territorial Legislature in L. Bradford Prince, "Pinkerton Investigation of the Attempted Assassination of J. A. Ancheta, February–August, 1891" (microfilm; Territorial Archives of New Mexico, State Records Center and Archives, Santa Fe, N.Mex.), reel 121, frames 680–847. (These records will hereafter be cited as Ancheta Shooting Investigation, TANM.) Telegram, Prince to Pinkerton's National Detective Agency, Feb. 7, 1891; W. A. Pinkerton to Prince, Feb. 7, 1891; James McParland to Prince, Feb. 10, 1891; Feb. 7, 1891; James McParland to Prince, Feb. 10, 1891; and Prince to C. T. Leon, Feb. 11, 1891, in ibid.

3. McParland to Prince, Feb. 20 and Mar. 6, 1891; Edward L. Bartlett to Prince, Feb. 24, 1891; and Siringo to Prince, July 7, 1891, in Ancheta Shooting Investigation, TANM; Siringo, *A Cowboy Detective*, 121; idem, *Riata and Spurs*, 154; Keleher, *The Fabulous Frontier*, 113–14; F. Stanley, *Ciudad Santa Fe, Territorial Days, 1846–1912*, 204–205 (quotation); Twitchell, *Leading Facts of New Mexican History*, II, 509–10, 509 n.428. In a "Statement With Regard to New Mexico," sent to President Benjamin Harrison on June 11, Prince stated that the White Caps were a separate, highly organized order within the Knights of Labor who commit depredations "like clock-work" for three months and then "lie low" for the rest of the year. Donlon, "LeBaron Bradford Prince," 254–55.

4. Siringo, *A Cowboy Detective*, 117, 118 (first three quotations), 119–24; Siringo to Prince, Mar. 13, 18, Apr. 4, 10, 30, and July 8, 1891 (fourth quotation); McParland to Prince, Mar. 30 and Apr. 8, 1891, all in Ancheta Shooting Investigation, TANM; Siringo, *Riata and Spurs*, 154–56.

5. John Gray to Prince, Apr. 25, 1891; Siringo to Prince, May 4 and 9, 1891, in Ancheta Shooting Investigation, TANM; Siringo, *A Cowboy Detective*, 124.

6. Siringo, *A Cowboy Detective*, 125–31; McParland to Prince, May 26 and June 1, 1891, in Ancheta Shooting Investigation, TANM; McParland to Bartlett, June 2, 1891, in the Edward L. Bartlett Papers, State Records Center and Archives, Santa Fe, N.Mex. (This archive will hereafter be cited as NMSA.) Contrary to Siringo's belief, it is unlikely that he contracted smallpox when

he helped bury the Mexican woman who had died from the disease. When Charlie arrived in Santa Fe on April 30, he wrote Governor Prince the next day, saying that he was ill with a "high fever." By May 4 he had recovered sufficiently to depart for Lamy Junction, and from there he continued on to Cow Springs, arriving May 9. On Sunday of the following week (May 17) he helped bury the smallpox victim, and by the end of that week (May 23), he became ill. Since smallpox has an incubation period of ten to fourteen days, Siringo was probably exposed to the disease after being debilitated with a form of ague in Santa Fe and just before his arrival in Cow Springs. See Siringo to Prince, May 1 (quotation) and 9, 1891; and McParland to Prince, July 20, 1891, in Ancheta Shooting Investigation, TANM; Siringo, *Riata and Spurs,* 156–57.

7. McParland to Prince, Apr. 18, July 20, 1891 (first two quotations), in Ancheta Shooting Investigation, TANM. Although an examination of the Pinkerton expense sheets shows that Siringo spent freely in currying favor with those whom he suspected, his expenses for hotel room and board were only ten dollars a week, hardly an immodest sum by standards of the time. The agency's bill to Prince for the first seven weeks of investigation, including the eight dollars per day for the operative, came to a total of $723.80. Deducting the $40 for the horse and saddle and Siringo's room and board leaves $221.80 in other expenses. Pinkerton's National Detective Agency to Prince, "Statement of Expenses," Apr. 11, 1891, for the period from Feb. 10 through Apr. 7, in ibid.

8. Prince to McParland, July 25, 1891; McParland to Prince, July 27, 1891; and Siringo to Prince, July 16, 1891, in ibid.; Siringo, *A Cowboy Detective,* 133; Keleher, *The Fabulous Frontier,* 114.

9. "Expenditures, Ancheta Reward & Investigation," TANM, reel 121, frame 844.

10. Keleher, *The Fabulous Frontier,* 112, 114 (quotation); Donlon, "LeBaron Bradford Prince," 256; Twitchell, *Old Santa Fe,* 418–19, 418 n.760; idem, *Leading Facts of New Mexican History,* II, 510 n.428 and 511–13 n.429; Siringo, *A Cowboy Detective,* 117, 132ff.; idem, *Two Evil Isms,* 32–33; idem, *Riata and Spurs,* 153, 156.

11. Siringo to Prince, July 8, 1891, in Ancheta Shooting Investigation, TANM; David H. Stratton, ed., "The Memoirs of Albert B. Fall," *Southwestern Studies* Monograph No. 15 (1966), 49–52; Siringo, *A Cowboy Detective,* 116; idem, *Riata and Spurs,* 153. Immediately after the shooting the *Daily New Mexican* (Santa Fe), Feb. 7, 1891 (quoting the *Albuquerque Citizen*) had speculated that the motives might have been over the fight to pass the public school bill. See Donlon, "LeBaron Bradford Prince," 252.

12. Siringo, *A Cowboy Detective,* 133 (quotations), 135, passim. Siringo's patent was in the name of C. Leon Allison, the alias he was using in 1891 when he filed his land claim. In 1914, following the death of his mother (see idem, *A Lone Star Cowboy,* 37), he filed a deposition to change the registration in

order to consolidate his mother's 140-acre patented homestead under his own name. Charles A. Siringo to the Hill Binding Company, July 18, 1914; Siringo to Alois B. Renehan, Dec. 17, 1914; and Affidavit of Charles A. Siringo, Aug. 31, 1914, Santa Fe, N.Mex., all in the Alois B. Renehan, Charles A. Siringo correspondence (Manuscript Collection, Box 6, M72-5/18), History Library, Museum of New Mexico, Santa Fe, N.Mex. (These records and archives are hereafter cited as the Renehan Papers, LMNM.) Last Will & Testament of Bridgit Siringo, Feb. 2, 1910, Office of the Probate Judge, Santa Fe, N.Mex. The complete *Abstract of Title No. 3858* to Siringo's Sunny Slope Ranch can be found in the Tony Albert Papers, Lischke Estate, NMSA.

Chapter 4

1. Siringo, *A Cowboy Detective*, 135–37; idem, *Riata and Spurs*, 158–59. The Coeur d'Alene violence was part of the widespread labor unrest during the last year of the Harrison administration. For a brief survey of that period and a discussion of Siringo's attitude, see the introduction. A history of the Coeur d'Alene dispute from the viewpoint of the labor movement is given in Richard E. Lingenfelter, *The Hardrock Miners: A History of the Mining Labor Movement in the American West, 1863–1893*, 196–218. See also Robert Wayne Smith, *The Coeur d'Alene Mining War of 1892: A Case Study of an Industrial Dispute*. Some of the accounts by participants, other than Siringo, include John Hays Hammond, *The Autobiography of John Hays Hammond*, I, 188–95; James H. Hawley, ed., *History of Idaho: The Gem of the Mountains*, I, 245–51; and William T. Stoll, *Silver Strike: The True Story of Silver Mining in the Coeur d'Alenes*.

2. Siringo, *A Cowboy Detective*, 136–37; idem, *Riata and Spurs*, 158–59; Lingenfelter, *The Hardrock Miners*, 198.

3. John Hays Hammond, "Strong Men of the Wild West," *Scribner's Magazine* 77 (Feb.–Mar., 1925), 122 (first quotation); Siringo, *A Cowboy Detective*, 136–38, 140 (second quotation); idem, *Riata and Spurs*, 159. In *Two Evil Isms* (37), Siringo said that in order to join the union he had to take a Molly Maguire oath to bleed and die for the order, and that death would be his reward if he ever turned traitor and gave away any union secrets.

4. Lingenfelter, *The Hardrock Miners*, 196–99.

5. Stoll, *Silver Strike*, 179–85; Hammond, "Strong Men of the Wild West," 122.

6. Siringo, *Two Evil Isms*, 38 (first quotation); idem, *A Cowboy Detective*, 138–39, 140 (second quotation); Stoll, *Silver Strike*, 185–88. The distance between Burke and Thompson's Falls, the first habitation, was thirty miles. Heavy winter snow accumulations of from four to twenty feet added to the difficulty and suffering of those forced to make the trek. Idem, *Two Evil Isms*, 38.

7. Siringo, *A Cowboy Detective*, 140–41; idem, *Riata and Spurs*, 159–62.

Except as indicated by the notes, the summary that follows is from Siringo's *A Cowboy Detective*, 138–87; idem, *Two Evil Isms*, 37–42; and idem, *Riata and Spurs*, 159–83.

8. Lingenfelter, *The Hardrock Miners*, 203–204. William Stoll, who was an attorney for the MOA, described Siringo's ability with weapons: "he was deadly with a Colt's 45, a weapon he carried at all times. I have thrown up an empty can and watched him, shooting from his hip, riddle it in flight; yet he had never, so far as anyone knows, taken a human life . . . Siringo's ability with a revolver was, if anything, excelled by his skill with [the bowie knife]. I have seen him, from the saddle, snip the head of a rattler coiled along the trail." Stoll, *Silver Strike*, 183, 199.

9. Griffin had helped blow up two Tuscarora, Nevada, mine owners but had managed to escape capture and prosecution. For an account of Siringo's work on the Prinz and Pelling case, see Siringo, *A Cowboy Detective*, 91–113; and idem, *Riata and Spurs*, 142–51. In *Two Evil Isms* (39) Siringo spelled Griffin's name "Griffith."

10. Siringo, *A Cowboy Detective*, 148 (first quotation), 149 (second quotation).

11. For a brief account of the union riots at the Homestead "works" in Pennsylvania and their consequences, see the introduction.

12. Siringo, *Riata and Spurs*, 165. He quotes a slightly different response in *A Cowboy Detective*, 151.

13. Siringo, *A Cowboy Detective*, 162.

14. Stoll, *Silver Strike*, 225–26, 242ff. Lingenfelter, in *The Hardrock Miners* (199, 206), suggests that Siringo was an agent provocateur, and that the strikers' lawlessness and violence were deliberately instigated in order to justify the MOA's call for federal intervention. His only proof, apparently, rests on his accusation that the miners took up arms because of their discovery that Siringo was a Pinkerton spy, and that his successful evasion of the miners' retribution only added to their frustrations. Although his charge in this instance is absurd, the idea that the violent excesses of the early labor movement were due to agents provocateurs employed by capitalists is commonly expressed by twentieth-century historians. For example: "Management frequently employed Pinkerton agents who did not hesitate to promote violence in order to discredit the labor movement and frame and convict union leaders" (W. E. Hollon, "Pinkerton Detective Agency," in Howard R. Lamar, ed., *The Reader's Encyclopedia of the American West*, 939–40).

15. Lingenfelter, *The Hardrock Miners*, 207–209; Stoll, *Silver Strike*, 227–48; *Spokane Review*, July 12, 1892. Lingenfelter described Dr. Sims (*The Hardrock Miners*, 209) as "a fiery little southerner 'cordially hated by every union man in the country.'" Lingenfelter does not mention that Dr. Sims was later shot to death as he emerged from a theater in Wallace (Siringo, *A Cowboy Detective*, 495).

16. Pettibone and the other union conspirators were sentenced to terms of fifteen months to two years in the federal penitentiary at Detroit. The case was appealed to the Supreme Court, and on Mar. 6, 1893, their convictions were reversed because of a defect in the indictment. Thus the convicted union leaders only served about eight months in prison. Stoll, *Silver Strike,* 247–48; Lingenfelter, *The Hardrock Miners,* 212–15.

17. Modern apologists for the violence associated with the early labor movement admit that many of its leaders preached Marxist ideology, usually referred to as a "doctrine of class warfare" (Horan, *The Pinkertons,* 466). Yet they try to justify it as being a reflexive response to the "brutality" of capitalism (Hofstadter, *Social Darwinism in American Thought,* 201–202), evoking the cliché of property rights opposing human rights. In the Molly Maguire case "the point of view of the property owners was well represented . . . [and the property owners] fought back with new tactics—and won." Broehl, *The Molly Maguires,* 359–60.

18. The Western Federation of Miners (WFM) was a direct outgrowth of the violent confrontations between labor and capital in the Coeur d'Alene in 1892. The next year representatives from local miners' unions throughout the West met in Butte, Mont., long a center for militant unionism, to found the WFM. After its establishment the WFM became a major factor in promoting the ideologies of class warfare and disruptive chaos throughout the mining regions of the West. Although the union's avowed purpose was to improve the lot of the working miner, many of its gains were negated or offset because of the radicalism of its early leaders such as "Big Bill" Haywood, Charles A. Moyer, and George Pettibone. See Richard Maxwell Brown, "The Western Federation of Miners," in Lamar, ed., *Reader's Encyclopedia of the American West,* 1254–55; and Lingenfelter, *The Hardrock Miners,* 219–25ff.

Chapter 5

1. Siringo, *A Cowboy Detective,* 185 (quotations), 189–91.

2. Ibid., 193, 197–230; idem, *A Lone Star Cowboy,* 229; idem, *Riata and Spurs,* 184–96. Lillie Thomas, born in Champian, Mich., was married to Charles Siringo on Nov. 11, 1893 (Carol Siringo McFarland to author, Nov. 10, 1976 [2nd quotation]).

3. Siringo, *A Lone Star Cowboy,* 229. Lee Roy Siringo was born in Denver on Jan. 28, 1896. At his christening his grandfather supplied the name William Lee Roy. However, he was never called William, and he went almost entirely by his middle name, Lee Roy. The name suggestion had to have come from Siringo, as Lee Roy (or sometimes LeRoy) was a favorite name he often used as an alias in his detective work. See idem, *A Cowboy Detective,* 275, 360, passim; also, Sawey, *Charles A. Siringo,* 65.

4. Siringo, *A Lone Star Cowboy,* 230.

5. Siringo, *A Cowboy Detective*, 267, 292ff., 313, 364–65; idem, *Two Evil Isms*, 92; "Evelyn Lischke of Peaceful Siringo Ranch," *Santa Fe Scene*, May 16, 1959, 12–13, in the Tony Albert Papers, Lischke Estate, NMSA. In 1914 Siringo leased his ranch to a Mr. H. M. Martin of Joplin, Mo., who added two rooms to the house. Charles A. Siringo to the Hill Binding Company, July 18, 1914, Renehan Papers, LMNM.

6. Siringo, *A Cowboy Detective*, 248, 249 (first quotation), 251 (second quotation); idem, *Riata and Spurs*, 92, 196–98.

7. Siringo, *A Cowboy Detective*, 250 (first quotation), 251–52, 253 (second quotation); idem, *Riata and Spurs*, 198.

8. Siringo, *A Cowboy Detective*, 253.

9. Ibid., 253–67 (quotations); idem, *Riata and Spurs*, 199–201.

10. Siringo, *A Cowboy Detective*, 305–24; idem, *Riata and Spurs*, 209–18; Sawey, *Charles A. Siringo*, 118–21; James D. Horan, *Desperate Men: Revelations from the Sealed Pinkerton Files*, 203–19, 243–49.

11. Horan, *Desperate Men*, 219. Both Eugene Manlove Rhodes and Raymond Thorp, who knew Siringo personally, said that his eyes were brown.

12. Horan, *Desperate Men*, 220, 249–52; Siringo, *A Cowboy Detective*, 329–80; idem, *Riata and Spurs*, 221–51; Sawey, *Charles A. Siringo*, 118–28. Sawey evaluates the several accounts concerning Cassidy's and Longbaugh's survival or demise (127–28). See also, Garry L. Roberts, "Butch Cassidy," in Lamar, ed., *Reader's Encyclopedia of the American West*, 169.

13. Siringo, *A Cowboy Detective*, 358, 487; idem, *Riata and Spurs*, 244.

14. Siringo, *A Cowboy Detective*, 488–91 (quotations); petition for divorce in *Charles A. Siringo, Plaintiff vs. Grace Siringo, Defendant*, Case No. 6439, Feb. 17, 1909, District Court of the First Judicial District of Territory of New Mexico, County of Santa Fe.

15. Horan, *The Pinkertons*, 454–77, 478 (quotation).

16. Siringo, *A Cowboy Detective*, 510–12; idem, *Riata and Spurs*, 257–61. Pettibone had recruited Orchard and instructed him in the art of making bombs and detonating them. When Idaho Chief Justice Gabbert was marked for execution by the WFM, Orchard planted a bomb in Gabbert's path while Pettibone looked on from a safe distance. By a quirk of fate, a mining engineer unexpectedly appeared instead of Gabbert and was blown to bits as Orchard and Pettibone watched. Siringo, *A Cowboy Detective*, 512; Horan and Swiggett, *The Pinkerton Story*, 300.

17. Horan and Swiggett, *The Pinkerton Story*, 300–306; Broehl, *The Molly Maguires*, 354–357; Horan, *The Pinkertons*, 478 (quotations), 479; Sawey, *Charles A. Siringo*, 112–13; W. E. Borah, *Haywood Trial: Closing Argument of W. E. Borah*, 130 pp. Siringo maintained that the not guilty verdict was the result of threats to jurors made by a fellow juror who was in the em-

ploy of the WFM (Siringo, *Riata and Spurs*, 259–60). Siringo's utter contempt for the WFM leaders and their lawlessness is revealed in his characterization "the Western Federation of Dynamiters" and "that blood-thirsty dynamiting bunch, who some well-meaning people believe are angels" (*A Cowboy Detective*, 493, 515). Broehl, in *The Molly Maguires* (354–57), treats the Steunenberg case as a postscript in the life of James McParland and implies that Orchard's confession was obtained, and perhaps even manufactured, by coercion. Omitting mention of the vast amount of evidence linking Orchard to the murderous schemes of the WFM leaders, Broehl leads his readers to believe that their innocence was affirmed by the jury's verdict. Yet Clarence Darrow, whom no one can accuse of being an unbiased participant, never denied the guilt of his clients but simply asserted that Orchard's testimony was uncorroborated, and that all of the evidence was circumstantial (Clarence Darrow, *The Story of My Life*, 147–56). For a much more balanced account of this sensational trial, see Horan, *The Pinkertons*, 454–79.

18. Siringo, *Riata and Spurs*, 257–61; Horan, *The Pinkertons*, 479; Darrow, *The Story of My Life*, 170. Despite the national notoriety of the labor cases that have been touched upon in this narrative, organized labor in the United States represented only a very small fraction of the total work force. In fact, the labor union movement did not make any significant headway in the nineteenth or the early twentieth centuries. Not until the administration of Franklin Delano Roosevelt in the 1930s and 1940s, when the unions were empowered by government, did the labor unions make any major gains. Perhaps the most compelling reason for unionism's slow growth is that, until fifty or sixty years ago, the main thrust of American society was profoundly individualist. It is no accident that the early labor union activists preached an ideology of class consciousness and promoted a policy of class warfare. Unionism requires a collectivist framework within which to operate, and the class struggle, a doctrine derived from socialism, is the linchpin of union ideology. Although union leaders today are not as publicly strident or anarchistic as their early counterparts, and although most American union members do not subscribe to socialism's revolutionary goals, the class conflict thesis remains an implicit although muted axiom in the labor union vernacular. For further study of the economics and history of labor unions in the United States, see Richard Maxwell Brown, "Labor Movement," in Lamar, ed., *Reader's Encyclopedia of the American West*, 628–30; Bernstein, *Turbulent Years*, 432, 445, 452; Carson, *Organized Against Whom?*, 78–82, 154, 243; Tarbell, *The Nationalization of Business, 1878–1898*, 156, 160–61.

19. Siringo, *A Cowboy Detective*, 516–17; idem, *Riata and Spurs*, 263; petition for divorce in *Charles A. Siringo vs. Grace Siringo*. Siringo had applied for a copyright of his proposed title to the book he intended to write in March, 1907, while still in the employ of the agency. Library of Congress, No. 170665, Registration of Title for Copyright to Charles A. Siringo, March 9, 1907, in the Renehan Papers, LMNM.

Chapter 6

1. Siringo, *A Cowboy Detective*, 516; idem, *A Lone Star Cowboy*, 234; idem, *Riata and Spurs*, 263–67; petition for divorce in *Charles A. Siringo vs. Grace Siringo*, and Final Decree Order, Apr. 15, 1909, District Court of the First Judicial District of Territory of New Mexico, for the County of Santa Fe.

2. Siringo, *A Lone Star Cowboy*, 234, 240; idem, *Riata and Spurs*, 267–68.

3. Yankee Doodle, Croppy, Comanche, Damfido, Satan, and Glen Alpine, Jr., are the names of some of the horses ridden by Siringo through the years. One of the early favorites was Whiskey-Peet (sometimes spelled Whiskey-peat), who carried Siringo through many of the pages in *A Texas Cowboy*. See Sawey, *Charles A. Siringo*, 45, 48, 53ff.; Siringo, *A Texas Cowboy*, 86, 92, 113. In *A Lone Star Cowboy*, 55, 99, 120, passim, he spelled the horse's name Whiskey-Pete.

4. Siringo, *A Texas Cowboy* (1886), [326]–336. For an excellent commentary on Siringo's "Addenda," see Sawey, *Charles A. Siringo*, 79–84.

5. Siringo, *A Cowboy Detective*, 457–59, 464; idem, *A Lone Star Cowboy*, 254–55; idem, *Riata and Spurs*, 254–55.

6. Siringo, *A Cowboy Detective*, 487; idem, *A Lone Star Cowboy*, 253–54; B. B. Dunne, "Charles Siringo, Called Most Famous Cowboy Detective, was Picturesque, Modest Figure," Santa Fe *New Mexican*, Oct. 23, 1928, p. 5. Eat 'em Up Jake died suddenly in 1913, while being patted on the head by Mrs. H. M. Martin. Siringo was gone at the time but upon his return his foreman, George Tweedy, told him he had given the dog a decent burial. Jumbo, one of E.E.U.J.'s pups, remained to take his place.

7. Siringo, *A Cowboy Detective*, 517.

8. "The Rocky Road the Cowboy Detective book had to Travel before Coming from the Press" (statement by Siringo accompanying his letter of Feb. 17, 1926, to Ferris Greenslet), HMC Records, HLHU; Agreement between A. B. Renehan and C. A. Siringo, Nov. 10, 1909; W. B. Conkey Company to A. B. Renehan, Feb. 4, 1910, in the Renehan Papers, LMNM. In 1896 Renehan paid Siringo $150 for stock he proposed to issue in his Sweet Cabin Home Gold Mining & Prospecting Company. This was one of several gold and copper mining claims he had staked out in the Glorieta Canyon. Contract between Siringo and Renehan, Santa Fe, Aug. 10, 1896; Siringo to Renehan, Mar. 27, 1916, in ibid.

9. Governors' Papers: L. Bradford Prince, 1889–93, letter of introduction, A. B. Renehan to L. B. Prince, Aug. 25, 1892, in roll 112, frame 653, TANM; Keleher, *The Fabulous Frontier*, 154; Twitchell, *Leading Facts of New Mexico History*, IV, 96; idem, *Old Santa Fe*, 475–76; Resolution of Tribute to A. B. Renehan by the Santa Fe County Bar Association, May 10, 1928, File No. 13037, District Court Records, Santa Fe, N.Mex. Renehan wrote a book of poetry, *Songs From the Black Mesa* (Santa Fe, 1900), and later authored a

treatise on the Pueblo Indians and their land grants in New Mexico. See Lyle Saunders, *A Guide to Materials Bearing on Cultural Relations in New Mexico,* 229.

10. Ramon F. Adams, *Six-Guns and Saddle Leather: A Bibliography of Books and Pamphlets on Western Outlaws and Gunmen,* 586. A copy of one of the later posters, advertising Siringo's *A Cowboy Detective,* is in the Governors' Papers: L. Bradford Prince, 1889–93, TANM; also in the author's collection.

11. Adams, *Six-Guns,* 586; Siringo to Ira Rich Kent, Feb. 3, 1927, HMC Records, HLHU; Temporary Injunction Decree by Judge Arthur H. Chetlain in *Pinkerton's National Detective Agency vs. Charles A. Siringo and the W. B. Conkey Company,* Chancery No. 277903, Court Records, Superior Court of Cook County, Chicago, Ill., 1910–11 (hereafter cited as Court Records, 1910–11).

12. W. B. Conkey Company to Siringo, Mar. 2, 1910; newspaper clipping: "Pinkerton Ban Put on Book" (Chicago, n.d.), in the Renehan Papers, LMNM.

13. Charles A. Siringo to William A. Pinkerton, Mar. 7, 1910, in Renehan Papers, LMNM. See advertisement for Gregg's Peerless Hotel, corner of Don Gaspar and Water streets, in the Santa Fe *New Mexican,* Mar. 11, 1910, p. 4.

14. Siringo to Pinkerton, Mar. 6 [*sic*], 1910, Renehan Papers, LMNM. Since Siringo's handwritten letter obviously preceded Renehan's typewritten revision, one of the dates shown must be incorrect, although both letters were probably written on the same day.

15. Decree of Richard E. Burke, Judge in the Superior Court of Cook County in Chancery, Dec. 12, 1911, Court Records, 1910–11.

16. "Deposition Is Taken in Pinkerton Case," Santa Fe *New Mexican,* July 17, 1911, p. 1; statement by A. B. Renehan in "Cowboy Detective Declares He Will Fight Extradition," ibid., Apr. 19, 1915, p. 8; Siringo, *Two Evil Isms,* 107–108; Siringo to Kent, Feb. 3, 1927, HMC Records, HLHU; Petition by the Complainants in *Pinkerton's National Detective Agency, a partnership composed of William A. Pinkerton and Allan Pinkerton, Complainants, vs. Charles A. Siringo, Defendant,* Mar. 8, 1915, in Court Records, Chancery No. 277903, Superior Court of Cook County, Chicago, Ill., 1914–15 (hereafter cited as Court Records, 1914–15).

17. Siringo, *A Cowboy Detective,* 19 ("the tiger blood in me began to boil"); idem, *Two Evil Isms,* 107–108; Renehan to John A. Brown, Nov. 24, 1914, "Exhibit F," in Court Records, 1914–15; Renehan to Siringo, Apr. 5, 1916, Renehan Papers, LMNM; Siringo to Greenslet, Feb. 17, 1926, HMC Records, HLHU.

18. Siringo, *Two Evil Isms,* 107–108; Siringo to Greenslet, Feb. 17, 1926, HMC Records, HLHU. Attorney Brown's buckram bound copy of the galley proofs, consisting of 519 single printed pages with his penciled emendations throughout, is in the author's collection. In my copy of *A Cowboy Detective,*

which Siringo inscribed to Erskine Clement, one of the owners of the LX Ranch for whom he had worked thirty years before, he wrote: "The Superior Court of Chicago compelled me to use the names of 'Dickenson' for Pinkerton, 'Tim Corn' for Tom Horn, and 'Jas. McCartney' for Jas. McParland in this volume."

19. Siringo, *A Cowboy Detective*, 5 (quotation from preface); Decree of Judge Richard E. Burke, Dec. 12, 1911, in Court Records, 1910–11. Ramon Adams erroneously states (in *Six-Guns*, 586) that after *A Cowboy Detective* was published, the Pinkertons again found names and references to confidential information which they did not want revealed, and that they obtained another injunction for the book's suppression. Adams probably confused the temporary injunction of Feb. 28, 1910, with the permanent injunction levied by Judge Burke on Dec. 12, 1911.

20. Siringo, *A Cowboy Detective*, 9, 486; Peavy, *Charles A. Siringo, A Texas Picaro*, 14; Adams, *Six-Guns*, 586; pictorial envelope advertising "Pinkerton's Cowboy Detective" in the author's collection.

21. Siringo, *A Cowboy Detective*, 293–94, 487; idem, *Riata and Spurs*, 263; B. B. Dunne, "Charles Siringo, Called Most Famous Cowboy Detective . . . ," 5; Raymond W. Thorp, "Cowboy Charley Siringo," *True West* 12 (Feb., 1965): 32; Harlan P. Euler to author, Nov. 11, 1976, and Jan. 12, 1977. Euler, of Sandia Park, N.Mex., was born on Siringo's ranch in 1902 and lived there until he was twelve years old.

22. Siringo, *A Lone Star Cowboy*, 244–53 (quotations); Siringo to Renehan, Feb. 17, 1913, Renehan Papers, LMNM.

23. Siringo, *A Lone Star Cowboy*, 251–53; petition for divorce in *Charles A. Siringo, Plaintiff vs. Ellen P. Siringo, Defendant*, Case No. 8073, Sept. 15, 1913, in the District Court, Santa Fe, N.Mex. See Ruth Pierce and A. B. Pierce, Jr., *Deming's Bridge Cemetery 1850–1898, Tres Palacios Baptist Church 1852–1898, Hawley Cemetery 1898–1978, Matagorda County, Texas*, 2nd ed., 84, 92; and Siringo, *A Lone Star Cowboy*, 16, for mention of the Partains.

24. Petition for divorce in *Charles A. Siringo vs. Ellen P. Siringo*; Ruth H. Pierce to author, June 24, 1981.

25. "Evelyn Lischke of Peaceful Siringo Ranch," *Santa Fe Scene* (May 16, 1959): 13; response of Mrs. Ellen P. Siringo to petition for divorce in *Charles A. Siringo vs. Ellen P. Siringo*, Case No. 8073, filed Sept. 23, 1913; and Order for Divorce, Final Decree, Case 8073, Oct. 16, 1913, District Court records, Santa Fe, N.Mex. Being a woman of some property and means, Ellen took time to have a new will drawn up during her brief marriage to Charlie. In it she bequeathed $2,000 to Siringo and provided for the distribution of $26,000 to thirteen other beneficiaries. She also stipulated that a fund of $3,000 be established, the proceeds from which were to be used "for the benefit of worthy, wornout Methodist ministers in the state of Texas." Last Will & Testament of Ellen Partain Siringo, Santa Fe, Aug. 14, 1913, in the Renehan Papers, LMNM.

Chapter 7

1. Siringo to Renehan, Feb. 17, 1913; Hill Binding Company to Siringo, June 19, 1914, quoted in Siringo to Hill Binding Company, July 18, 1914; Siringo to Renehan, Dec. 17, 1914; and Promissory Note, Siringo to Alonzo E. Compton for $625 for two years at 10 percent interest per annum, secured by mortgage deed on two parcels of land held by Siringo under patent from the United States government, Santa Fe, N.Mex., Sept. 1, 1914, in the Renehan Papers, LMNM; also, *Abstract of Title No. 3858* for Evelyn Lischke, p. 52, in the Tony Albert Papers, Lischke Estate, NMSA. Nearly two months after negotiating the $625 loan, Siringo mortgaged his mother's 140-acre patented homestead (she had died earlier that year) along with a 300-front-foot lot on Cerrillos Road to Compton for $300 at 12 percent interest per annum, payable in two years. Book P, p. 49, Mortgage Records, Oct. 23, 1914, Records of the County Clerk, Santa Fe, N.Mex.

2. Raymond W. Thorp, "A Tamer of the Old West," *Triple-X Magazine,* Mar., 1926, p. 141. Siringo told an interviewer that he ordered his Frontier model six-shooter, triple silver plated, engraved with pearl grips, at a cost of $36, from Colt's Patent Firearms Manufacturing Company in Hartford, Conn., in 1880. "Detective Who Fought Wild West Desperadoes Now Hollywood Citizen," Los Angeles *Times,* Apr. 12, 1925, pt. II-A, p. 3.

3. Charles A. Siringo, *A Cowboy Detective* (1914), pictorial wrappers; Siringo to Renehan, Dec. 17, 1914, Renehan Papers, LMNM. Siringo retailed the paperback edition of *A Cowboy Detective* for twenty-five cents a copy. Renehan to the Economy Bookshop, June 24, 1916, in ibid.

4. A copy of the typewritten manuscript of *Two Evil Isms* is in the Renehan Papers, LMNM.

5. B. B. Dunne, "Charles Siringo, Called Most Famous Cowboy Detective, Was Picturesque, Modest Figure," Santa Fe *New Mexican,* Oct. 23, 1928, p. 5 (first quotation); Siringo to John A. Brown, July 3, 1915 (second and third quotations), in "Petition of Pinkerton's National Detective Agency," Case 277903, filed July 14, 1915, p. 4, in Court Records, 1914–15.

6. Deposition of J. O. Watkins in *Pinkerton's National Detective Agency, (et al.), Complainants, vs. Charles A. Siringo, Defendant,* pp. 6–8; and Siringo to General Manager, P.D.A., Oct. 17, 1914, p. 7, Court Records, 1914–15; and pictorial front cover to Charles A. Siringo, *Two Evil Isms.*

7. *Two Evil Isms,* passim; Brown to Siringo, Nov. 11, 1914, "Exhibit A"; Brown to Renehan, Nov. 11, 1914, "Exhibit C"; and Brown to W. B. Conkey Company, Nov. 11, 1914, "Exhibit D," all in *Pinkerton's National Detective Agency vs. Charles A. Siringo,* filed Mar. 18, 1915, in Court Records, 1914–15.

8. Renehan to Brown, Nov. 24, 1914, "Exhibit F," in *Pinkerton's National Detective Agency vs. Charles A. Siringo,* Mar. 18, 1915, Court Records, 1914–1915.

9. Siringo to Renehan, Dec. 17, 1914 (quotation), Renehan Papers, LMNM; Siringo, *Riata and Spurs,* 257–61.

10. Siringo to Renehan, Dec. 17, 1914, Renehan Papers, LMNM.

11. Siringo to Renehan, Jan. 22, 1915, in ibid.

12. Renehan to Siringo, Jan. 25, 1915, in ibid.

13. Siringo to Renehan, December 17, 1914, and January 22, 1915, in ibid. Renehan later estimated his outlay on *A Cowboy Detective,* counting the fees he paid Dobyns and the special master, etc., to be in excess of $1,700. Renehan to Siringo, April 5, 1916, ibid.

14. A daughter, Margaret May, was born to Viola and Joseph Reid on May 4, 1907, in New Mexico Territory. In 1916 the Reids moved from Prescott, Ariz., to California, where they later separated (Death Certificate, Margaret May [Reid] Sherbank, Nov. 18, 1972, San Diego, in the State Registrar of Vital Statistics, Sacramento, Calif. Mary Armer Earwood, interview with author, Feb. 10, 1982 [Mrs. Earwood, of Sonora, Texas, was Margaret May's aunt]).

15. Quitclaim Deed, Charles A. Siringo to Mrs. Joseph W. Reid, on 360 acres in the County of Santa Fe, as described in Book P-1, CQD, p. 222, dated Feb. 12, 1915, and notarized in Cook County, Ill., Feb. 15, 1915; Mortgage Deed, Charles A. Siringo to Alonzo E. Compton, on 220 acres of land in Santa Fe County, as described in Book P, Mortgages, p. 41, Sept. 1, 1914; Mortgage Deed, Charles A. Siringo to H. S. Kaunne & Company, on 220 acres in Santa Fe County, as described in Book P, Mortgages, p. 100, Oct. 20, 1914, all in the Deed Records of the County Clerk, Santa Fe County Courthouse, Santa Fe, N.Mex. Both the mortgages of Mrs. Reid and H. S. Kaunne were secondary to the first mortgage given Alonzo Compton. Viola's mortgage on the 140-acre portion of her father's ranch that had been her grandmother's patented homestead was also secondary to the first mortgage of Compton. See also, *Abstract of Title No. 3858* for Evelyn Lischke, pp. 52–53, 55, in the Tony Albert Papers, Lischke Estate, NMSA; Siringo to Renehan, Dec. 17, 1914, and Siringo to Renehan, Dec. 14, 1916, Renehan Papers, LMNM.

16. Deposition of J. O. Watkins, Mar. 18, 1915, pp. 11–13, 15, in Court Records, 1914–15.

17. Deposition of [operative] Edwin Bihn, Mar. 24, 1915 (quotation), in ibid.

18. Deposition of [operative] Maurice Wolff, Mar. 24, 1915, in ibid. Will F. Read was the uncle of Siringo's first wife, Mamie (Siringo, *A Cowboy Detective,* 116, 358), and Charlie was using his name with a different spelling as an alias. As Will F. Reed [*sic*] of Kingman, Ariz., Siringo had deposited two boxes on Feb. 19 with the storage company. These boxes, along with several packages he had deposited on Mar. 1 and Mar. 12, contained a large number of copies of *Two Evil Isms* and the plates used for its printing. "Answer of the Garfield Park Storage Company," Mar. 30, 1915, in Court Records, 1914–15.

19. *Petition of Pinkerton's National Detective Agency . . . Complainants, vs. Charles A. Siringo, Defendant,* No. 277903, Mar. 25, 1915; and Order of Judge Charles M. Foell, Mar. 30, 1915, in Court Records, 1914–15.

20. "Cowboy Detective Declares He Will Fight Extradition," Santa Fe *New Mexican,* Apr. 19, 1915, p. 8.

21. Affidavit of John A. Brown in *Petition of Pinkerton's National Detective Agency vs. Charles A. Siringo,* filed July 14, 1915, Court Records, 1914–15.

22. "Siringo Arrested on Libel Charge, Report," Santa Fe *New Mexican,* Apr. 17, 1915, p. 1; "Pinkertons' Game to Grab Man Is Blocked" (Chicago, n.d.), newspaper clipping accompanying Siringo's letter of May 20, 1915, to William E. Hawks, original letter and clipping in the author's collection; "Cowboy Detective Declares," p. 8; "Before the Governor of the State of New Mexico" (arguments presented by Renehan and Wright, attorneys for Charles A. Siringo in opposition to an extradition request by the governor of the state of Illinois), n.d., in the Renehan Papers, LMNM.

23. "Governor Hearing Argument in Effort to Secure Siringo," Santa Fe *New Mexican,* Apr. 21, 1915, p. 5; "Governor Refuses Extradition for Charles A. Siringo, Requisition Faulty," Santa Fe *New Mexican,* Apr. 22, 1915, p. 4; "Before the Governor of . . . New Mexico," Renehan Papers, LMNM; Dunne, "Charles Siringo, Called Most Famous Cowboy Detective," p. 5 (first quotation); "Cowboy Detective Declares," p. 8 (second quotation); Siringo, *A Lone Star Cowboy,* 274; idem, *Riata and Spurs,* 80.

24. Dunne, "Charles Siringo, Called Most Famous Cowboy Detective," p. 5 (quotations); Attorney General Frank W. Clancy to Gov. W. C. McDonald, Apr. 22, 1915, in the Governors' Papers: William C. McDonald, 1912–16, Letters Received, NMSA. That same day, McDonald wrote to Illinois governor Edward F. Dunne conveying his reason for denying the extradition request. Dunne replied promptly with the acknowledgment that McDonald had acted properly in following the advice of his attorney general. "This is my practice," he added, "and it should be the practice of every Governor of every state in the Union." McDonald to E. F. Dunne, Apr. 22, 1915, Letters Sent; and Dunne to McDonald, Apr. 26, 1915, Letters Received, in ibid. Years later, Pinkerton attorney John Brown would claim that it was Siringo's friendship with the New Mexico governor that was solely responsible for the extradition refusal. Although the friendship between Siringo and McDonald may have been a factor, the faulty nature of the extradition request, not to mention the absence of any indictment, suggests that the request was prompted by W. A. Pinkerton's influence among high Illinois state officials. Renehan correctly perceived that the libel charge was simply a ruse to get Siringo back to Chicago where he could be tried for violating the injunction. See John A. Brown to Houghton Mifflin Company, May 27, 1927, in HMC Records, HLHU.

25. Siringo to William E. Hawks, May 20, 1915, author's collection. William E. Hawks, an alumnus of Yale Business College in the 1880s, ranched on

the Snake River in Idaho in the 1890s. He took permanent residence in Bennington, Vt., around 1900, where he built a collection of western memorabilia and contributed newspaper and magazine articles in the spirit of "correcting" the romantic misrepresentations about the history of the West. Siringo, *A Lone Star Cowboy*, 289.

26. Deposition of [operative] Maurice Wolff, Mar. 24, 1915, Court Records, 1914–15; Siringo to Hill Binding Company, July 18, 1914; Siringo to Renehan, Dec. 14, 1916, Renehan Papers, LMNM.

27. Siringo to Brown, July 3, 1915, p. 4, in Court Records, 1914–15. Siringo's remark, concerning "that big bluff you worked on me," referred to the Pinkerton's contrived attempt to extradite him to Chicago on libel charges.

28. Ibid.

29. Order of Judge Charles M. Foell, July 16, 1915, in ibid. *Two Evil Isms* is the rarest of all of Siringo's books, with the possible exception of the first edition of *A Texas Cowboy* in paper wrappers. Of the eleven hundred copies that were printed, most were handed to the Pinkertons by court order, thereby assuring their destruction. Only those copies that Siringo had sold to Chicago bookstores and newsstand dealers, plus the copies he carried with him to Santa Fe, got into circulation; and the Pinkertons bought up many of former. When the Steck-Vaughn Company reprinted the book in 1967, the Library of Congress copyright copy was used as a model.

30. Siringo to Renehan, Dec. 14, 1916, Renehan Papers, LMNM. For an account of Fred Harvey, the entrepreneur who fed travelers and crews on the Santa Fe Railroad and whose food and hotel service was state of the art, see L. L. Waters's excellent study, *Steel Trails to Santa Fe*, 261–85.

Chapter 8

1. Siringo, *A Lone Star Cowboy*, 273–74; idem, *Riata and Spurs*, 271–72; B. B. Dunne, "Charles Siringo, Called Most Famous Cowboy Detective, Was Picturesque Modest Figure," Santa Fe *New Mexican*, Oct. 23, 1928, 5.

2. Siringo, *A Lone Star Cowboy*, 273–74; idem, *Riata and Spurs*, 271–72. See also, Ben E. Pingenot, "Charlie Siringo: New Mexico's Lone Star Cowboy," *Cattleman* 63 (Nov., 1976): 56–57, 122–28, for an account of Siringo's experiences as a ranger with the Cattle Sanitary Board of New Mexico.

3. Siringo, *A Lone Star Cowboy*, 276.

4. Ibid., 276–77.

5. Ibid., 278–79. See also, Siringo to Renehan, Aug. 16, 1916, Renehan Papers, LMNM. Clarence Siringo Adams tells of a similar hazardous experience Siringo had at Encinoso involving a justice of the peace who was allied with the cattle thieves, and a mob that was bent on hanging him. In Adams's story, Siringo escapes the mob and makes his way to Carrizozo and later returns with several deputies to make his arrest. Although Adams's account contains

some parallel elements, it still differs from Siringo's in *A Lone Star Cowboy*. See Clarence Siringo Adams, "Fair Trial at Encinoso," *True West* 13 (Mar.–Apr., 1966): 32–33, 50–51; and idem, *For Old Times' Sake*, 19–20.

6. Siringo, *A Lone Star Cowboy*, 280–81 (quotations); Eve Ball, "Charlie Siringo and 'Eat Em Up Jake,'" *True West* 16 (May–June, 1969): 46–47.

7. Ball, "Charlie Siringo and 'Eat Em Up Jake,'" 36.

8. Ibid., 46; Siringo, *A Lone Star Cowboy*, 281–82, 284–87. See also George Washington Coe, *Frontier Fighter: The Autobiography of George W. Coe, Who Fought and Rode with Billy the Kid*.

9. Siringo to Joseph B. Hayward, Oct. 2, 13, and 14, 1916; Hayward to Siringo, Oct. 4 and 18, 1916, in the Jennie M. Avery Papers, NMSA; Siringo, *A Lone Star Cowboy*, 288.

10. Hayward to Siringo, Oct. 10 and Dec. 4, 1916; and Siringo to Hayward, Oct. 13 and 20, 1916, both in Jennie M. Avery Papers, NMSA.

11. Hayward to Siringo, Sept. 15 and Nov. 21, 1916, ibid.; Promissory Note: Charles A. Siringo to Alonzo E. Compton, Sept. 1, 1914, in the amount of $625 at 10 percent per annum, in the Renehan Papers, LMNM; Petition of Alonzo E. Compton to intervene in District Court case No. 8477, *Tom Williams, Plaintiff vs. Charles A. Siringo* [and] *Mrs. Joseph W. Reid, Defendants*, filed Nov. 20, 1919, pp. 6ff., in Records of the District Clerk, Santa Fe, N.Mex. See also, *Abstract of Title No. 3858* for Evelyn Lischke, 59–72, in the Tony Albert Papers, Lischke Estate, NMSA.

12. Siringo to Renehan, Mar. 27 and Dec. 14, 1916 (quotation); Renehan to Siringo, Apr. 5, 1916, Renehan Papers, LMNM. When a Chicago book dealer made an inquiry concerning *A Cowboy Detective*, Renehan replied that there were approximately one thousand copies of the clothbound edition on hand, which if the dealer would take the entire lot he would sell at fifty cents each. Renehan to The Economy Book Shop, June 24, 1916, in ibid.

13. Siringo's original title was "Reminiscences of A Lone Star Cowboy," which he had hoped Rand McNally & Company would publish. Siringo to William E. Hawks, May 20, 1915, original letter in the author's collection. Siringo, *A Lone Star Cowboy*, [1], [v]; Charles A. Siringo, *The Song Companion of a Lone Star Cowboy: Old Favorite Cow-Camp Songs*. See Peavy, *Charles A. Siringo, A Texas Picaro*, 10–11; and J. Frank Dobie, "Charlie Siringo, Writer and Man," in Siringo, *A Texas Cowboy* (1950), xiv–xv, for a comparative study of Siringo's writing style.

14. Siringo to Greenslet, Feb. 17, 1926, HMC Records, HLHU; Siringo to O. W. Nolen, June 30, 1922, in O. W. Nolen, "Charley Siringo, Old-Time Cowboy, Rancher, Detective and Author," *Cattleman*, 38 (Dec., 1951): 54.

15. Peavy, *Charles A. Siringo, A Texas Picaro*, 35. See also chap. 11, this volume.

16. Siringo, *A Cowboy Detective*, 273–74; idem, *Riata and Spurs*, 202–203; Raymond W. Thorp, "'Old Colt's Forty-Five,' Letters of Charley Si-

ringo," *Western Sportsman* 5 (Aug., 1940): 32. Dobie, in his introduction to the 1950 reprint of *A Texas Cowboy*, said that Siringo had an inclination to write about women but suppressed it. Dobie was mistaken, of course, even though probably correct in assuming that whatever Charlie might have had to say on the subject would not have been news. Dobie, "Charlie Siringo, Writer and Man," x.

17. Harlan P. Euler to author, Jan. 12, 1977. Euler was born on Siringo's ranch in 1902 and lived there until he was twelve years old. He later married the daughter of Matias Nagel, who also was a friend of Siringo's (Euler to the author, Nov. 11, 1976); Ball, "Charley Siringo and 'Eat Em Up Jake,'" 47; Clarence Siringo Adams, "Charley Siringo—The Cowboy Detective," *New Mexico Magazine,* Oct., 1967, p. 18; Clarence Siringo Adams to the author, Apr. 26, 1981. Adams says that Siringo, who was not related, visited his father, John "Shorty" Adams, on Aug. 8, 1920, at their homestead near Corona while doing historical research. Clarence Adams was one day old and to celebrate the occasion of Siringo's visit, his father added "Siringo" as his middle name. Ibid.; Adams to the author, May 23, 1981.

18. Pingenot, "Charlie Siringo: New Mexico's Lone Star Cowboy," 126; Dobie, "Charlie Siringo, Writer and Man," x; Siringo, *History of "Billy the Kid."*

19. Renehan to The Economy Book Shop, June 24, 1916; Siringo to Renehan, Oct. 21, 1923; and Renehan to Siringo, Nov. 5, 1923, in the Renehan Papers, LMNM. The New Mexican Publishing Company wholesaled much of its stock of *A Lone Star Cowboy* to Siringo's friend, the curio dealer J. F. Collins. See Siringo to Renehan, Apr. 19, 1923, in ibid.

Chapter 9

1. *Abstract of Title No. 3858* for Evelyn H. Lischke, 59–72, Albert Papers: Lischke Estate, NMSA; District Court Case No. 8477, *Tom Williams, Plaintiff vs. C. A. Siringo* [and] *Mrs. Joseph W. Reid, Defendants, Alonzo E. Compton, Intervenor,* Final Decree, Sept. 5, 1922, in Book S, p. 446, District Court records, Santa Fe, N.Mex.; Harlan P. Euler to the author, Jan. 12, 1977.

2. Henry F. Hoyt to Charles A. Siringo, June 9, 1921, Hoyt-Siringo Correspondence, Panhandle Plains Historical Museum, Canyon, Tex.: Charles A. Siringo, "John Chisum, Cattle King; Billy the Kid, Outlaw, Characters who made Lincoln County Celebrated; Charley Siringo tells Anecdotes of the Early Days," Santa Fe *New Mexican,* Sept. 7, 1921, p. 3. Henry F. Hoyt (1854–1930) was born in Minnesota, studied medicine in Saint Paul and in Chicago, and came to West Texas in 1877. He worked as a cowboy for the LX Ranch and was said to be the first physician to practice medicine at Tascosa. He later attended Columbus (Ohio) Medical College before becoming head of the Saint Paul Department of Health. From 1893 to 1898 he served as chief surgeon of Northern Railway Lines, the Chicago, Burlington and Northern Railway, and

the Eastern Minnesota Railway. During the Spanish-American War he served in the Philippines as a major and chief surgeon, United States Volunteers. Following the war he practiced medicine in El Paso until he moved to Long Beach in 1910. His book, *A Frontier Doctor,* detailed his youthful adventures on the West Texas Plains. Doyce B. Nunis, Jr., "Historical Introduction" to *A Frontier Doctor* (1979), xxi–xlix; Webb, Carroll, and Branda, eds., *The Handbook of Texas,* I, 856.

3. Hoyt to Siringo, June 17, 1921, original letter in the author's collection; Clarence Siringo Adams, "Charley Siringo—The Cowboy Detective," *New Mexico Magazine,* Oct., 1967, p. 36; Jon Tuska, *The Filming of the West,* 103–15; William H. Goetzmann and William N. Goetzmann, *The West of the Imagination,* 300.

4. William K. Everson and George N. Fenin, *The Western: From Silents to Cinerama,* 9ff.

5. Ibid., 47, 75ff.; Tuska, *The Filming of the West,* 30–32; Kevin Brownlow, *The War, the West, and the Wilderness,* 264–68; Goetzmann and Goetzmann, *The West of the Imagination,* 298–303.

6. Hoyt to Siringo, June 17, 1921; William S. Hart to Siringo, Sept. 21, 1920, reproduced on the back of a business card of Chas. A. Siringo, in the author's collection.

7. It was a year later, on June 30, 1922, that Siringo wrote O. W. Nolen he had just finished his novel entitled "Prairie Flower, or Bronco Chiquita." Nolen, "Charley Siringo, Old-Time Cowboy Rancher, Detective and Author," *Cattleman* 38 (Dec., 1951): 54.

8. Raymond W. Thorp to Orlan Sawey, Sept. 10, 1949, original letter in the author's collection; Siringo to Kent, Sept. 10, 1926, HMC Records, HLHU; Raymond W. Thorp, "Cowboy Charley Siringo," *True West* 12 (Jan.–Feb., 1965): 62; Siringo, *Riata and Spurs,* photo facing p. 274 shows Siringo on Sailor Gray fording the Rio Grande at Cochiti Pueblo. Postcard photograph of this same scene, addressed to O. W. Nolen: "Mounted on my favorite saddle horse, 'Sailor Gray,' crossing the Rio Grande river [*sic*] at the Cochiti Indian Pueblo in November, 1921." Siringo to O. W. Nolen, June 30, 1922, original postcard in the author's collection.

9. Thorp to Sawey, Sept. 10, 1949; Thorp, "Cowboy Charley Siringo," 62; Siringo, *Riata and Spurs,* 273.

10. Siringo's interests were still being represented by Renehan, and the attorney employed every legal device to delay the inevitable in the hope that through some stroke of fortune Siringo could pay off his indebtedness. Eventually the Sunny Slope Ranch was sold by a special master at an auction held in Santa Fe on Mar. 31, 1924. The successful bidder was Alonzo E. Compton with a bid of $1,465. Certificate of Sale, Apr. 14, 1924, in Book S Miscellaneous, p. 590, District Court records, Santa Fe, N.Mex. See also, *Abstract of*

Title No. 3858 for Evelyn H. Lischke, 64–81, Tony Albert Papers, Lischke Estate, NMSA.

11. Siringo to Joseph Haywood, Oct. 13, 1916, Jennie M. Avery Papers, NMSA; Siringo to Renehan, Sept. 12, 1923, Renehan Papers, LMNM.

12. Renehan to Fletcher Dobyns, Nov. 18, 1922; Leland C. Welts to Renehan, Nov. 27, 1922, Renehan Papers, LMNM.

13. Harlan P. Euler to the author, Jan. 12, 1977; Siringo, *Riata and Spurs,* 273.

14. Siringo, *Riata and Spurs,* 273–74. James H. (Jim) East (1853–1930) was born in Missouri and came to Texas about 1869, where he rode cattle for John Files Tom, Richard King, and Mifflin Kenedy. In 1880 he was employed on the LX Ranch, during which time he rode with Siringo in pursuit of Billy the Kid. In 1882 he was elected the second sheriff of Oldham County, and it was during his four years in office that he made his reputation as a lawman. In 1903 East moved to Douglas, Ariz., where he variously served as city marshal, chief of police, and police judge. Ibid., 75ff.; Webb, Carroll and Branda, eds., *The Handbook of Texas,* I, 533.

15. Siringo, *Riata and Spurs,* 273–74; Siringo to Renehan, Mar. 23 and Apr. 19, 1923, Renehan Papers, LMNM. In 1921 Siringo made a deal with the J. S. Ogilvie Company to use his electrotype plates and cuts to produce a paperback edition of *A Cowboy Detective* to sell for fifty cents a copy. Ogilvie persuaded Siringo to allow the company to issue the book in two volumes, being numbers 127 and 128 in the Railroad Series. Later, Charlie realized this was a mistake because people would buy the first volume, which carried the reader through page 246, but then fail to buy the second book entitled *Further Adventures of A Cowboy Detective.* Siringo to Greenslet, Feb. 17, 1926, HMC Records, HLHU.

16. Siringo to Renehan, Oct. 21 and Dec. 26, 1923, Renehan Papers, LMNM.

17. Siringo to William E. Hawks, Oct. 10, 1928 (first quotation), original letter owned by Michael Heaston, Rare Books & Manuscripts, Austin, Tex.; Siringo, *Riata and Spurs,* 274–75 (second quotation); Siringo to Renehan, May 20 and June 11, 1924 (third quotation), Renehan Papers, LMNM.

18. Brownlow, *The War, the West, and the Wilderness,* 290; Siringo, *Riata and Spurs,* 275 (quotation).

19. Siringo to Renehan, June 11, 1924 (quotation), Renehan Papers, LMNM. Henry Herbert Knibbs (1874–1945) was born in Clifton, Ont. Some of his works were *Songs of the Outlands* (1914), *Sundown Slim* (1915), *Riders of the Stars* (1916), *Saddle Songs* (1922), and *The Tonto Kid* (1936). His stories of western life were praised for their sense of character and dry humor. Of his poetry, William Rose Benét wrote: "Mr. Knibbs writes in an old western tradition, but he writes flashingly better than most celebrators of the cowboy." *Webster's Biographical Dictionary,* 1971 ed., 828; Stanley J. Kunitz and Vineta Colby, eds., *Twentieth Century Authors, First Supplement, A Biographical*

Dictionary of Modern Literature, 1955 ed., 528 (quotation). Two letters in the Huntington Library from Knibbs to Charles Fletcher Lummis highlight not only his friendship with that southwestern writer but his familiarity with Santa Fe and New Mexico as well. Harry Knibbs to C. F. Lummis, Sept. 12, 1922, and Mar. 6, 1923, in Knibbs-Lummis Correspondence, Huntington Library, San Marino, Calif. According to another letter that Knibbs wrote to Sara [Hughes] Cornell, he spent the winter of 1916 in Santa Fe. In ibid.)

20. W. H. Hutchinson, *A Bar Cross Man: The Life and Personal Writings of Eugene Manlove Rhodes,* 145–46.

21. Siringo to Renehan, Sept. 12, 1923; Renehan to Siringo, Oct. 11, 1923, in the Renehan Papers, LMNM; Warranty Deed, Charles A. Siringo to A. B. Renehan, Oct. 11, 1923, No. 27478 of record date Oct. 20, 1923, in Deed Records of the County Clerk, Santa Fe, N.Mex.

22. Siringo to Renehan, Oct. 21 and Nov. 5, 1923; and Renehan to Siringo, Nov. 5, 1923, Renehan Papers, LMNM. This might explain the origin of those copies of *A Lone Star Cowboy* that turn up, from time to time, in a red pictorial dust wrapper. All such jackets contain advertising for Siringo's *History of "Billy the Kid"* (which was published the year after *A Lone Star Cowboy*), and "Leonard's Hollywood Book Store, 6812–14 Hollywood Blvd., Hollywood, Calif." After acquiring the remaining copies of *A Lone Star Cowboy* and *History of "Billy the Kid"*, Cole probably wholesaled the books to Leonard's bookstore as a means of marketing them. Leonard then had the dust jackets made, not only to enhance the book's physical appearance but to serve as an advertisement for his bookshop.

23. Siringo to Renehan, Jan. 10, May 20, June 11, and July 3, 1924 (quotation), Renehan Papers, LMNM.

24. Fall had persuaded President Warren G. Harding to transfer government lands containing oil reserves from the Navy Department to the Department of the Interior. Once these lands were under his department's administration, he leased the Teapot Dome Naval Oil Reserve in Wyoming to petroleum magnate Harry F. Sinclair, and a similar oil reserve at Elk Hills, Calif., to Edward L. Doheny. A national scandal erupted when a Senate investigating committee revealed that Fall had lied about the source of $100,000 cash he had received from Doheny. Because of the protests of conservationists and others, Fall had already resigned as secretary of the interior. Later, he was tried and convicted of accepting a bribe from Doheny and was sent to prison. By some twist of justice, Doheny was tried and acquitted of the same charge that he had given a bribe to Fall. For an excellent account of these turbulent events, see Burl Noggle, *Teapot Dome: Oil and Politics in the 1920's,* 69, 74, 183, 210–11, passim. Fall's early life, as well as arguments in his defense, are treated in David H. Stratton, ed., "The Memoirs of Albert B. Fall," *Southwestern Studies,* Monograph 15, 3–11ff.

25. Siringo to Renehan, Nov. 10, 1924, Renehan Papers, LMNM.

26. Ibid.; Kenneth W. Leish, ed., *The American Heritage Pictorial History of the Presidents of the United States*, II, 747–63. For an insight to Siringo's political orientation, see Siringo, *A Cowboy Detective*, 481–82 (his opinion of union abuses), 503 (his naive attitude toward socialism), and 518 (his comments on "greedy capitalists and blood-thirsty labor union agitators"). Siringo to Renehan, Nov. 10, 1924 (quotation), Renehan Papers, LMNM. Nearly a year later Siringo wrote to an Austin, Tex., friend that his "Bad Man Cowboys of the Early West" manuscript was in the hands of a New York publisher. "If they don't get it out," he wrote, "[I] will do so myself this winter." Siringo to Frank Caldwell, Aug. 3, 1925, original letter in the author's collection.

27. "Detective Who Fought Wild West Desperados Now Hollywood Citizen," Los Angeles *Times*, Apr. 24, 1925, pt. II-A, p. 3; Siringo to Renehan, Apr. 24, 1925, Renehan Papers, LMNM; Brownlow, *The War, The West, and the Wilderness*, 270–71; Everson and Fenin, *The Western*, 91, 99–100; Tuska, *The Filming of the West*, 117.

28. Hart, *My Life East and West*, 3–11, 12 (quotation); Everson and Fenin, *The Western*, 75ff. 104; Brownlow, *The War, The West, and the Wilderness*, 264–65, 270–71; Tuska, *The Filming of the West*, 32, 118 (quotation), 122.

29. Thorp to Sawey, Sept. 10, 1949; Raymond W. Thorp, "'Old Colt's Forty-Five,': Letters of Charley Siringo," *Western Sportsman* 5 (July, 1940): 14; idem, "Cowboy Charley Siringo," 60 (quotation). Thorp, writing from memory, incorrectly stated in "Cowboy Charley Siringo" that this first meeting between Hart and Siringo occurred in the spring of 1924.

30. Siringo to Renehan, Apr. 24, 1925, Renehan Papers, LMNM.

31. Ibid.; Siringo to Renehan, Oct. 3, 1925, in ibid.; Thorp, "Cowboy Charley Siringo," 60; Siringo, *Riata and Spurs*, 274 (quotations).

32. Siringo to Renehan, Apr. 24, 1925 (quotations), Renehan Papers, LMNM; Stony Nagel, "When Siringo Was Marked for Death," *True West* 18 (Nov.–Dec., 1970): 31, 68–69; Siringo, *A Lone Star Cowboy*, 30–31; idem, *Riata and Spurs*, 18.

33. Siringo to Renehan, Apr. 24, 1925; and Renehan to Siringo, May 14, 1925, Renehan Papers, LMNM.

34. Ibid.

35. Siringo to Renehan, June 22, 1925 (first quotation), and Oct. 3, 1925 (second quotation), in ibid.; Brownlow, *The War, the West, and the Wilderness*, 269–71; Tuska, *The Filming of the West*, 118.

36. Siringo to Renehan, June 22, 1925, and Oct. 3, 1925, Renehan Papers, LMNM; Tuska, *The Filming of the West*, 32, 118–22; Brownlow, *The War, the West, and the Wilderness*, 271 (first and third quotations); Goetzmann and Goetzmann, *The West of the Imagination*, 309 (second quotation).

37. Hart, *My Life East and West*, 341–46; Everson and Fenin, *The Western*, 100, 101–102; Brownlow, *The War, the West, and the Wilderness*, 273–74; Tuska, *The Filming of the West*, 122. The original judgment won by Hart was for $190,480. When the case was finally settled in 1950, four years after the actor's death, the studio was ordered to pay $278,209, which included interest, to Hart's estate. Ibid.

38. Brownlow, *The War, the West, and the Wilderness*, 273–74; Everson and Fenin, *The Western*, 103–104. In 1939 *Tumbleweeds* was reissued with an eight-minute prologue by Hart (his only speaking role in motion pictures), which was filmed at Hart's Horseshoe Ranch at Newhall. William Everson said "it is unquestionably one of the most moving reels of film ever made . . . [that] of a man delivering his own obituary." Appearing in his old familiar western costume, Hart outlines the story of the opening of the Cherokee Strip, and then in a rich voice racked with emotion tells what film making had meant to him. Removing his hat, he closes by describing his vision of a phantom herd of trailing cattle, led by a pinto pony with an empty saddle. There are tears in his eyes and his voice falters, leaving no doubt he is describing his beloved horse Fritz. He hears that "much loved whinney" beckoning him to leave the drag and come ride point. "Can't you see," he hears Fritz implore, "my saddle is empty. The boys up ahead are calling. . . . They are waiting for you and me . . . to help drive this last great roundup into eternity. Adios, amigos. God bless you all, each and every one." The same speech rendered by another might have seemed maudlin, but from Hart every word is so thoroughly sincere that one has to be moved by its emotional impact. Bill Hart died seven years later on June 23, 1946 (Everson and Fenin, *The Western*, 103–104. William S. Hart's "Farewell to the Screen," from *Tumbleweeds* [1925], Blackhawk Films, Davenport, Iowa).

Chapter 10

1. Charles A. Siringo to Ferris Greenslet, Feb. 17, 1926, HMC Records, HLHU. Ferris Greenslet (1875–1959) was born in Glens Falls, N.Y. He was a Phi Beta Kappa graduate of Wesleyan University in 1897, and received the Ph.D. from Columbia in 1900. He became a literary advisor to Houghton Mifflin Company in 1907 after serving as an associate editor of the *Atlantic Monthly*. Three years later he was made a director of the Executive Committee and remained at that post until 1918, when he was named editor in chief. In 1933 he became general manager of the Trade Department and served until his retirement in 1947. He still continued as a director and was the senior member of the board. Greenslet was the author of several books, including his autobiography *Under the Bridge*, which was published in 1943. Houghton Mifflin Company records cited in Stella Easland, Assistant Editor, Trade Division, to author, Sept. 27, 1982; Ferris Greenslet, *Under the Bridge: An Autobiography*, 16; Hutchinson, *A Bar Cross Man*, 153n.

2. Greenslet to Siringo, Feb. 26, 1926 (quotation); Siringo to Greenslet, Feb. 17, 1926, HMC Records, HLHU. See John Hays Hammond, "Strong Men of the Wild West," *Scribner's Magazine* 77 (Feb. and Mar., 1925): 121–25. At the end of his article Hammond wrote "Siringo, brave man, is in his grave" (125). Charlie immediately wrote the publisher, commending Hammond's article, and calling their attention to the fact he was still alive. Siringo to Editor, *Scribner's Magazine*, Feb. 10, 1925; Scribner's to John Hays Hammond, Feb. 19, 1925; Scribner's to Siringo, Feb. 19, 1925, in Will James–Charles Siringo Correspondence, Charles Scribner's Sons Archives, Princeton University Library, Princeton, N.J.

3. Memorandum, Ira Rich Kent to Ferris Greenslet, Mar. 2, 1926, HMC Records, HLHU. Ira Rich Kent (1876–1945) was born in Calais, Vt., and was a graduate of Tufts College, class of 1899. He served as a member of the staff and editor of *Youth's Companion* from 1900 to 1925, when he became an editor of Houghton Mifflin Company. Kent served as managing editor and later became secretary of the board of directors. Kent's dominant presence at Houghton Mifflin was such that for several years following his death in 1945 his guiding influence was still being felt. His wife, Louise Andrews Kent, was a noted author of children's books. Houghton Mifflin records cited in Stella Easland to the author, Sept. 27, 1982; Hutchinson, *A Bar Cross Man*, 243; Austin Olney, General Manager, Trade Division, Houghton Mifflin Company, interview with author, Aug. 9, 1982.

4. Memorandum, Kent to Greenslet, Mar. 2, 1926; Greenslet to Siringo, Mar. 17, 1926; memorandum, Kent to Greenslet, July 1, 1926; Kent to Siringo, July 8, 1926, HMC Records, HLHU. In his memorandum of Mar. 2, Kent told Greenslet that the "Siringo stuff" was a pretty highly spiced meal for Houghton Mifflin to swallow. He thought that the shooting, robbing, hanging, and "all that sort of thing" was almost sickening or would be to many readers. He ended by saying he would oppose publication unless they could be allowed to do a certain amount of editing and elimination.

5. Greenslet to Siringo, Mar. 17, 1926, in ibid.

6. Memorandum, Kent to Greenslet, Mar. 2, 1926, in ibid.

7. Siringo to Renehan, Mar. 31, 1926; and Renehan to Siringo, Apr. 3, 1926, in Renehan Papers, LMNM.

8. Siringo to Greenslet, Apr. 14, 1926, HMC Records, HLHU.

9. Siringo to Houghton Mifflin Co., Apr. 26, 1926, in ibid.

10. Siringo to Renehan, May 7, 1926, Renehan Papers, LMNM; Lola Shelton, *Charles Marion Russell: Cowboy, Artist, Friend*, 208–15, 218–19. Two months later Russell was operated on at Mayo brothers' hospital in Rochester, Minn., and was told that he was terminally ill. He returned to his home at Great Falls, Mont., where he died three months later. Harold McCracken, *The Charles M. Russell Book: The Life and Work of the Cowboy Artist*, 230.

11. Memorandum, W. Whitman III to Greenslet, Apr. 28, 1926; and Siringo to Kent, July 29, 1926, HMC Records, HLHU.

12. Kent to Greenslet, May 4, 1926, in ibid.

13. Alois Renehan to William S. Hart, June 27, 1926; Siringo to Renehan, July 2, 1926, Renehan Papers, LMNM; Hart, *My Life East and West,* 349–50.

14. Siringo to Renehan, July 26, 1926, Renehan Papers, LMNM.

15. Siringo to Kent, July 29 and Aug. 31, 1926; Kent to Siringo, Aug. 25, 1926, HMC Records, HLHU.

16. Gifford Pinchot to Siringo, July 29, 1926, in ibid.; Siringo, *A Cowboy Detective,* 513; idem, *Riata and Spurs,* 258–62.

17. Siringo to Renehan, Sept. 14, 1926, Renehan Papers, LMNM; Siringo to Kent, Nov. 27, 1926, HMC Records, HLHU; Carol Siringo McFarland, interview with author, Oct. 13, 1976.

18. Pinchot to Siringo, Sept. 16, 1926; Memorandum, Kent to Greenslet, Sept. 27, 1926., HMC Records, HLHU.

19. Siringo to Kent, Sept. 22, 1926; Kent to Siringo, Sept. 29, 1926, in ibid.

20. Kent to Siringo, Nov. 18, 1926, in ibid.

21. Siringo to Kent, Nov. 27, 1926; Kent to Siringo, Dec. 23, 1926 (first quotation); Siringo to Kent, Dec. 30, 1926 (second quotation); Siringo to Kent, Jan. 5, 1927 (third quotation), in ibid.

22. Siringo to Kent, Dec. 29, 1926, and Jan. 5, 1927; Kent to Siringo, Jan. 17, 1927, in ibid. Alice Wines Apple (1875–1941), one of four girls in a family of five children, was the daughter of Charlie's sister, Catherine (Mrs. George Wines of Saint Louis, Missouri). Divorced from her husband, Charles H. Apple, Alice supported herself as a stenographer for the U.S. government. Siringo, *A Lone Star Cowboy,* 3; Death Certificate, Alice Apple, Apr. 3, 1941, Los Angeles, in the State Registrar of Vital Statistics, Sacramento, Calif.

23. Memorandum, Kent to Greenslet, Jan. 8, 1927, HMC Records, HLHU.

24. Kent to Siringo, Jan. 27, 1927, in ibid.

25. Siringo to Kent, Feb. 3, 1927, in ibid.; Siringo to William S. Hart, Feb. 14, 1927, in the Los Angeles County Museum of Natural History. (These letters between Hart and Siringo will hereafter be referred to as Hart Letters, CMNH.) A group photograph taken in Altadena on Jan. 30, 1927, including Siringo and ten others, was presented to Jack Cole by Orie Oliver Robertson. The original photograph is in the possession of Carol Siringo McFarland. Carol McFarland to author, Nov. 10, 1976. See Don Russell, *The Wild West or, A History of the Wild West Shows,* 11, 32–33ff., 114, 130 for mention of "Tex" Cooper and an account of Pawnee Bill's career; see also Glenn Shirley, *Pawnee Bill: A Biography of Major Gordon W. Lillie.*

26. Siringo to Kent, Feb. 3, 1927, HMC Records, HLHU. See, Siringo, *Riata and Spurs,* 22, wherein the story of Henry Brown and Ben Wheeler is related.

In Siringo, *A Cowboy Detective*, 14, Wiley Payne is spelled "Pain." For an account of the Medicine Lodge incident, see Miller and Snell, *Why the West Was Wild*, 76–80; and Leola Howard Blanchard, *Conquest of Southwest Kansas*, 223–27.

27. Miller and Snell, *Why the West Was Wild*, 514–15.

28. Siringo to Greenslet, Feb. 3, 1927; Greenslet to Siringo, Feb. 9, 1927, HMC Records, HLHU.

29. Roger L. Scaife to Siringo, Feb. 15, 1927; Siringo to Kent, Feb. 21, 1927 and Feb. 26, 1927 (quotation); Kent to Siringo, Mar. 3, 1927, in ibid.; Siringo to Hart, May 22, 1927, Hart Letters, CMNH; Stella Easland, Asst. Ed., Houghton Mifflin Co. to the author, Sept. 27, 1982. Harrison Leussler traveled Houghton Mifflin Company's entire western territory and was an avid devotee of everything pertaining to the Old West. His fervor and zeal resulted in the publication of some distinguished works of Western Americana by Houghton Mifflin. Hutchinson, *A Bar Cross Man*, 238n.

30. Siringo to Kent, Mar. 5, 1927, HMC Records, HLHU. This would be the third and final book dedicated to Alois Renehan by Siringo, the others being *A Cowboy Detective*, in which Renehan had a substantial investment, and *A Lone Star Cowboy*.

31. Greenslet to Siringo, Mar. 16, 1927, HMC Records, HLHU; Siringo to Bill Hart, Feb. 14, 1927, Hart Letters, CMNH. Siringo's face, seen in a photo clipped from an Los Angeles newspaper of Mar. 26, 1927 (in the Renehan Papers, LMNM), reveals the ravages of the disease that was afflicting him.

32. Siringo to Renehan, Mar. 26, 1927; text of telegram to Siringo cited in "Old Friends of Siringo Join Felicitations to Old Timer," clipping from a Los Angeles newspaper, Mar. 24, 1927, in the Renehan Papers, LMNM; Estelle Lawton Lindsey, "Chat with Ex-Cowboy, Hailed as Great Literary Find, Recalls Wild West Days," "Los Angeles *Evening Express*, Apr. 11, 1927, sec. 3, pp. 1, 4; Hutchinson, *A Bar Cross Man*, 228ff.

33. "Stirring Days when Six-shooters Ruled West Recalled," Los Angeles *Times*, Mar. 26, 1927, pt. II, p. 9, photo caption showing Siringo and other guests seated at the head table. See Hart, *My Life East and West*, 350, and Russell, *The Wild West*, 95, 132, for mention of Chief Standing Bear. Houghton Mifflin later published Chief Standing Bear's book entitled *My People the Sioux*.

34. Lindsey, "Chat with Ex-Cowboy," 4.

35. Siringo to Renehan, Mar. 26, 1927, Renehan Papers, LMNM; Siringo to Kent, Apr. 1, 1927, HMC Records, HLHU; Siringo to Hart, Apr. 7, 1927, Hart Letters, CMNH.

36. Will Rogers to Siringo, Mar. 27, 1927, HMC Records, HLHU; Siringo to Renehan, Apr. 14, 1927, Renehan Papers, LMNM.

37. Siringo to Hart, Apr. 7, 1927, Hart Letters, CMNH; Siringo to Kent, Apr. 1, 1927; Siringo to Kent, Western Union night letter, Apr. 3, 1927; and

Ira Kent, hand written memorandum scribbled on Siringo's telegram, Apr. 4, 1927, HMC Records, HLHU.

38. Siringo to Kent, Apr. 12, 1927, in HMC Records, HLHU; Siringo to Renehan, Apr. 14, 1927, Renehan Papers, LMNM.

39. Siringo to Kent, Apr. 21, 1927, HMC Records, HLHU.

Chapter 11

1. Kent to Siringo, Apr. 21, 1927, HMC Records, HLHU.

2. [Roger L. Scaife] to Siringo, Apr. 27, 1927; Siringo to Scaife, May 16, 1927, in ibid.; Owen P. White, "Six Shooters, Cinch Rings, Longhorns and Saloons," *New York Times Book Review,* May 9, 1927, p. 6.

3. William Rose Benét, "Quick on the Draw," *Saturday Review of Literature* 4 (Aug. 27, 1927): 69–70; Walter Prescott Webb, "Charlie Siringo Tells the Story of Thrilling Life on the Frontier," *Dallas Morning News,* May 8, 1927, sec. 3, p. 3. See also Jim Tully, review in the *New York World,* June 5, 1927, p. 7.

4. B. W. Smith, Jr., review in the *New York Post Literary Review,* May 9, 1927, p. 3.

5. J. Frank Dobie, "Old Charlie," *Nation* 125 (July 13, 1927): 4. For an appraisal of *Riata and Spurs* along with a critical analysis of its attendant book reviews, see Sawey, *Charles A. Siringo,* 131–40.

6. [Roger L. Scaife] to Siringo, Apr. 27, 1927, HMC Records, HLHU.

7. Siringo to Kent, May 1, 1927, in ibid.

8. Ibid.

9. Siringo to Scaife, May 16, 1927, in ibid.

10. Kent to Siringo, May 7, 1927, in ibid.

11. Siringo to Kent, Apr. 27, 1927, in ibid. This was not the only time Siringo graphically symbolized the handshake. When Charlie visited El Alisal, the home of Charles Fletcher Lummis, he signed the house book "To my friend, Mr. Charles Fletcher Lummis, Here's my [followed by a sketch of a hand] shake! Charles A. Siringo" (Keith Lummis to the author, Aug. 7 and 30, 1982).

12. Siringo to Kent, Apr. 27, 1927; Dr. Henry F. Hoyt to Kent, May 24, 1927, HMC Records, HLHU.

13. Renehan to Siringo, May 2, 1927, Renehan Papers, LMNM. Siringo did give Renehan an inscribed copy of *Riata and Spurs,* for on July 11 he wrote Charlie to thank him for it. In ibid.

14. Siringo to William S. Hart, May 22, 1927; Hart to Siringo, May 25, 1927, Hart Letters, CMNH.

15. John A. Brown to Houghton Mifflin Co., Chicago, May 27, 1927, HMC Records, HLHU.

16. Greenslet to J. D. Phillips, May 31, 1927, Postal Telegraph night letter, in ibid.

17. Phillips to Greenslet, May 31, 1927, Western Union telegram, in ibid.

18. Brown to B. H. Ticknor, office manager, Houghton Mifflin Co., Boston, June 21, 1927, telegram, in ibid. An investigation in the Pinkerton archives in New York concerning the agency's action against Houghton Mifflin in 1927 also revealed a paucity of information. A copy of the original edition of *Riata and Spurs* with red pencil marks on the pages to be deleted in the revised edition and a copy of the 1911 injunction decree were the only items in their files. (George F. O'Neill, Assistant Vice President and Director of Personnel, Pinkerton's, Inc. to author, Sept. 1, 1982).

19. Ira Kent to Asher Rossetter, June 20, 1927, HMC Records, HLHU.

20. Brown to Ticknor, June 23, 1927, telegram; Siringo, "The Rocky Road the Cowboy Detective book had to Travel before Coming from the Press," Feb. 17, 1926; Rossetter to Ticknor, June 27, 1927, in ibid.

21. Earl Alonzo Brininstool (1870–1957) was born in Warsaw, N.Y. He came to Los Angeles in 1895 and worked variously for the Los Angeles *Times,* Los Angeles *Record,* and Los Angeles *Examiner.* He wrote more than five thousand poems, mostly about cowboy and ranch life, and he became noted as one of the authorities on the Battle of the Little Big Horn, Mont., June 25, 26, 1876. "The Personal Library of E. A. Brininstool," *Western Americana: Catalogue 438,* Dawson's Book Shop, June, 1976.

22. Siringo to Bill Hart, May 30, 1927, Hart Letters, CMNH; Siringo, *Riata and Spurs,* 253. Brininstool's inscribed copy of *Riata and Spurs,* now in the author's collection, contains a photo tipped in of Miss Ramey, Siringo, and Smith on the roof of the Alexandria Hotel, with Brininstool's notes, dated June 16, 1927.

23. Memoranda, Frank Bruce to Kent, July 12 and July 13, 1927 (quotations), HMC Records, HLHU.

24. Kent to Siringo, July 13, 1927, in ibid.

25. Kent to Siringo, July 15, 1927, in ibid.

26. Siringo to Kent, July 19, 1927, in ibid.; Siringo to Renehan, July 20, 1927 (quotations), Renehan Papers, LMNM. Will Rogers (1879–1935), humorist, entertainer, actor, and writer, was born near Oologah, Cherokee Nation, Indian Territory (present-day Oklahoma). Rogers worked as a cowhand in Texas in 1898 and later traveled to Argentina to work as a gaucho. In 1903 he began working with Wild West shows, during which he perfected his riding and trick-roping act. With his wit and southwestern drawl, he turned to vaudeville, where he soon became a star attraction. By 1916 he was a headliner with the Ziegfeld Follies, and later he began to combine stage appearances with motion picture acting. During the 1920s Rogers's popularity with the nation, and the world, created a demand for newspaper and magazine articles, lecture tours, radio broadcasts, books, and more movies. In all, he starred in over fif-

teen movies and wrote seven books and over a thousand newspaper and magazine articles. Rogers's unique talent, which made him so immensely popular,
was his ability to utilize his homespun wit and perspective in his commentary
on everyday affairs. Guy Logsdon, "Will Rogers," in Lamar, ed., *Reader's Encyclopedia of the American West*, 1032.

27. Siringo to Kent, July 19, 1927, HMC Records, HLHU. When Fletcher
Dobyns's office advised Renehan in 1922 that the old indictment against Siringo had been "disposed of," Charlie may have thought that this included the
injunction as well. However questionable Siringo's belief that his old antagonists had rolled over, his presentation had convinced the editors at Houghton Mifflin, who had gone ahead and published an unexpurgated account of
his detective experiences. See Welts (for Dent, Dobyns & Freeman) to A. B.
Renehan, Nov. 27, 1922, in the Renehan Papers, LMNM.

28. Siringo to Renehan, July 20, 1927; Renehan to Siringo, July 29, 1927,
Renehan Papers, LMNM.

29. Houghton Mifflin to Siringo, July 21, 1927, telegram; Siringo to Kent,
July 22, 1927, Postal Telegraph night letter, HMC Records, HLHU.

30. Kent to Rossetter, July 21, 1927, in ibid.

31. Rossetter to B. H. Ticknor, July 22, 1927, in ibid.

32. Siringo to Kent, July 20, 1927, and Greenslet to Siringo, July 26, 1927,
in ibid. Siringo had resigned himself to what was inevitable, as evidenced by a
letter he wrote to an Austin, Tex., friend just a month before the release of the
revised edition of *Riata and Spurs*. After relating the actions of the Pinkertons
that were forcing the revision, he said the publisher thought the "new *Riata
and Spurs*" would be an even better book than the old one. "Hope so" was his
unenthusiastic comment. Siringo to Frank Caldwell, Sept. 14, 1927, original
letter in the author's collection.

Chapter 12

1. Siringo to Hart, May 22, 1927, Hart Letters, CMNH; Siringo to Kent,
July 1, telegram, and July 4, 1927, HMC Records, HLHU.

2. Siringo to Greenslet, Aug. 2, 1927; Siringo to Houghton Mifflin, Aug. 7,
1927, HMC Records, HLHU; Siringo to Hart, Aug. 9, 1927, Hart Letters, CMNH.

3. Kent to Siringo, Sept. 7, and Oct. 10, 1927, HMC Records, HLHU.

4. Siringo to Kent, Oct. 17, 1927, in ibid.

5. Ibid. This was a modification of his earlier title, "Prairie Flower, or
Bronco Chiquita."

6. Ibid.

7. Greenslet to Siringo, Oct. 22, 1927, in ibid.

8. Kent to Siringo, Oct. 22, 1927, in ibid.

9. Siringo to Kent, Aug. 31, 1927, in ibid.; Siringo to Hart, Nov. 31, 1927, Hart Letters, CMNH.

10. Siringo to Renehan, Nov. 21, 1927; Renehan to Siringo, Nov. 25, 1927, Renehan Papers, LMNM. When William S. Hart read Burns's *Saga of Billy the Kid,* he noticed striking similarities between it and Siringo's *History of "Billy the Kid",* which preceded it by several years. Even Siringo's misspelling of a Spanish surname was repeated in Burns's book. When Hart called Charlie's attention to these duplications, Siringo wrote Alois Renehan to seek his advice. Renehan, in turn, wrote Burns's publisher, Doubleday, Page & Company, a three-page letter detailing the conspicuous similarities between the two books. The publisher's reply was a clever combination of double-talk and dissimulation. In reality, both Siringo and Burns had borrowed extensively from Ash Upson, who had supposedly ghost written Pat Garrett's *The Authentic Life of Billy, the Kid.* Both accounts follow the Garrett book very closely, and in fact Siringo even admitted as much in a letter of June 19, 1926, to Renehan. Siringo to Renehan, May 6 and June 19, 1926; Renehan to Doubleday, Page & Co., June 15, 1926; Renehan to Hart, June 27, 1926, in the Renehan Papers, LMNM; Patrick Floyd Garrett, *The Authentic Life of Billy, the Kid, the Noted Desperado of the Southwest.* See also, Adams, *Six-Guns and Saddle Leather,* 244–45. In his reply to Siringo, Renehan said he had advised Doubleday, Page & Company "to save [yourselves from] the necessity for a suit by making an adjustment [now]." The publisher chose to ignore Renehan's advice and that ended the matter. Renehan to Siringo, Nov. 25, 1927, Renehan Papers, LMNM.

11. Siringo to Renehan, Nov. 10, 1927, Renehan Papers, LMNM; Keith Lummis to the author, Aug. 7, 1982. Siringo signed Lummis's El Alisal house book on Nov. 13, 1927, according to a photocopy provided by Lummis's son, Keith. Frank B. Putnam (1895–1962) lived just a few blocks from the home of Charles F. Lummis and at that time was assistant cashier of the Farmers & Merchants National Bank of Los Angeles. Later, he served as historian for the Security Pacific Bank. Throughout his life, Putnam was active in the Historical Society of Southern California. Doyce B. Nunis, Jr., to the author, Jan. 13, 1981; F. B. Putnam to Siringo, June 1, 1927, HMC Records, HLHU.

12. Siringo to Houghton Mifflin Company, Oct. 28, 1927; Kent to Siringo, Oct. 31, 1927; *Chicago Daily News* to Siringo, Oct. 31, 1927; Dale Warren to Siringo, Nov. 4, 1927, all in HMC Records, HLHU.

13. Siringo to Warren, Dec. 9, 1927, ibid.; Siringo to Hart, Nov. 31, 1927, Hart Letters, CMNH. A number of these postcards are in the Renehan Papers, LMNM, indicating that Charlie had also sent a quantity to the Santa Fe attorney to distribute.

14. Greenslet to Siringo, Dec. 21, 1927; Siringo to Greenslet, Dec. 29, 1927, HMC Records, HLHU.

15. Siringo to Houghton Mifflin Company, Dec. 24, 1927; Siringo to

Greenslet, Dec. 29, 1927; Greenslet to Siringo, Jan. 6, 1928; Siringo to Greenslet, Jan. 10, 1928 (quotations), all in ibid.

16. Siringo to Greenslet, Feb. 26, 1928 (quotation), and Mar. 2, 1928, in ibid.

17. J. Marvin Hunter to Siringo, Mar. 11, 1928 (quotations); Siringo to Greenslet, Mar. 2 and 15, 1928, all in ibid.

18. Kent to Siringo, Mar. 31, 1928, in ibid.

19. H. A. McComas to Siringo, Mar. 5, 1928; Siringo to Greenslet, Mar. 10, 1928, in ibid.; Siringo to William E. Hawks, Apr. 17, 1928, Michael D. Heaston, Rare Books & Manuscripts, Austin, Tex. Early in his dealings with Houghton Mifflin, Siringo had written them that he was writing a new book entitled "Flashes from a Cowboy's Pen." He said it would be made up of "short fact stories, never before in print," and that he was using flashes instead of chapters. The titles for his first nine "flashes" were "Heaven and Hell," "Thunder and Lightning," "Hydrophobia Skunks," "Good and Bad Snakes," "Ghosts and Superstitions," "Alligators and Dog Meat," "Panthers and Wildcats," "Treed by a Wild Boar," and "A Twelve Year Old Cowboy wears his burial Clothes and Makes Play Boats out of his Coffin." Siringo to Kent, Sept. 21, 1926, HMC Records, HLHU.

20. Siringo to Hart, June 11, 1928, Hart Letters, CMNH; Siringo to William E. Hawks, Oct. 10, 1928, Michael Heaston, Rare Books & Manuscripts, Austin, Tex.

21. Siringo to Will Rogers, July 12, 1928, HMC Records, HLHU; Siringo to Hart, July 4, 1928 (quotation), Hart Letters, CMNH.

22. Ibid.; greeting card, copyright 1928, by Siringo, in the author's collection.

23. Siringo to E. A. Brininstool, July 6, 1928, original letter in the author's collection; Siringo to Will Rogers, July 12, 1928; Siringo to Houghton Mifflin Company, July 16, 1928, and Houghton Mifflin to Siringo, July 20, 1928, in HMC Records, HLHU; Siringo to Hart, July 4, 1928, Hart Letters, CMNH. In his letter to Bill Hart, Siringo enclosed a copy of "Prairie Fires" and asked the actor, if he thought favorably of his essay, to write him a letter giving his opinion, which he could then use to influence Houghton Mifflin. "Of course," he added, "if you don't think 'Prairie Fires' is O.K. don't write me the letter. Just return the typed copy." Hart did write Siringo a letter praising "Prairie Fires." Hart to Siringo, [July, 1928], Hart Letters, CMNH.

24. Siringo to Greenslet and Scaife, July 26, 1928, HMC Records, HLHU; Carol Siringo McFarland, interview with author, Oct. 14, 1976; Mary Armer Earwood, interview with author, Feb. 10, 1982.

25. "A. B. Renehan Dies in Dayton, Ohio," Santa Fe *New Mexican,* Apr. 21, 1928, p. 1; Siringo to Stella Canny, undated letter, and Canny to Siringo, July 17, 1928, Renehan Papers, LMNM; Last Will & Testament of Charles A. Siringo,

July 24, 1928, Superior Court Records, Los Angeles County, Los Angeles, Calif. In his will Siringo provided that his four nieces and one nephew each receive the sum of five dollars. He directed that his personal debts to George T. Cole, to William J. Ramey, and to his daughter Miss Evelyn Ramey (Bronco Chiquita) be paid. He further directed that his Lodge, No. 2, Knights of Pythias in Santa Fe, be notified of his death; also, the Woodmen of the World with headquarters in Denver, in which order his life was insured for $3,000. The rest of his estate he divided evenly between his daughter, Mrs. Viola Reid, and his son, Lee Roy Siringo. Finally, he appointed his friends, actor William S. Hart, writer Henry Herbert Knibbs, and banker Frank B. Putnam to serve as executors without bond.

26. Siringo to Ferris Greenslet and Roger Scaife, July 26, 1928; Greenslet to Siringo, Aug. 3, 1928, HMC Records, HLHU.

27. Siringo to Hawks, Oct. 10, 1928, Michael Heaston, Rare Books & Manuscripts, Austin, Tex.; Death Certificate of Charles A. Siringo, Oct. 18, 1928, California Registrar of Vital Statistics, Sacramento, Calif. Since Siringo's death occurred late on the evening of the eighteenth, the news of it did not reach the Los Angeles papers until the next day. Although the date of his death was generally reported correctly, the wire services somehow picked it up and reported it as having occurred on the nineteenth. Thereafter, virtually all accounts of Siringo's death incorrectly report it as October 19. (For example, see J. Frank Dobie, "Charlie Siringo, Writer and Man," introduction to *A Texas Cowboy* [1950], ix; Raymond W. Thorp, "Cowboy Charley Siringo," *True West* 12 [Jan.–Feb. 1965]: 62; Roy E. Appleman, *Charlie Siringo, Cowboy Detective*, 2; J. Evetts Haley, "Charles A. Siringo," *Dictionary of American Biography*, IX, 191; and "Charlie Siringo, Cowboy Chronicler," *The Shamrock* [Spring, 1962]: 15; Chester Newton Hess, "Sagebrush Sleuth, The Saga of Charlie Siringo," *Cattleman* 41 [Jan., 1955]: 82; and "Cowboy Author, Known Here, Dies," *Hollywood Citizen News*, Oct. 20, 1928, vol. 24, no. 173, p. 2, all give Oct. 19, 1928, as the date of Siringo's death.) Reporting his death date correctly were the Los Angeles *Evening Express* and the Los Angeles *Times*. The Los Angeles *Examiner* simply carried a death notice in the classified advertisements. "Chas. Siringo, Cowboy and Author, Dead," Los Angeles *Evening Express*, Oct. 19, 1928, vol. 58, no. 178, p. 3; "Last Rites for Plainsman Set," Los Angeles *Times*, Oct. 21, 1928, vol. 47, pt. II, p. 5.

28. Roger L. Scaife to Lee Roy Siringo, Oct. 19, 1928, HMC Records, HLHU.

29. Siringo's remains were taken to the mortuary of W. A. Brown at 1815 South Flower Street, where services were conducted at 2:00 P.M. Monday, before interment in Inglewood Cemetery. Death Certificate of Charles A. Siringo, Oct. 18, 1928, State Registrar of Vital Statistics, Sacramento, Calif.; notation of E. A. Brininstool that he was a pallbearer, along with a sympathy acknowledgment from Lee Roy Siringo and Viola Reid, in his copy of *Riata and Spurs*, now in the author's collection; "Last Rites for Plainsman Set," Los Angeles *Times*, Oct. 21, 1928; Carol Siringo McFarland to the author, Dec. 14, 1976;

Will Rogers and Bill Hart to Lee Roy Siringo, Oct. 20, 1928, Western Union telegram, in the author's collection. Although Rogers shared equally with Hart in the telegram to Lee Roy Siringo, its brief but aureate composition is vintage William S. Hart.

Chapter 13

1. Showing on *Riata and Spurs,* undated; and Greenslet to Siringo, Oct. 22, 1927, HMC Records, HLHU; Charles A. Siringo, *Riata and Spurs: The Story of a Lifetime Spent in the Saddle as Cowboy and Ranger.* Bibliographers, such as Ramon Adams, have contributed to the myth by writing that "only a few copies of the original printing survived, hence its scarcity." Adams, *Six-Guns,* 587.

2. Decree of Richard E. Burk, Dec. 12, 1911, Court Records, 1910–11; Siringo, *A Cowboy Detective,* 9, 486.

3. Horan, *The Pinkertons,* 457ff.; John Hays Hammond, "Strong Men of the Wild West," *Scribner's Magazine* 77 (Feb.–Mar., 1925): 121–25; Stoll, *Silver Strike,* 183–248. See also Sawey, *Charles A. Siringo,* 88.

4. Siringo to Greenslet, Feb. 17, 1926, HMC Records, HLHU.

5. *A Cowboy Detective,* 22–23. Siringo's reaction and attitudes to situations arising from nineteenth-century ethics are discussed in my introduction, this volume.

6. Siringo, *Two Evil Isms,* 7.

7. Ibid., 6–7; idem, *A Cowboy Detective,* 22.

8. John A. Brown to Houghton Mifflin Company, May 27, 1927; Siringo to Greenslet, Feb. 17, 1926, HMC Records, HLHU; Peavy, introduction to *Two Evil Isms,* iii.

9. Siringo, *A Lone Star Cowboy,* 226–27, 234.

10. William A. Pinkerton remained as head of the agency following the death of his brother, Robert, in 1907, with his nephew, Allan Pinkerton, associated as his partner. In the winter of 1923, at the age of seventy-seven, he was still active and preparing a national tour of agency branch offices. In December he arrived in Los Angeles, where he was to preside over a series of conferences, but on the eleventh he suffered a heart attack and died in his hotel room. Horan, *The Pinkertons,* 493, 501–502.

11. Horan, *The Pinkertons,* 502–503; Greenslet to Phillips, May 31, 1927, telegram (quotation); Brown to Houghton Mifflin Co., May 27, 1927, in HMC Records, HLHU. Ferris Greenslet, in all probability, had been unaware of Charlie's having written *Two Evil Isms,* much less having ever read it.

12. Kent to Rossetter, June 30, 1927, HMC Records, HLHU. See, e.g., Greenslet to Siringo, Oct. 22, 1927, in which he referred to "a legal flaw in the title to the property represented by the first edition of *Riata and Spurs,*" in ibid.

13. Kent to Siringo, Oct. 10, 1927; Greenslet to Siringo, July 26, 1927, in ibid. The die had been cast by July 15 when Kent wrote Siringo that they wanted to get out the revised book just as quickly as possible "without wasting time asking for explanations now." Kent to Siringo, July 15, 1927, in ibid.

14. Rowan, *The Pinkertons*, 326, 336; Horan and Swiggett, *The Pinkerton Story*, 343; James D. Horan, *Desperate Men*, 219–20, 249–52; idem, *The Pinkertons*, 364, 457–58.

15. Horan, *The Pinkertons*, 326; idem, *Desperate Men*, 249ff.; Rossetter to Ticknor, June 27, 1927, HMC Records, HLHU; Siringo, *Two Evil Isms*, 83, 87; W. A. Pinkerton to James McParland, Dec. 22, 1899, quoted in ibid., 105 (first two quotations); Hammond, "Strong Men of the Wild West," 121 (third quotation).

16. Eugene Manlove Rhodes to Ferris Greenslet, Apr. 1, 1927, in Hutchinson, *A Bar Cross Man*, 247; O. W. Nolen, "Charley Siringo, Old-Time Cowboy Rancher, Detective and Author," *Cattleman* 38 (Dec., 1951): 56 (first quotation); Ben E. Pingenot, "Charlie Siringo: New Mexico's Lone Star Cowboy," *Cattleman* 63 (Nov., 1976); 124; Siringo, *A Lone Star Cowboy*, 274 (second quotation); J. Frank Dobie, "Charlie Siringo, Writer and Man," introduction to *A Texas Cowboy* (1950), xviii–xix; see "Pawnee Bill" incident, chapter 10, this volume.

17. J. Frank Dobie, "Old Charlie," *Nation* 125 (July 13, 1927): 4 (first quotation); Siringo, *Riata and Spurs*, 263 (second quotation). Siringo's explanation for refusing advancement, as given in *Two Evil Isms* (93), is more candid to say the least: "Had I wanted to learn red tape, corruption and graft, I would have accepted a position as superintendent." Ramon F. Adams, *Burs Under the Saddle: A Second Look at Books and Histories of the West*, 463–74; idem, *Six-Guns and Saddle Leather*, 587–88. For a critical examination of Siringo's writing style, see Peavy, *Charles A. Siringo, A Texas Picaro*, 11–12; and Sawey, *Charles A. Siringo*, 133–39.

18. Frank Dobie, in "Charlie Siringo, Writer and Man" (xi), wrote that the virtue of *A Texas Cowboy* was "that it was written and published without benefit of respectability"; Goetzmann & Goetzmann, *The West of the Imagination*, 300–301. See also, J. Evetts Haley, "Charles A. Siringo," *Dictionary of American Biography*, XVII, 191–92.

19. Hart to Siringo, July 6, 1928, Hart Letters, CMNH.

20. Raymond W. Thorp, "Cowboy Charley Siringo," *True West* 12 (Jan.–Feb., 1965): 59.

21. Hart to Siringo, May 25, 1927; Siringo to Hart, May 30, 1927, in Hart Letters, CMNH.

22. Rhodes' purpose in writing an article on Siringo was to help promote *Riata and Spurs* for his friend. He told Ira Kent that there was "No man alive—and few dead—with such a wealth of experience" as Siringo. E. M. Rhodes to Ira Kent, Mar. 10, 1927, in Hutchinson, *A Bar Cross Man*, 246–47.

23. Eugene Manlove Rhodes, "He'll Make a Hand," *Sunset Magazine,* 63 (June, 1927): 23.

24. Neil M. Clark, "Close Calls: An Interview with Charles A. Siringo," *American Magazine* 107 (Jan., 1929): 129 (quotation). J. Evetts Haley, who interviewed Siringo in Venice while doing research for his biography of Charles Goodnight, was later to personally know Ferris Greenslet and Ira Rich Kent when Houghton Mifflin undertook publication of his book. Haley recalled that Kent was "a kindly, portly gentleman," and he described Greenslet as a "sturdy, tough-fibered Easterner." Although both were no-nonsense business-men, their dealings with him were always pleasant and tempered by sympathetic understanding. J. Evetts Haley, interview with author, March 7, 1981.

25. Peavy, *Charles A. Siringo, A Texas Picaro,* 36.

26. *A Lone Star Cowboy,* 291; *Riata and Spurs,* 275–76. This is an adaptation of the poem, "The Old Cow Man," in Charles Badger Clark, Jr., *Sun and Saddle Leather,* 54–56.

27. Known as Inglewood Cemetery at the time of Siringo's death, the cemetery was later renamed Inglewood Park Cemetery. R. J. Brodt, for Inglewood Park Cemetery, to author, Oct. 25, 1976; Loring Campbell to author, Sept. 22, 1976.

Epilogue

1. Carol Siringo McFarland to author, Nov. 10, 1976; Lee Roy Siringo to Orlan Sawey, July 27, 1946, in the author's collection; Dawson's Book Shop, Catalogue 142, Apr. 1940, p. 8. Eighteen items that had belonged to Siringo, including the table and portrait, were offered at the lot price of $30. The books included copies of *A Lone Star Cowboy* and *History of "Billy the Kid",* both presentation-inscribed to Siringo's son; *A Cowboy Detective* in original wrappers with the Santa Fe, 1914, imprint; *A Texas Cowboy,* Chicago, [1886]; and Thorp's *Songs of the Cowboys* with Siringo's bookplate. In Dawson's Book Shop, Catalogue 142.

2. Dawson's Bookshop, Catalogue 142, p. 8; Glen Dawson to author, Sept. 21, 1976; Glen Dawson, interview with Nancy Nakasone, Apr. 12, 1981, and Nakasone to author, May 11, 1981.

3. Mary Armer Earwood, interview with author, Feb. 10, 1982, (Mrs. Earwood, of Sonora, Tex., was Margaret Sherbank's aunt); R. J. Brodt (for Inglewood Park Cemetery) to author, Oct. 25 and Nov. 1, 1976; Death Certificate, Viola Reid, July 31, 1960, in Los Angeles; Death Certificate, Margaret May Sherbank, Nov. 18, 1972, in San Diego; and Death Certificate, William Lee Roy Siringo, Oct. 21, 1955, in Laguna Beach, Calif., State Registrar of Vital Statistics, Sacramento, Calif.; Orlan Sawey to author, Apr. 24, 1978.

4. Betty Siringo Kent to author, Mar. 15, 1981; Carol Siringo McFarland to author, Nov. 10, 1976. One gift Siringo presented to Thornton, still owned

by the family, was the book *A Tribute to the Dog* by Gustav Kobbe, dated Dec. 25, 1923. Carol McFarland to author, Nov. 10, 1976. See also Siringo, *A Lone Star Cowboy,* 230.

5. Ruth H. Pierce, interview with author, May 21, 1981; Ruth H. Pierce to author, June 24, 1981; Mrs. Arnold Burton to author, July 5, 1981; Last Will & Testament of Ellen Partain Siringo, Aug. 14, 1913, in the Renehan Papers, LMNM; Ruth Pierce and A. B. Pierce, Jr., *Deming's Bridge Cemetery 1850– 1898,* 96.

6. Siringo to Bill Hart, Apr. 24, 1928, Hart Letters, CMNH; Death Certificate, William J. Ramey, Apr. 3, 1941, and Death Certificate, Evelyn Elizabeth Ramey, Feb. 7, 1964, both in Los Angeles, in State Registrar of Vital Statistics, Sacramento, Calif.

7. Hutchinson, *A Bar Cross Man,* 237–38 (quotation); [Santa Fe], *City Street Guide and Santa Fe Area Map* (Santa Fe: Chamber of Commerce, 1975).

BIBLIOGRAPHY

ARCHIVAL SOURCES

Tony Albert Papers, Lischke Estate, New Mexico State Records Center and Archives, Santa Fe, N. Mex.

Jennie M. Avery Papers, New Mexico State Records Center and Archives, Santa Fe, N. Mex.

Edward L. Bartlett Papers, New Mexico State Records Center and Archives, Santa Fe, N. Mex.

James H. East, transcript of personal interview with J. Evetts Haley, September 27, 1927, Panhandle Plains Historical Museum, Canyon, Tex.

Governors' Papers: William C. McDonald, 1912–16, New Mexico State Records Center and Archives, Santa Fe, N. Mex.

Governors' Papers: L. Bradford Prince, 1889–93, New Mexico State Records Center and Archives, Santa Fe, N. Mex.

William S. Hart, Charles A. Siringo Correspondence, History Division, Los Angeles County Museum of Natural History, Los Angeles, Calif.

Will James, Charles A. Siringo Correspondence, Charles Scribner's Sons Archives, Princeton University Library, Princeton, N.J.

Henry Herbert Knibbs, Charles Fletcher Lummis Correspondence, Huntington Library, San Marino, Calif.

Matagorda County Records, 1860, Eugene C. Barker Texas History Center, University of Texas at Austin, Austin, Tex.

Cal Polk Manuscript, a copy from the original in the Panhandle Plains Historical Museum, Canyon, Tex.

Alois B. Renehan, Charles A. Siringo Correspondence, History Library, Museum of New Mexico, Santa Fe, N. Mex.

Charles A. Siringo File, Houghton Mifflin Company Records, Houghton Library, Harvard University, Cambridge, Mass.

Charles A. Siringo Collection: Consisting of original letters, photographs, post cards, and related memorabilia in the author's private library.

Charles A. Siringo, Plaintiff, vs. W. P. Cox and C. C. Rushing et al., in the Promissory Note hereinafter described, Case No. 6604, filed May 16, 1910, final judgment November 2, 1910, District Court Records, Territory of New Mexico, New Mexico State Archives and Records Center, Santa Fe, N. Mex.

Territorial Archives of New Mexico: L. Bradford Prince, "Pinkerton Investigation of the Attempted Assassination of J. A. Ancheta, February–August, 1891," microfilm, New Mexico State Archives and Records Center, Santa Fe, N. Mex.

Tumbleweeds, starring William S. Hart and Barbara Bedford, piano score by William Perry, with William S. Hart's "Farewell to the Screen," United Artists (1925), Black Hawk Films, Davenport, Iowa.

PUBLIC RECORDS

Death Certificates: Alice Apple, Frank B. Putnam, Evelyn E. Ramey, William J. Ramey, Viola Reid, Margaret May Sherbank, Charles A. Siringo, and William Lee Roy Siringo, State Registrar of Vital Statistics, Department of Health, Sacramento, Calif.

Deed Records, Office of the County Clerk, Santa Fe County, Santa Fe, N. Mex.

Last Will and Testament of Bridgit Siringo, February 2, 1910, Office of the Probate Judge, Santa Fe, N. Mex.

Last Will and Testament of Charles Angelo Siringo, July 24, 1928, Probate Court Records, Los Angeles County, Los Angeles, Calif.

Pinkerton's National Detective Agency, Plantiff, vs. *Charles A. Siringo and W. B. Conkey Company, Defendants,* 1910–1911; and *Pinkerton's National Detective Agency . . .* vs. *Charles A. Siringo . . . ,* 1914–15, Chancery No. 277903, Court Records, Superior Court of Cook County, Chicago, Ill.

Resolution of Tribute to A. B. Renehan by the Santa Fe County Bar Association, May 10, 1928, File No. 13037, District Court Records, Santa Fe, N. Mex.

Charles A. Siringo, Plaintiff, vs. *Ellen P. Siringo, Defendant,* Divorce, Case No. 8073, September 15, 1913, and October 16, 1913, First Judicial District Court Records, Santa Fe County, N. Mex.

Charles A. Siringo, Plaintiff, vs. *Grace Siringo, Defendant,* Case No. 6439, February 17, 1909, and April 15, 1909, First Judicial District Court Records, Santa Fe County, N. Mex.

Tom Williams, Plaintiff, vs. C. A. Siringo, Mrs. Joseph W. Reid, Defendants, Case No. 8477, filed August 4, 1915; Petition of Alonzo E. Compton to intervene in District Court Case No. 8477, filed November 20, 1919, Records of the District Court, Santa Fe County, Santa Fe, N. Mex.

INTERVIEWS AND LETTERS

Adams, Clarence Siringo, to author, April 26 and May 23, 1981.

Brodt, R. J., Vice President, Inglewood Park Cemetery, Los Angeles, Calif., to author, October 25 and November 1, 1976.

Burton, Mrs. Arnold, Palacios, Tex., to author, July 5, 1981.

Campbell, Loring, Burbank, Calif., to author, September 22, 1976.

Dawson, Glen, Los Angeles, Calif., to author, September 21, 1976.

Earwood, Mary Armer, Sonora, Tex., interview with author, February 10, 1982.

Easland, Stella, Assistant Editor, Houghton Mifflin Company, Boston, Mass., to author, September 27, 1982.

Euler, Harlan P., Sandia Park, N. Mex., to author, November 11, 1976, and January 12, 1977.

Haley, J. Evetts, El Paso, Tex., interview with author, March 7, 1981.

Hoyt Henry F., to Charles A. Siringo Correspondence. June 9, 1921, in the Panhandle Plains Historical Museum, Canyon, Tex.; and June 21, 1921, original letter in the author's collection.

Kent, Betty Siringo, El Paso, Tex., interview with author, March 6, 1981.

Kent, Betty Siringo, Westlake Village, Calif., to author, March 15 and May 31, 1981, and April 24, 1982.

Lummis, Keith, San Francisco, Calif., to author, August 7, 1982, and August 30, 1982.

McFarland, Carol Siringo, Whittier, Calif., interviews with author, October 13, 1976, March 6, 1981, and March 11, 1981.

McFarland, Carol Siringo, Whittier, Calif., to author, November 10, and December 14, 1976; January 21, March 12 and April 29, 1981.

Nakasone, Nancy N., Torrance, Calif., to author, May 11, 1981.

Nunis, Doyce B., University of Southern California, Los Angeles, Calif., to author, January 13, 1981.

Olney, Austin, Manager, Trade Division, Houghton Mifflin Company, Boston, Mass., interview with author, August 9, 1982.

O'Neill, George F., Asst. Vice President, Pinkerton's, Inc., New York, N.Y., to author, September 1, 1982.

Pierce, Ruth H., Blessing, Tex., interview with author, May 21, 1981.

Pierce, Ruth H., Blessing, Tex., to author, June 24, 1981.

Potter, Colonel Jack, Clayton, N. Mex., to Orlan Sawey, October 16, 1947. Original letter in the author's collection.

Sawey, Orlan, Truth or Consequences, N. Mex. to author, April 24, 1978.

Siringo, Charles A., to William E. Hawks Correspondence. May 20, 1915, original letter in the author's collection. Two letters: April 17 and October 10, 1928, owned by Michael Heaston, Rare Books & Manuscripts, Austin, Tex.

Siringo, Lee Roy, San Bernardino, Calif., to Orlan Sawey, July 27, 1946. Original letter in the author's collection.

Thorp, Raymond W., Los Angeles, Calif., to Orlan Sawey, September 10, 1949. Original letter in the author's collection.

NEWSPAPERS

Caldwell Journal (Caldwell, Kans.), February 19 and October 8, 1885.

The Daily New Mexican (Santa Fe), February 6 and 7, 1891.

Dallas Morning News, May 8, 1927.

Hollywood Citizen News, October 20, 1928.

Los Angeles *Evening Express,* April 11, 1927; October 19, 1928.

Los Angeles *Examiner,* October 21, 1928.

Los Angeles *Times,* April 12, 24, 1925; March 26, 1927; October 21, 1928.

New York Times, May 3, 1927.

New York World, June 5, 1927.

Santa Fe *New Mexican,* March 11, 1910; July 17, 1911; April 17, 19, 21, and 22, 1915; September 7, 1921; April 21 and 23, 1928.

Spokane Review, July 12, 1892.

CHRONOLOGY OF BOOKS BY SIRINGO

A Texas Cow Boy or, Fifteen Years on the Hurricane Deck of a Spanish Pony. Taken from Real Life by Chas. A. Siringo, An Old Stove Up "Cow Puncher," Who Has Spent Nearly Twenty Years on the Great Western Cattle Ranches. Chicago: M. Umbdenstock & Co., 1885.

A Texas Cow Boy. . . . Second edition, enlarged. Chicago: Siringo & Dobson, Publishers, 1886.

A Texas Cowboy. . . . Introduction by J. Frank Dobie and Bibliography of Siringo's Writings. Drawings by Tom Lea. New York: William Sloan Associates, 1950.

A Cowboy Detective: A True Story of Twenty-Two Years with a World-Famous Detective Agency. Chicago: W. B. Conkey Company, 1912.

A Cowboy Detective. . . . Facsimile reprint in pictorial wrappers. [Chicago: Hill Binding Company] Santa Fe, New Mexico, 1914.

A Cowboy Detective. . . . New York: J. S. Ogilvie Publishing Company, [1912]. No. 127 in the Railroad Series. Pictorial wrappers, actually published between 1921 and 1924.

Further Adventures of a Cowboy Detective. New York: J. S. Ogilvie Publishing Company, [1912]. No. 128 in the Railroad Series. Pictorial wrappers, actually published between 1921 and 1924.

Two Evil Isms, Pinkertonism and Anarchism. By a Cowboy Detective Who Knows, as He Spent Twenty-Two Years in the Inner Circle of Pinkerton's National Detective Agency. Chicago: Charles A. Siringo, Publisher, 1915.

Two Evil Isms. . . . Facsimile reprint with an introduction by Charles D. Peavy. Austin: Steck-Vaughn Company, 1967.

A Lone Star Cowboy, Being Fifty Years Experience in the Saddle as Cowboy, Detective and New Mexico Ranger, on Every Cow Trail in the Wooly Old West. Santa Fe, N. Mex.: Charles A. Siringo, 1919.

The Song Companion of A Lone Star Cowboy: Old Favorite Cow-Camp Songs. Santa Fe: Chas. A. Siringo, 1919. Printed pictorial wrappers.

History of "Billy the Kid": The True Life of the Most Daring Young Outlaw of the Age. Santa Fe: Chas. A. Siringo, 1920. Pictorial wrappers.

History of "Billy the Kid." Facsimile edition, with an introduction by Charles D. Peavy. Austin: Steck-Vaughn Company, 1967.

Riata and Spurs: The Story of a Lifetime Spent in the Saddle as Cowboy and Detective. Boston and New York: Houghton Mifflin Company, 1927.

Riata and Spurs: The Story of a Lifetime Spent in the Saddle as Cowboy and Ranger. Revised edition. Boston and New York: Houghton Mifflin Company, 1927.

BOOKS

Adams, Clarence Siringo. *For Old Times' Sake.* Roswell, N. Mex.: Hall-Poorbough Press, 1980.

Adams, Ramon F. *Burrs under the Saddle: A Second Look at Books and Histories of the West*. Norman: University of Oklahoma Press, 1964.

————. *Six-Guns and Saddle Leather: A Bibliography of Books and Pamphlets on Western Outlaws and Gunmen*. New edition, revised and enlarged. Norman: University of Oklahoma Press, 1969.

Appleman, Roy E. *Charlie Siringo, Cowboy Detective*. Washington, D.C.: Potomac Corral, The Westerners, 1968.

Bernstein, Irving. *Turbulent Years*. Boston: Houghton Mifflin, 1970.

Blanchard, Leola Howard. *Conquest of Southwest Kansas*. Wichita, Kans.: Wichita Eagle Press, [1931].

Borah, W. E. *Haywood Trial: Closing Argument of W. E. Borah*. Boise, Idaho: The Statesman Shop, (1907).

Branch, Douglas. *The Cowboy and His Interpreters*. New York: D. Appleton, 1926.

Broehl, Wayne G., Jr. *The Molly Maguires*. Cambridge, Mass.: Harvard University Press, 1964.

Brownlow, Kevin. *The War, the West, and the Wilderness*. New York: Alfred A. Knopf, 1978.

Burns, Walter Noble. *The Saga of Billy the Kid*. Garden City, N.Y.: Doubleday, Page, 1926.

Carson, Clarence B. *Organized Against Whom? The Labor Unions in America*. Alexandria, Va.: Western Goals, 1983.

Chamberlain, John. *The Enterprising Americans: A Business History of the United States*. New York: Harper & Row, 1963.

Clark, Charles Badger, Jr. *Sun and Saddle Leather*. Boston: Richard G. Badger, 1917.

Clemens, Samuel L. *Adventures of Huckleberry Finn*, by Mark Twain. New York: Charles L. Webster, 1885.

————. *Following the Equator: A Journey around the World*. Hartford: American Publishing, 1897.

Coe, George Washington. *Frontier Fighter: The Autobiography of George W. Coe, Who Fought and Rode with Billy the Kid*. Boston: Houghton Mifflin, 1934.

Darrow, Clarence. *The Story of My Life*. New York: Charles Scribner's Sons, 1932.

David, Henry. *The History of the Haymarket Affair*. New York: Russell & Russell, 1936, 1938.

DeArment, Robert K. *Bat Masterson: The Man and the Legend*. Norman: University of Oklahoma Press, 1979.

Dobie, J. Frank. *Guide to Life and Literature of the Southwest*. Dallas: Southern Methodist University Press, 1965.

Dykstra, Robert R. *The Cattle Towns*. New York: Alfred A. Knopf, 1968.

Everson, William K., and George N. Fenin. *The Western: From Silents to Cinerama*. New York: Orion Press, 1962.

Garrett, Patrick Floyd. *The Authentic Life of Billy, the Kid, the Noted Desperado of the Southwest*. Santa Fe: New Mexican Printing and Publishing, 1882.

Ginger, Ray. *The Age of Excess: American Life from the End of Reconstruction to World War I*. New York: Macmillan, 1965.

Goetzmann, William H., and William N. Goetzmann. *The West of the Imagination*. New York: W. W. Norton, 1986.

Greenslet, Ferris. *Under the Bridge: An Autobiography*. Boston: Houghton Mifflin, 1943.

Hammond, John Hays. *The Autobiography of John Hays Hammond*. 2 vols. New York: Farrar and Reinhart, 1935.

Hart, William S. *My Life East and West*. Boston: Houghton Mifflin, 1929.

Hawley, James H., ed. *History of Idaho: The Gem of the Mountains*. 3 vols. Chicago: S. J. Clarke Publishing, 1920.

Hofstadter, Richard. *Social Darwinism in American Thought*. Rev. ed. Boston: Beacon Press, 1955.

Horan, James D. *Desperate Men: Revelations from the Sealed Pinkerton Files*. Rev. and enlarged ed. Garden City, N.Y.: Doubleday & Company, 1962.

———. *The Pinkertons: The Detective Dynasty That Made History*. New York: Crown, 1967.

Horan, James D., and Howard Swiggett. *The Pinkerton Story*. New York: G. P. Putnam's Sons, 1951.

Hoyt, Henry F. *A Frontier Doctor*. Introduction by Frank B. Kellogg. Boston: Houghton Mifflin, 1929.

———. *A Frontier Doctor*. Historical introduction by Doyce B. Nunis, Jr. Chicago: The Lakeside Press, 1979.

Hutchinson, W. H. *A Bar Cross Man: The Life and Personal Writings of Eugene Manlove Rhodes*. Norman: University of Oklahoma Press, 1956.

Jenkins, John H. *Basic Texas Books: An Annotated Bibliography of Selected Works for a Research Library*. Austin, Tex.: Jenkins Publishing, 1983.

Kaplan, Justin. *Mark Twain and His World*. New York: Simon and Schuster, 1974.

———. *Mr. Clemens and Mark Twain*. New York: Simon and Schuster, 1966.

Keleher, William A. *The Fabulous Frontier: Twelve New Mexico Items*. Santa Fe, N. Mex.: Rydal Press, 1945.

Lamar, Howard R., ed. *The Reader's Encyclopedia of the American West*. New York: Thomas Crowell, 1977.

Leish, Kenneth W., ed. *The American Heritage Pictorial History of the Presidents of the United States*. 3 vols. New York: American Heritage Publishing, 1968.

Lingenfelter, Richard E. *The Hardrock Miners: A History of the Mining Labor Movement in the American West, 1863–1893*. Berkeley: University of California Press, 1974.

McCracken, Harold. *The Charles M. Russell Book: The Life and Work of the Cowboy Artist*. Garden City, N.Y.: Doubleday, 1957.

Metz, Leon. *Pat Garrett: The Story of a Western Lawman*. Norman: University of Oklahoma Press, 1974.

Miller, Nyle H., and Joseph W. Snell. *Why the West Was Wild. A Contemporary Look at the Antics of Some Highly Publicized Kansas Cowtown Personalities*. Topeka: Kansas State Historical Society, 1963.

Noggle, Burl. *Teapot Dome: Oil and Politics in the 1920's*. New York: W. W. Norton, 1965.

Peavy, Charles D. *Charles A. Siringo, A Texas Picaro*. Southwest Writers Series No. 3. Austin, Tex.: Steck-Vaughn, 1967.

Pierce, Ruth, and A. B. Pierce, Jr. *Deming's Bridge Cemetery 1850–1898, Tres Palacios Baptist Church 1852–1898, Hawley Cemetery 1898–1978, Matagorda County, Texas*. 2nd ed. Palacios, Tex.: Hawley Cemetery Association, Blessing Historical Foundation, 1977.

Renehan, Alois B. *Songs from the Black Mesa*. Santa Fe: New Mexican Printing Company, 1900.

Riegel, Robert E. *America Moves West*. Rev. ed. Titusville, N.J.: Holt, Rinehart & Winston, 1947.

Rowan, Richard Wilmer. *The Pinkertons, A Detective Dynasty*. Boston: Little, Brown, 1931.

Russell, Don. *The Wild West or, A History of the Wild West Shows*. Fort Worth, Tex.: Amon Carter Museum of Western Art, 1970.

Saunders, Lyle. *A Guide to Materials Bearing on Cultural Relations in New Mexico*. Albuquerque: University of New Mexico Press, 1944.

Sawey, Orlan. *Charles A. Siringo*. Twayne's United States Authors Series No. 376. Boston: Twayne, 1980.

Shelton, Lola. *Charles Marion Russell: Cowboy, Artist, Friend*. New York: Dodd, Mead, 1962.

Shirley, Glenn. *Pawnee Bill: A Biography of Major Gordon W. Lillie.* Albuquerque: University of New Mexico Press, 1958.

Smith, Robert Wayne. *The Coeur d'Alene Mining War of 1892: A Case Study of an Industrial Dispute.* Corvallis: Oregon State University Press, 1961.

Spence, Clark C. *Mining Engineers and the American West: The Lace-Boot Brigade, 1849–1933.* New Haven: Yale University Press, 1970.

Standing Bear, Luther. *My People the Sioux.* Edited by E. A. Brininstool. Boston: Houghton Mifflin, 1928.

Stanley, F. *Ciudad Santa Fe: Territorial Days, 1846–1912.* Pampa, Tex.: Pampa Print Shop, 1965.

Stoll, William T., as told to H. W. Shicher. *Silver Strike: The True Story of Silver Mining in the Coeur d'Alenes.* Boston: Little, Brown, 1932.

Taft, Phillip. *Organized Labor in American History.* New York: Harper & Row, 1964.

Tarbell, Ida M. *The Nationalization of Business, 1878–1898.* New York: Macmillan, 1936.

Tuska, Jon. *The Filming of the West.* New York: Doubleday, 1976.

Twitchell, Ralph Emerson. *Leading Facts of New Mexican History.* 5 vols. Cedar Rapids: The Torch Press, 1911–1917.

———. *Old Santa Fe: The Story of New Mexico's Ancient Capital.* Santa Fe: New Mexico Publishing, 1925.

Waters, L. L. *Steel Trails to Santa Fe.* Lawrence, Kans.: University of Kansas Press, 1950.

Webb, Walter Prescott, H. Bailey Carroll, and Eldon Stephen Branda, eds. *The Handbook of Texas.* 3 vols. Austin: Texas State Historical Association, 1952, 1976.

Wright, Robert M. *Dodge City: The Cowboy Capital and the Great Southwest in the Days of the Wild Indian, the Buffalo, the Cowboy, Dance Halls and Bad Men.* [Wichita, Kans.: Wichita Eagle Press, 1913.]

BOOK REVIEWS, ARTICLES, AND MISCELLANY

Adams, Clarence Siringo. "Charley Siringo—The Cowboy Detective." *New Mexico Magazine*, October, 1967, 18–19, 36–40.

———. "Fair Trial at Encinoso." *True West* 13 (March–April, 1966): 32–33, 50–51.

Ball, Eve. "Charlie Siringo and 'Eat Em Up Jake.'" *True West* 16 (May–June, 1969): 36–37, 46–47.

Benét, William Rose. "Quick on the Draw." *Saturday Review of Literature* 4 (August 27, 1927): 69–70. Review of *Riata and Spurs*.

Clark, Neil M. "Close Calls: An Interview with Charles A. Siringo." *American Magazine* 107 (January, 1929): 38–39, 130–31.

Dobie, J. Frank. "Bibliography of Siringo's Writings," in *A Texas Cowboy*. New York: William Sloan Associates, 1950.

———. "Charlie Siringo, Writer and Man," introduction to *A Texas Cowboy*. New York: William Sloan Associates, 1950.

———. "Old Charlie." *Nation* 125 (July 13, 1927): 41. Review of *Riata and Spurs*.

Dunne, B. B. "Charles Siringo, Called Most Famous Cowboy Detective, Was Picturesque, Modest Figure." Santa Fe *New Mexican*, October 23, 1928, p. 5.

"Evelyn Lischke of Peaceful Siringo Ranch." *The Santa Fe Scene*, May 16, 1959, pp. 12–13.

Haley, J. Evetts. "Charlie Siringo, Cowboy Chronicler." *Shamrock* [Spring, 1962], pp. 5–7, 15.

———. "Charles A. Siringo." *Dictionary of American Biography*, edited by Dumas Malone, IX, 191–92. New York: Charles Scribner's Sons, 1964.

———. "Jim East, Trail Hand and Cowboy." *Panhandle Plains Historical Review* 4 (1931): 52–55.

Hammond, John Hays. "Strong Men of the Wild West." *Scribner's Magazine* 77 (February–March, 1925): 215–25, 246–56.

Hess, Chester Newton. "Sagebrush Sleuth, The Saga of Charlie Siringo." *Cattleman* 41 (January, 1955): 36–37, 64–82.

Holmes, Oliver W. "Allan Pinkerton." *Dictionary of American Biography*, edited by Dumas Malone, VII, 623. New York: Charles Scribner's Sons, 1964.

"Henry Herbert Knibbs." *Twentieth Century Authors, First Supplement, A Biographical Dictionary of Modern Literature*, edited by Stanley J. Kunitz and Vineta Colby, 528. New York: H. W. Wilson, 1955.

Lindsey, Estelle Lawton. "Chat with Ex-Cowboy, Hailed as Great Literary Find, Recalls Wild West Days." Los Angeles *Evening Express*, April 11, 1927, sec. 3, pp. 1–2.

Nagel, Stony. "When Siringo Was Marked for Death." *True West* 18 (November–December, 1970): 31, 68–69.

Nolen, O. W. "Charley Siringo, Old-Time Cowboy Rancher, Detective and Author." *Cattleman* 38 (December, 1951): 50–56.

Nunis, Doyce B., Jr. "Historical Introduction" to *A Frontier Doctor*. Chicago: The Lakeside Press, 1979.

Peavy, Charles D. "Introduction" to *Two Evil Isms: Pinkertonism and Anarchism*. Facsimile ed. Austin: Steck-Vaughn, 1967.

——. "Introduction" to *History of "Billy the Kid"*. Facsimile ed. Austin: Steck-Vaughn, 1967.

Pingenot, Ben E. "Charlie Siringo: New Mexico's Lone Star Cowboy." *Cattleman* 63 (November, 1976): 56–57, 122–28.

Renehan, Alois B. *Songs From the Black Mesa*. Santa Fe: New Mexican Printing Company, 1900.

Rhodes, Eugene Manlove. "He'll Make a Hand." *Sunset Magazine* 63 (June, 1927): 23, 89–91.

[Santa Fe]. *City Street Guide and Santa Fe Area Map*. Santa Fe, N. Mex.: Chamber of Commerce, 1975.

Sawey, Orlan. "Charlie Siringo, Reluctant Propagandist." *Western American Literature* 7 (Fall, 1972): 203–10.

Smith, B. W., Jr. Review of *Riata and Spurs*. *New York Post Literary Review*, May 8, 1927, p. 3.

Stratton, David H., ed. "The Memoirs of Albert B. Fall." *Southwestern Studies* 4 (1966), Monograph No. 15. El Paso: Texas Western Press, University of Texas at El Paso.

"Thirty-fifth Anniversary Catalogue No. 142." Dawson's Book Shop, April, 1940, p. 8. Offers for sale eighteen books and related items from the library of Charles A. Siringo.

Thompson, George G. "Bat Masterson: The Dodge City Years." *Fort Hays Kansas State College Studies*, No. 1. Topeka: Kansas State Printing Plant, 1943.

Thorp, Raymond W. "A Tamer of the Old West." *Triple-X Magazine*, March, 1926, p. 141.

——. "Cowboy Charley Siringo." *True West* 12 (January–February, 1965): 32–33, 59–62.

——. "'Old Colt's Forty-Five': Letters of Charley Siringo." *Western Sportsman* 5 (July, 1940): 13–14, 40–41, and (August, 1940): 21–22, 32.

Webb, Walter Prescott. "Charlie Siringo Tells the Story of Thrilling Life on the Frontier." *Dallas Morning News*, May 8, 1927, sec. 3, p. 3. Review of *Riata and Spurs*.

"Western Americana: The Personal Library of E. A. Brininstool." Dawson's Book Shop, catalogue 438 (June, 1976). Contains a brief biographical sketch of Brininstool.

White, Owen P. "Six Shooters, Cinch Rings, Longhorns and Saloons." *New York Times Book Review*, May 9, 1927, p. 6. Review of *Riata and Spurs*.

UNPUBLISHED

Donlon, Walter John. "Le Baron Bradford Prince, Chief Justice and Governor of New Mexico Territory, 1879–1893." Ph.D. dissertation, University of New Mexico, 1967. Typescript copy in the State Archives and Records Center, Santa Fe, N. Mex.

INDEX

Siringo was composed into type on a Linotron 202 digital photo-typesetter in ten point Sabon with two points of spacing between the lines. The book was designed by Cameron Poulter, typeset by G & S Typesetters, Inc., printed offset by Thomson-Shore, Inc., and bound by John H. Dekker & Sons. The paper on which the book is printed is designed for an effective life of at least three hundred years.

TEXAS A&M UNIVERSITY PRESS : COLLEGE STATION